The New Ryan

Development and History of the Ryan ST and SC

by
Ev Cassagneres

FLYING BOOKS
by
 Historic Aviation

The New Ryan
Development and History of the Ryan ST and SC
By Ev Cassagneres

Published as part of the
"HISTORIC AIRCRAFT SERIES"

FLYING BOOKS INTERNATIONAL, Publishers & Wholesalers
1401 Kings Wood Rd., Eagan, MN 55122-3811
612/454-2493
James B. Horne, Publisher

The "Historic Aircraft Series" is published to document the careers and service of the men and machines that gave America Wings. Other titles in this series from Historic Aviation are:

Piper: A Legend Aloft
by Edward H. Phillips

Beechcraft, Pursuit of Perfection
by Edward H. Phillips

Cessna, A Master's Expression
by Edward H. Phillips

Travel Air, Wings Over the Prairie
by Edward H. Phillips

Wings of Cessna, Model 120 to the Citation X
by Edward H. Phillips

Speed, the Biography of Charles Holman
by Noel Allard

The 91 Before Lindbergh
by Peter Allen

DH-88: The Story of DeHavilland's Racing Comets
by David Ogilvy

Of Monocoupes and Men
by John Underwood

The Stinsons
by John Underwood

T-Hangar Tales
by Joseph P. Juptner

Aircraft Service Manual Reprints
Piper J-3 Cub
Aeronca 7AC Champ
Aeronca 11AC Chief
Taylorcraft BC-12D
Ercoupe

Aircraft Flight Manual Reprints
F-51D Mustang
B-29 Superfortress
Vultee BT-13

The New Ryan
Development and History of the Ryan ST and SC

Flying Books International,
Publishers & Wholesalers.
1401 Kings Wood Rd.,
Eagan, MN 55122 U.S.A.

©1995 Ev Cassagneres

Library of Congress Cataloging in Publication Data
Cassagneres, Ev
The New Ryan
Development and History of the Ryan ST and SC
Aviation History

Library of Congress Catalog No. 95-61927
ISBN 0-911139-20-6 Softcover

Printed and bound in the United States of America
Art Director, Noel Allard
Cover Artist, Don Carlson
Publisher, James B. Horne

Acknowledgments

There is no question that this book has not been written by just me. The various abilities of many people, — friends, fellow pilots, writers and authors, historians, Ryan airplane owners, former Ryan owners, and organizations — have contributed and become part of what ever success this work may represent. Their cooperation and interest is without parallel. One might say that they are true collaborators. By way of their generous gifts of time, talent, experience and encouragement in different ways and in varying degrees, have been a source of immense help and inspiration.

I truly owe these special individuals and groups my deepest gratitude and appreciation, for without them I could not possibly have put this book together.

And may I offer a final bow and thanks to all names I have freely used in some of the yarns and other interesting accounts of flying these beautiful Ryan airplanes.

T. Claude Ryan
William Wagner
Ed Morrow
"Dapper" Dan Burnett
Jon Harme van der Linde
Mrs. Will Vandermeer
Millard C. Boyd
Mrs. John Fornasero
William Emmenschuh
Elizabeth Ferguson
Douglas Corrigan
Al Menasco
Dr. Paul E. Garber
Paul Wilcox
Harvey Gray
William "Doc" Sloan
Mel Thompson
O.J. Whitney
Fred L. Barber
William T. Larkins
Peter M. Bowers
Richard Sanders Allen
John Underwood
Paul R. Matt
Woody Edmonson
Virginia Fiore
Alan Wheeler
George Hardie
John C. Barbery
Roberta "Bobby" Lupton
Bettie Lund Cary
Bill Hodges
Drina Welch Abel
Alan Abel
Hans & Ruth Bauer
Peter Dana
Richard M. Bueschel
Dick Wood
Kenneth D. Wilson
Robert C. Baker
William Backus
Mr. & Mrs. Diar Clark
Robert L. Scott, Jr.
Eugene Hershey
Virginia & Bill Welch
Paul Stevens

Peter Boisseau
David Bilodeau, Yale Univ.
William Rose
Andy Spak
Richard Switlik
Hal Schnerr
"Toots" Womack
Foster Lane
N.A. Nabel, Jr.
Stan Solecki
Chet Wellman
Dorr C. Carpenter
Jim Flatland
Jack Tweed
Franklin Farrel
Eline O. Cassagneres
C.R. Patist, Netherlands
H.J. Broekhuizen, Netherlands
Theo J. M. Wesselink, Netherlands
F.N.M. Emmink, Netherlands
Alfred Damen, Netherlands
John P. Redder (NASA)
Walter C. Hill
Lennart Johnsson, Sweden
Peter R. Keating, England
Kenneth Meehan, New Zealand
John Hopton, Australia
A. Bovert, Australia
Steve J. Gilbetson, Australia
Geoff Goodall, Australia
D.J. Bourke, Australia
E.R. Burnett-Read, Australia
John Bange, Australia
Graham Hosking, Australia
Santiago Flores Ruiz
Daniel P. Hagedorn
Ted Babbini
Remo Galeazzi
William W. Halverson
Ed Power, Jr.
Ed Bowman
Ray Wagner
Donald Carter
Bob Fergus
Jimmie Leeward
Kirk Leeward

James R. Bassett
Dave Masters
Willis M. Allen, Jr.
Jerry Ryan
Steve Pitcairn
Howard Levy
Warren Shipp
Ted Koston
Edgard Hoet, Venezuela
Alberto A. Anido, Phillipines
Gerald J. Casius
Ralph Romaine, Edo Corp.
William H. Greenhalgh
Bud Bodding
Roger Beseker
Kenneth M. Sumney
Harvey C. Lippincott
H. Glenn Buffington
Bob Clark
Melvin Rice
Olive Wolcott
Janet Wolcott Barone
George Wolcott
Cole Palen
James Bursey
William Greisemer
C. V. Glines, Col. USAF Pentagon
Charles G. Worman,
    Historian USAF Wright-Patterson AFB
Robert A. Webb, Lt. Col. USAF Pentagon
Lynn Wendl
Steve Freeman
Bill Ahern
Chot Zock
John Richards
Jim Dewey
Ron Johnson
Mike Wilson
Brad Larson
Mark Hoskins
Rick Farrell
Doug Koeppen
William Dodd
Buck Hilbert
James R. Bassett

John Gosney
Roger Thiel
Franklin T. "Hank" Kurt
Tom Poberezny
Norman Petersen
Dennis Parks
Jack Cox
Bill Feeney
Robert T. Smith
Bill Sweet
Muriel Harris

James Horne
Jack Newton
Bryan Ev Cassagneres
Kirsten Joy Cassagneres
Harold Duarte
Ernie Moore
Marcus Bates
Louis B. Briasco
Frank Greene
Walter Bohrer
William M. Foley

R.F. Haywood
Judith Schiff, Yale University
George Collier
C.E. Galloway
Les Reissner
Thomas B. Scott, Jr.
Dawn Fitzpatrick
Walter M. Jefferies, Jr.
Dilys Pierson
Frank J. Recupido

ASSOCIATIONS - ADMINISTRATIONS - INSTITUTIONS - ARMED FORCES

American Aviation Historical Society
Experimental Aircraft Association
Aircraft Owners & Pilots Association
Federal Aviation Administration
United States Air Force
United States Navy
United States Army
National Air & Space Museum
Ryan Aeronautical Library
San Diego Aero Space Museum
Ryan Aeronautical Company
Teledyne Ryan Aeronautical
National Archives

United States Air Force Museum
Wright-Patterson Air Force Base
Langley Research Center
National Aeronautic Association
National Aeronautics & Space Administration
Yale University, Sterling Library
Ministerie van Defensie Marine (Holland)
Dept. of Civil Aviation of Australia
Wheelock Mardin & Co. Ltd. Hong Kong, China
Pentagon - Office of the Assistant Secretary of Defense
(Grover Heiman, Jr. Col. USAF)
Connecticut Aeronautical Historical Association
U.S. Air Force Association, Charles A. Lindbergh Chapter

DEDICATED TO

**Eline, Kirsten & Bill, Leslie & Bryan
with appreciation and admiration.**

Preface

Over recent years there has been a renewed interest in the history of America and its heritage, aviation history in particular. Much emphasis has been on the achievements and design of military aircraft in recent wars, especially WW I and WW II, yet in the intervening years of peace have produced their share of great aircraft and heroic fliers as well.

During the thirties I was part of the great air-minded throng of young Americans who would run outdoors and gaze upward at any airplane that would pass overhead. And I would not take my eyes off the plane until it passed over the horizon and clear out of sight. Its shape, its sound, its direction and altitude would be deeply recorded in my memory. I kept scrapbooks, built both solid and flying (wood and paper) models, and would ride my trusty bicycle many miles to the local airports to watch the aviators fly those beautiful aircraft.

Clear in my mind are those years that I came home from school each day to work on building both a solid scale and wood and paper model of the classic Ryan ST airplane. It was sometime in the summer of 1937. The Ryan ST had been in production already since 1934.

I also recall my parents taking me to the local New Haven Municipal Airport here in Connecticut, where I live, each summer to watch famous aviators flying in the annual air show. Men like Alex Papana flying a Bucker Jungmeister and Al Williams stand out in my mind. But the one airplane to really catch my eye was a beautiful silver open cockpit airplane known as the Ryan ST, flown by local pilot Jack Tweed. There it was, in the flesh, just like the ones I was building after school each day. Wow.

It was some years later when all of this thrill was to resurface. In fact it was about 1956. I know only a pilot would even think of taking his date to see an airport. But the attractive secretary whom I had met at a ski club did accept my offer of an after-hours tour of the Bridgeport Airport. Having flown out of New Haven for ten years, I was familiar enough with the airport in Bridgeport to find my way around and attempt to make it interesting enough for my date. We strolled along in the darkness as I talked about airplanes. A thin slice of light from a nearby hangar caught my attention. Someone had slipped through one of the hangar's sliding doors and left it open, I thought. Knowing this particular hangar had a reputation for boarding experimental and antique/classic type aircraft from time to time, I stuck my head in through the open space. In one corner of the hangar beneath a couple of night lights, a man stood, busily sorting packages for shipment the following morning

on a local commercial flight. Surrounded by the baggage he raised his head to notice the two figures standing in the twilight outside his wire cage and then went on with his work.

Alone in the rest of the nearly darkened hangar, we could make out the shapes of several aircraft. Though I was able to identify them all at the time, I can only be sure of the details of one of them now — the one whose memory has blurred the memory of the others. Sitting alone in a corner, its outline stirred up recollections as a young model builder back in the 1930s when I had been so enchanted by the lines of the sporty "Ryan ST." I still have both of those models I built back then. Could I be looking at an ST through the dusk of this hangar?

Pressing through the semidarkness, I knew at once I was standing before a genuine and well-preserved edition of the now classic plane. As the "silver bullet," this plane quickly rose to pre-eminence among the sports craft of the late '30s. For a generation of pilots weaned on the bulky fabric-covered biplane, the Ryan ST's single set of low-slung wings and sleek metallic fuselage prefigured the revolution in the aircraft design clearly seen in the military fighters of World War II.

My blond date must have sensed the presence of an intruder on my attentions. From the shout of my surprise at the moment of discovery there was little else on my mind the rest of the evening. A real love affair had begun. The next day I drove the 20 miles from New Haven, introduced myself to Don Sullivan, the hangar's operator, and found out that the aging but still beautiful Ryan belonged to a local club of pilots who rightly called themselves the "Ryanites." Now thoroughly captivated by the possibility of even flying the airplane, I persuaded another date that evening to visit the airport with me. The hangar door still open, I impulsively feigned the job of discovery and shouted, "Look, there's a Ryan ST." From across the room a voice announced, "Yeah, that's what you said last night with another girl." Caught off guard, I stumbled for something to say, mumbling a few words of self defense as I hastily retreated in embarrassment, but not permanently.

Before a month was up, I found the fifty dollars for the membership fee. I became "associate" member to club president Al Wheeler, a pilot whom I had admired for some time. I still know the day I joined — November 11, 1956. The Ryanites turned out to be a poor man's club with a wealthy man's airplane. Without money to pay for a mechanic's time, we spent nearly every weekend of that winter readying the plane for her annual licensing. She presided over a

Sunday court with a dozen devotees who usually managed to sandwich in two or three hours of serious work along with flying stories, food and talk of the upcoming maneuvers in the open cockpit plane.

When spring came in 1957, and after a 30 minute "check ride" with president Wheeler, I was caught up in the joy of flying a real airplane. What bliss it was. Difficult to handle anywhere near or on the ground, but absolute ecstasy in the air, the spirited ST polished this pilot's sense of feel to such a degree that even years later I was able to quickly accustom myself to unfamiliar high performance aircraft. The following year the flying club broke up and our 1936 "Silver Bullet" was sold. I vowed at the time that I would buy her back myself someday and I did, after saving up $1700 in 3 years.

With the ST in my possession, I became interested in her prior history since leaving the Ryan plant. Before long I was badgering the company for more information. I tried to pry into the history of every single Ryan ST built, then on to the earlier Ryan Broughams, the M-1 mail ships, Claude Ryan, the Ryan Aeronautical Company, and of course to the greatest plane Ryan ever built, the "Spirit of St. Louis." Little by little photographs, anecdotes and technical data began to come in the mail and pile upon my desk. By late 1961, I found myself being recognized by others interested in aviation history as the "Ryan Man." The original file — a tiny cardboard box — eventually grew into two 5-drawer file cabinets with separate folders for correspondence, clippings and photographs of every plane assembled by Ryan between 1924 and 1941 that I could get any information on. By the end of 1978, the project had amassed to what I understand to be the world's largest collection of memorabilia and technical data on the Ryan Aeronautical Company and Lindbergh's "Spirit of St. Louis."

Incidentally, the Ryan ST I happened across that evening in Bridgeport was s/n 117, NC14985, built in 1936, and now the only remaining original "ST" left in the world.

In June of 1968, the Ryan Aeronautical Company flew me out to San Diego to spend 3 weeks doing research on the company's history. Part of that time was devoted to searching out and interviewing many former employees who actually worked on Ryan aircraft production lines, engineering, and experimental test and production test flying. Others were flight instructors in Ryan airplanes at either the Ryan school or the later CPTP program and military flight schools.

Some of these people have "gone west" since that 1968 trip, and some are still with us, and I would like herewith to name them individually in tribute to the dedicated and skilled work they did to produce these beautiful airplanes.

They are — Millard C. Boyd, Jon Harme van der Linde, Ed Morrow, "Dapper" Dan Burnett, George Hammond, Clare Rand, Mrs. John Fornasero, Paul Wilcox, Mrs. Earl (Adelaide) Prudden, Mrs. Will Vandermeer, William P. "Doc" Sloan, Mrs. Helen Hendrix, O. R. McNeal, Bill Wagner — retired V. P. of the company, and of course, Claude Ryan.

This book therefore is being written to help aviation enthusiasts, aviators, model builders, and historians to understand and appreciate the trials and tribulations of those who were involved in the early days of aviation, having to do with one of the most beautiful airplane designs ever to fly in the skies of our great country.

History has a way of being distorted over time as stories are handed down. This writer therefore has spent countless hours in exhaustive research to determine what really happened and why. It is a never ending process, and as long as I am alive and well, this research will continue. Although it has its frustrations, over the whole I have to admit it's a lot of fun and rewarding in many ways, ways not always seen on the surface. I suppose the most rewarding aspect of all this for me has been the wonderful family of aviation people I have met over the past 40 years. As Lindbergh once said — "Science, freedom, beauty, adventure. What more could you ask of life? Aviation combined all the elements I loved."

Having spent many hours as pilot in command in the cockpit of Ryan STs, I can honestly say that it is one of the nicest, most challenging, and yet most fun and exciting airplanes I have ever flown.

And I must add that due to the Ryan ST being so sensitive an airplane to fly, it has fine-tuned my flying skills to such a degree that I have never had a problem checking out in any other airplane, be it an early antique or classic or modern sophisticated prop jet type. I have often wondered if it would not be wise for our present day flying schools to consider having this type of airplane on their training aircraft flight line. I think if this were to happen we might just eliminate the ground-loop once and for all. Let's not forget what that rudder was originally designed for, the Ryan ST has proven that.

EV CASSAGNERES

Foreword

by William P. "Doc" Sloan

This book is about two airplanes. It is a book about two of the finest airplanes ever designed and built before World War II. And it is a book written by Ev Cassagneres, a professional pilot and aviation historian who is probably the most knowledgeable authority on the classic Ryan STs (Sport Trainer) and SCs (Sport Cabin), with some background on the Ryan PTs thrown in as a bonus.

After more than fifty years, the STs and the SCs still fill Webster's definition of a classic which reads, "Classic — of recognized value; serving a standard of excellence; traditional and enduring; characterized by simple tailored lines in fashion year after year.

❖❖❖❖❖❖❖❖❖

Aside from bygone myths — Icarus and ill-fated flight too near the sun — aside from daVinci's early designs for potential flying machines — and including the Montgolfier brothers' first ascension in their wondrous hot air balloon, the dream of flight has intrigued venturous men to risk their lives in attempting to soar into the sky and no longer be earthbound.

It is a far cry from Montgolfiers' ascension to today's unbelievable technology wherein man has conquered space to go on to the moon, sent exploratory missions to far planets — with aircraft that can exceed the speed of sound, can circumnavigate the globe with pin-point accuracy and can be flown hands-off from takeoff to landing by computerized controls.

The evolution of the Wright brothers' crude machine to the sophisticated aircraft of today has produced thousands of inventions for conquering the sky. However, there have been relatively few designs that have satisfied the individual dream of flight to capture the freedom of the sky. Before today's pilot reached the end goal of his desired proficiency, he began his training in a small airplane and will always remember his first solo — alone for the first time — and experiencing the initial culmination of an adventurous aspiration.

In pre-war days of the late thirties, a few of us were fortunate enough to experience the rapture of flying the classic Ryan ST – Sport Trainer. With underpowered biplanes or high-wing rag-sheet and tubing aircraft available for initial training, the ST entered the scene to become the forerunner of today's modern design.

From conception to production by Claude Ryan in 1934, the ST was the result of two years of design, testing, re-design and more flight testing until Claude was satisfied with the creation of an airplane years ahead of existing models.

Not fully content with the design of the ST, he simultaneously began his second creation. By 1937 with the Ryan SC (Sport Cabin), the transition from open cockpit to enclosed cabin was completed, again years ahead of the state-of-the-art. The complete history of that development and the struggles it entailed are both accurately depicted in this book.

Tracing the history of these magnificent birds from the first production through World War II and up to the present has been a monumental task. However, it is apparently not an undesirable chore but a labor of love by Ev Cassagneres. Anyone who has ever flown one, or even yearned to fly one, will find this yarn a delightful history of these remarkable airplanes.

My own acquaintance with the ST took place in 1937 as a student at the Ryan School of Aeronautics in San Diego. As a flight instructor after receiving my transport license, I became intimately familiar with this bird. As a fledgling neophyte I ferried an STM from San Diego to Honduras in 1938, using charts indicating "unexplored" terrain below me. Later, with the Army Air Corps in California and Arizona, my log book shows hundreds of hours spent in the front cockpit. During WW II, as a relief from herding B-24s, I was able to give check rides in STM-2As to Chinese students in Lajoe, in a remote corner of northern India. In post war years I found STs and PTs tucked away in corners of hangars throughout the United States.

Claude's keen insight to the future of aviation resulted in the design and fabrication of the PT series which not only trained thousands of pilots to fly, but contributed eventually to the successful outcome of World War II. Unfortunately, the Menasco-powered bird was the victim of hurried mass-production, and the Kinner powerplant was used for the bulk of the trainers during the war. While the radial engine was a reliable substitute, her beautiful stream-lined profile disappeared. A dancing ballerina metamorphosed into a somewhat stodgy dowager. Kinner-equipped PT-22s still survive and are a source of pride and joy to their owners, but those fortunate pilots who own the few classic STs still in existence will continue to know the ecstasy of flying one of the greatest airplanes ever built.

A Tribute

In an early memo from T. Claude Ryan to William Wagner, he had the following to say about his first inspiration to design a "Sport Trainer" airplane . . . "Bill, I read this story (about Jimmy Doolittle and the Gee Bee racer) with fascination. I, of course, knew most of the individuals and watched the air races described, except that last one. Incidentally, these and other racers of that period were the inspiration to me for the configuration of the ST."

The man who made it all possible, T. Claude Ryan, next to his beautiful creation, s/n 101.   RYAN AERON. CO.

T. Claude Ryan with a model of the Spirit   RYAN AERON. CO.
of St. Louis — where it all began.

T. Claude Ryan, at 74, in the cockpit of   TELEDYNE-RYAN AERON. CO.
restored Ryan STM, s/n 184, NC17360, May 7, 1972.

Introduction

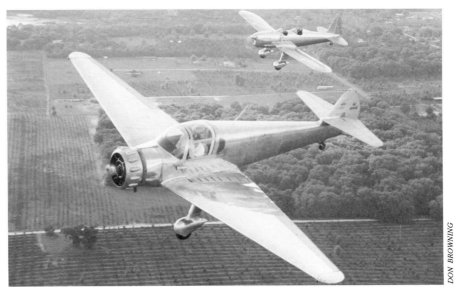

Beautiful air view of Ryan SC-W, s/n 202, and Ryan STA Special (STM) s/n 184, over Ocala, Florida, 1991.

When Claude Ryan was flying forest patrol duty in Oregon, he became friends with Millard C. Boyd, a young, slightly-built, sandy-haired engineer, who years before had built his own airplane and taught himself to fly. They met again in the summer of 1922, at a small flying strip near Santa Ana. It was not until one warm day in August, 1933, that Boyd and a friend, Will Vandermeer, also an engineer, met again. Both came to San Diego seeking a job with Ryan. They had just completed the engineering on a new airplane for Kinner Airplane & Engine Company (also known as Security National Aircraft Corporation), of Downey, California.

About this time, designer Ryan envisioned a new low-wing sport trainer, termed the "new Ryan", and desperately needed a full-time engineer. They asked Claude if he could afford to pay $200 a month for their services. Ryan did not think so, considering that would come to a total of $400. However, when Boyd explained it would be a *total* of $200 for *both* engineers, Ryan could not resist. It was still a lot of money in those days, but he was willing to take a chance in order to make his dream plane become a reality.

But Claude Ryan was a man with insight when it came to business ventures as well as envisioning a new airplane design. T. Claude Ryan, a farm boy from Parsons, Kansas, and son of William Marion Ryan and Ida Ziegler Ryan, formed the original Ryan Flying Company as a flying service in 1922. His original base of operations was a small field at the foot of Broadway, in San Diego, where an old Curtiss Jenny was used for joy-rides, and occasionally, flight instruction and charter trips. The next year he moved the operation to Barnett Avenue, where a hangar was constructed and the business expanded. One of his pupils was B. F. Mahoney, who eventually became a business partner.

In March, 1925, the firm added the name Ryan Airlines, Inc., and daily commercial passenger service was inaugurated between San Diego and Los Angeles — the first of its kind in the United States to offer year-round regularly scheduled passenger service.

In 1926, the U.S. Government prepared to award Contract Air Mail Routes to private contractors. A demand for new airplanes developed, and Ryan responded by designing and building the M-1 and M-2 mail and passenger parasol monoplanes.

Eventually Claude Ryan sold his interest to B. Franklin Mahoney and the company became the B.F. Mahoney Aircraft Corporation, although the name Ryan continued to be used in advertising and the aircraft produced were known as Mahoney-Ryan airplanes.

As an outgrowth of the business, one of the most famous Ryan airplanes was built in 1927 for Charles A. Lindbergh, and is known as the "Spirit of St. Louis."

With the success of Lindbergh's flight from New York to Paris, France, the company achieved international prominence as a builder of quality airplanes.

Ryan had a deep interest in operating both a flying school and aircraft design and manufacture. Joined in this operation by the dynamic Earl D. Prudden in 1928, they ran an extremely modern flight training school. While the financial depression was at its peak in 1931, the Ryan School of Aeronautics, Ltd., was organized. The corporate name was changed in 1934 to The Ryan Aeronautical Company and the Ryan School of Aeronautics continued as a wholly-owned subsidiary.

Contents

Chapter One

A Star is Conceived

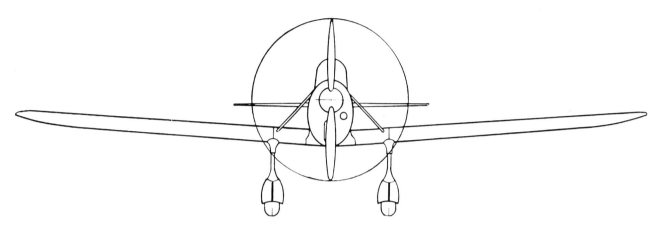

During the few years preceding 1935, the T.C. Ryan Flying School used Great Lakes biplanes in their training program. However, long experience had shown that these planes did not have all the qualities desirable in a good training machine. To overcome these deficiencies, the Ryan company decided to design and manufacture an advanced primary trainer of their own. Thus was created the Ryan ST or Sport Trainer. It would emerge as an entirely new design and become one of the great classic aircraft of the "thirties".

After the hiring of Millard C. Boyd and Will Vandermeer, Claude Ryan was not about to lose the design rights to someone else and had to protect himself against such a loss. He did not forget his unfortunate experience with the Ryan Mechanics Monoplane Company and the William Waterhouse incident and M-1 deal in 1925 (see the book, "The Spirit of Ryan" by Ev Cassagneres, TAB Books, Inc., 1982).

Mr. Ryan did not wish to get himself trapped into a similar situation. He drew up an "Agreement" in 1933 which read, "Memoranda of Agreement made and entered into at San Diego, California, this August 21st, 1933, by and between Millard C. Boyd of Santa Ana, California, a qualified aeronautical engineer, hereinafter referred to as 'Boyd' and T. Claude Ryan of San Diego, California, hereinafter referred to as 'Ryan'".

(Continued on Page 7)

(Contract appears in Appendix 1)

T. Claude Ryan and Ryan Flying School student posing with a Cirrus-powered Great Lakes 2T-1.

EXHIBIT "A"

SPECIFICATIONS

Name of Airplane: Ryan Super Sportster

Type:

Two place tandem, open cockpit, low wing, wire braced monoplane

Construction:

Fuselage — Metal monocoque (Aluminum alloy 17ST or 24ST)
Wings — Wood spars, metal or wood ribs, fabric covered.
Control Surfaces — Metal frames, fabric covered.

Motor:

American Cirrus, 95 hp
Menasco C-4, 125 hp
Kinner K-5, 100 hp, or
Kinner B-5, 125 hp

Dimensions:

Wing Span	30'
Length overall	21'10" (approx.)
Height overall	7'2" (approx.)
Wing chord	56"
Dihedral	4 1/2°
Wing area (including ailerons)	120 sq ft
	(effective area)

Weights:

Calculated gross weight	1,550 lbs
Useful load	532 lbs
Calculated weight empty	1,018 lbs
Wing loading	12.4 lbs per sq ft
Power loading	16.3 lbs/hp
	(@ 1,550 lbs gross wt)

PERFORMANCE SPECIFICATIONS

High Speed at Sea Level	142 mph	Service Ceiling	15,500'
Cruising Speed	122 mph	Absolute Ceiling	17,650'
High Speed at 10,000 ft.	129 mph	Climb to 10,000 ft. in	18.1 min
Rate of Climb at Sea Level	808 fpm	Fuel Capacity	25 gallons
Rate of Climb at 10,000 ft.	351 fpm	Cruising Range	420 miles
		Landing Speed	44 mph

(Original specs per T. Claude Ryan)

RYAN SUPER SPORTSTER
SUMMARY OF PERFORMANCES

	Cirrus (95 hp)	Menasco C-4 (125 hp)
High Speed at Sea Level	142 mph	152 mph
Cruising Speed	122 mph	131 mph
High Speed at 10,000 feet	129 mph	142 mph
Rate of Climb at Sea Level	808 fpm	1,220 fpm
Rate of Climb at 10,000 feet	351 fpm	660 fpm
Service Ceiling	15,500 ft	19,450 ft
Absolute Ceiling	17,650 ft	21,200 ft
Climb to 10,000 feet in minutes	18.1 min	11.0 min
Landing Speed	44 mph	44 mph
Gas Capacity	25 gallons	25 gallons
Cruising Range	440 miles	400 miles

(Original specs per T. Claude Ryan)

RYAN SUPER SPORT - TRAINER
SUMMARY OF PERFORMANCES

ENGINE	Kinner K-5 100 hp	Kinner B-5 125 hp	Cirrus 95 hp	Menasco C-4 125 hp
High Speed @ sea level	140 mph	152 mph	140 mph	148 mph
Cruising Speed	120 mph	132 mph	120 mph	128 mph
High Speed @ 10,000 ft.	127 mph	141 mph	127 mph	140 mph
Rate of Climb @ sea level	930 fpm	1,235 fpm	766 fpm	1,160 fpm
Rate of Climb @ 10,000 ft.	370 fpm	640 fpm	310 fpm	586 fpm
Service Ceiling	14,800 ft	19,100 ft	14,600 ft	18,450 ft
Absolute Ceiling	16,600 ft	20,800 ft	16,800 ft	20,200 ft
Climb to 10,000 ft. in minutes	17 min	11 min	19.7 min	11.9 min
Gas Capacity	20 gallons	20 gallons	20 gallons	20 gallons
Cruising Range	380 miles	328 miles	376 miles	300 miles
Landing Speed	47 mph	47 mph	47 mph	47 mph

COMPARISON OF TANDEM
AND SIDE-BY-SIDE SEATING ARRANGEMENT FOR
SMALL TWO PLACE OPEN COCKPIT AIRPLANE

	Tandem	Side by Side
Vision	Superior	
Comfort	More room for each psgr. No interference.	
Efficiency, Aerodynamic	Superior — by wide margin in combination with in-line engine.	
Appearance	Superior Lines	
Sociability		Superior

Suitability as Training Plane:
    (a)   Ease of getting feel
          for student   Superior
    (b)   Ease of Communication
          between student & instructor   Superior
    (c)   Suitability for performing
          advanced maneuvers   Superior
    (d)   Instilling self-reliance   Superior

This was probably the design just before it was finalized into what the first was constructed to look like.

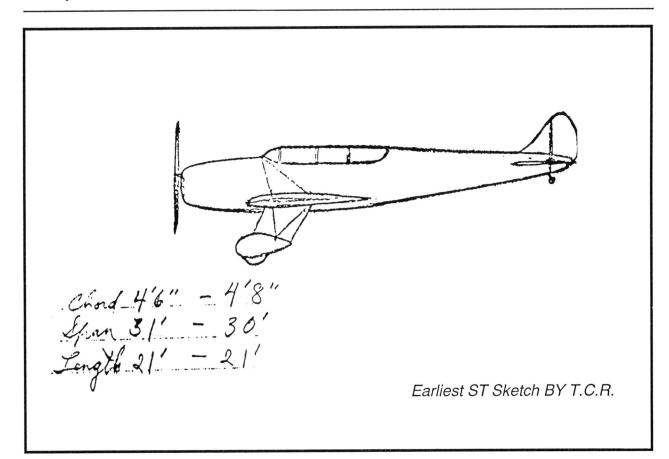

Chord 4'6" – 4'8"
Span 31' – 30'
Length 21' – 21'

Earliest ST Sketch BY T.C.R.

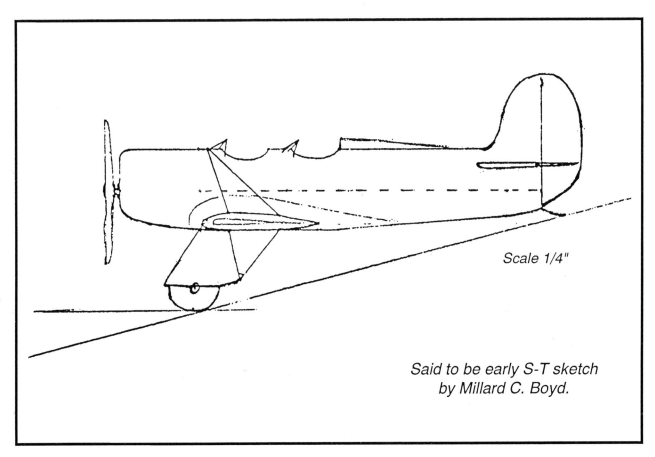

Scale 1/4"

*Said to be early S-T sketch
by Millard C. Boyd.*

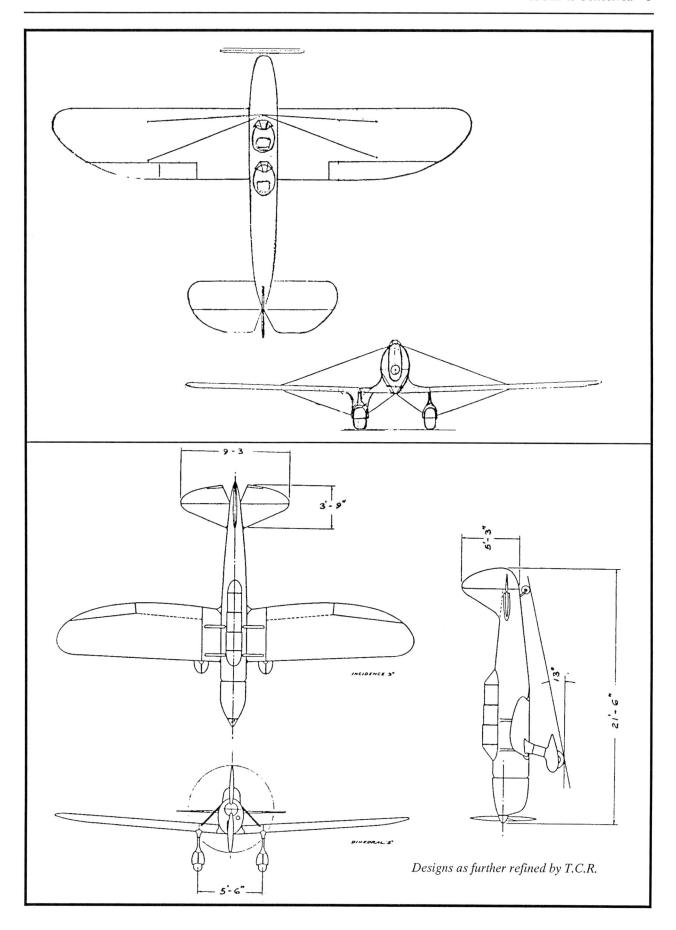

Designs as further refined by T.C.R.

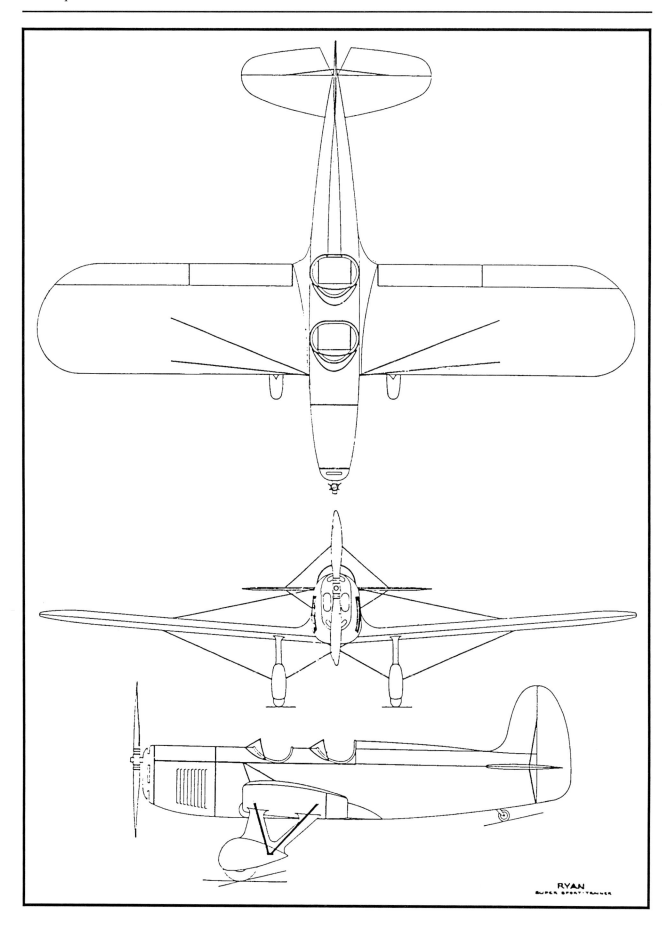

RYAN
SUPER SPORT TRAINER

(Continued from Page 1)

This was probably the last conceptual design just before it was finalized into what the first Ryan Super Sport-Trainer was constructed to look like. Notice the narrow pants, wider vertical fin and rudder, large radius wing to fuselage fillet, and short fuselage which was extended in the final production model or version.

With this initial concept worked out, the team was ready to begin the serious engineering design phase of the development of the airplane.

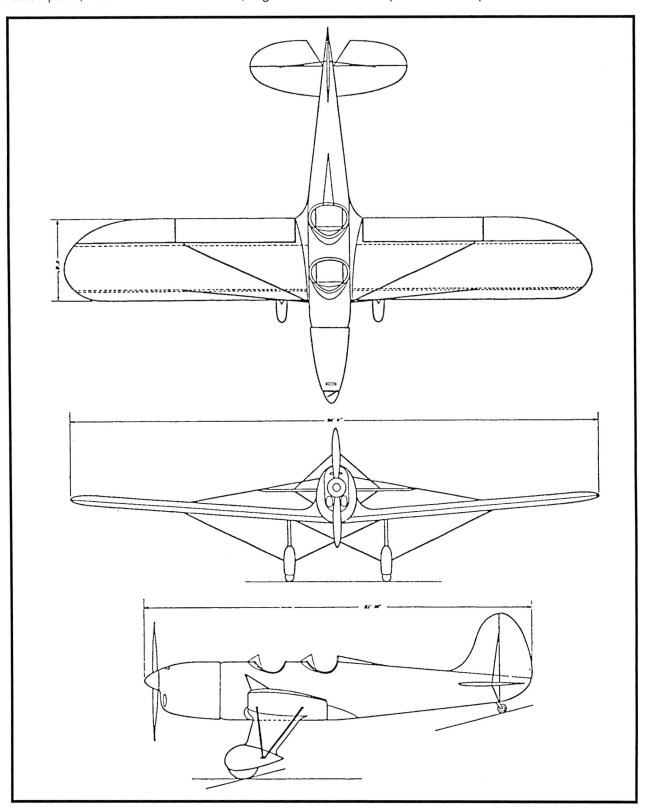

OPERATOR'S PROFITS *Soar* WITH **RYAN S-T** *

Sport Trainer

NC 16039

These Operators Know the Answers

Brown of Los Angeles:
"Took in $6000 first nine months, with first ship." Now has two Ryan's in operation.

Stockert of South Bend:
"190 hours and not a penny for maintenance. Soloed 47 students."

Demorr of Philadelphia:
"Never knew a ship could have such an appeal to students."

Lyon of San Francisco:
"Too busy with students to send details except to say business is beyond expectations."

Extracts taken at random from a few of many letters from Ryan operators.

The very features that make the RYAN S-T preferred by commercial operators make it THE sport ship for private owners.

Students Demand Modern Ships No Less than Airline Patrons

Imagine airlines bidding for traffic today with old time Fords or Fokkers. Silly? No more so than operators soliciting students and rentals with equipment just as obsolete. Many operators still fly ships 5 to 10 years old and yet wonder why those who have modernized with Ryan Sport Trainers get all the gravy. ★ Wise up to a ship with eye appeal and real performance, that's *modern* from prop to tail, has an all-metal monocoque fuselage, wing flaps, trimming tabs and dual brakes. Powered with a Menasco in-line engine it cruises at 125, races at 150; lands at 40 m.p.h. Maintenance is practically nil. In its power class it's a miser with fuel and oil. Stays in the air making profits because it's the kind of a ship *everybody wants to fly*. You get the idea. Now write, wire or phone *today* for our deal.

Ryan

RYAN AERONAUTICAL CO., LINDBERGH FIELD, SAN DIEGO, CALIFORNIA

Chapter Two

Initial Engineering Design

RYAN AERONAUTICAL CO.

From left to right: John Fornasero, test pilot; T. Claude Ryan, designer; Millard C. Boyd, engineer; Will Vandermeer, engineer/draftsman. Serial number 101, X14223.

As can be seen in the first sketches by Claude Ryan and Millard Boyd, the airplane took on a rather angular and boxy fuselage with predominantly straight lines. Actually, the first sketch by Ryan was a bit sleeker than the Boyd concept.

Claude Ryan, with a keen sense of the aesthetic, sharpened his pencil and modified these initial sketches to give the airplane a more graceful appearance to the basic lines. This was, of course, to make the fuselage more compatible with the streamlined nose cowl covering the in-line engine, as yet to be selected. A longer, more graceful, and narrower wing was also created.

Ryan, Boyd and Will Vandermeer worked without regard to the hour, changing and revising the many details as they went along. Vandermeer and Boyd did all the stress analysis and drawings and even made the blueprints. Boyd borrowed an old blueprint frame, the

kind used out in the sun, and together they made the blueprints, which they developed in the bathtub in Vandermeer's house and hung up to dry on a clothesline. Then they cut and folded the prints and sent them to the Department of Commerce for approval.

Any avid aviation historian or old airplane buff will agree that with some new designs often there has been a similar configuration that might suggest a possible relationship or similar philosophy of design thinking. Take for instance the Lockheed Models 10 and 12 "Electra" and the Beechcraft D-18 "Twin Beech."

One airplane that comes to mind while thinking of a Ryan ST counterpart is the fairly unknown and rare Cairns. Built in Naugatuck, Connecticut, from about 1930 to 1935, only five or so were constructed. The Cairns was a single-engine, two-place open-cockpit monoplane. It was all metal with a monocoque (inverted "heart shaped" section) fuselage, low wing (internally

Cairns model AG-4 at Bethany, Connecticut, June 7, 1936. Pilot is Gus Graf. Could be cousin of the Ryan ST. This ship also flew with the in-line Scorpion engine.

GEORGE COLLIER

braced) with a fixed landing gear faired in from strut to wheel. The airplane had a tail skid rather than a tail wheel.

One of the Cairns, the model AG-4, was powered for a while with a 4 cylinder, 110 hp, in-line upright, air cooled "Scorpion" engine, similar in configuration to the Menasco.

All of the Cairns have disappeared, apparently, although rumor says one may still exist in the White Plains, New York, area.

Now that the basic Ryan airframe design had been worked out, the question arose as to what presently- available engine they would use that would fit the sleek nose cowl concept. Ryan liked the in-line concept since it provided greater streamline possibilities and therefore much better forward visibility for the pilot, and, of course, the instructor in the forward cockpit.

The Great Lakes airplanes they had been using in the flying school were powered with the American Cirrus 4 cylinder inverted in-line engine. However, these had developed a bad habit of swallowing valves, so Claude Ryan quickly gave up that possibility and began to look elsewhere for the right engine.

Other possibilities were the Wright 90 hp Gypsy and the Menasco B-4 of 95 hp or the C-4 of 125 hp, known as the "Pirate." The de Havilland Gypsy was manufactured under license in the United States by the Wright Corporation, and would have been quite suitable for the ST. Because, the Wright company was located way back east in New Jersey, a bit removed from San Diego, deliveries and liaison could be costly and much time consumed.

It looked as though Menasco was the answer, for several reasons. Al Menasco had made an excellent reputation building specialized engines for small racing airplanes and was anxious to get into the more lucrative commercial market. The Menasco firm and plant was located in nearby Los Angeles, which afforded easier scheduling of deliveries. Coordinating service and engineering developments was likewise simplified.

It so happened that the Los Angeles brokerage

firm of G. Brashears and Company later handled the initial financial arrangements of several aircraft firms in the Southern California area during this time, including Ryan and Menasco. The overall financial condition being what it was, it was quite natural that there would be some rapport between Claude and Al in the matter. In reviewing the new commercial version of the B-4 engine and its proposed subsequent development, Claude felt it would work well. Financially and technically, the situation was ideal and the ST now had an engine.

They settled on the 95 hp B-4 and the 125 hp C-4 and D-4 "Pirate" engines for initial production. By early 1934, the design had been finalized and construction of the prototype begun. The first ST was the project of the students of the Ryan School of Aeronautics, led by a crew consisting of Mel Thompson, Ed Morrow, Bob Kerlinger, Bert Mathews and "Dapper" Dan Burnett.

Mass production of the little sport trainer was Ryan's goal from the outset. However, this meant assembly line construction which, in turn, dictated definite design requirements to fit the necessary manufacturing methods. Ryan's original specifications and general arrangements, dated August 21, 1933, were turned over to the capable engineering ability of Millard C. Boyd, now Chief Engineer, and Will Vandermeer, assistant Chief Engineer, for design on a production basis.

Mel Thompson was an artist in metal sculpturing. He would take a piece of aluminum, a few measurements from the drawings, and go out on the hangar floor with his hammer and other tools and go to work. The sheet of metal would look terrible for some time, but he would continue to pound away. Eventually, it would take shape and come out as a work of modern beauty, as if it had been poured over a mold.

Ed Morrow, a welder by trade, made all the jigs and fixtures, while "Dapper" Dan Burnett worked closely with Thompson in forming the metal and making up fittings and other final-assembly chores. It was the first metal-fuselage airplane they had ever built, so there was much to learn. The first ST was virtually hand built — right up to the day that Boyd cut the cockpit openings with a hacksaw and file.

Claude Ryan worked out a deal with Admiral Towers at North Island Naval Air Station across the bay to do the heat-treating. Claude would hop in a plane and fly over there for this work, the trip taking less than five minutes.

First bulkheads (formers) for s/n 101 fuselage.

Serial number 101 fuselage at start of assembly — shown in jig, being mated to center section.

Shows aft fuselage "cone" being skinned. This is s/n 102, NC14909.

The old Ryan Broughams were built of tubing and fabric, an accepted process of the day, but with the development of the stressed-skin metal plane for airline use, Claude Ryan was quick to perceive the possibilities in light airplanes built by the new process.

The ST represented rugged simplicity in design and construction. The fuselage was full monocoque in construction with only eight bulkheads employed. The stressed skin, of 18 and 20 gage 24ST Alclad, was riveted directly to the drop-hammer formed dural bulkhead rings. No fore or aft members, such as longerons or stringers, were used, except to two "U" channels riveted inside the skin, running from the upper engine mount at the firewall to just aft of the rear cockpit. These strategically placed members were designed to carry the loads around the cockpit openings. Except for the engine cowling, wing fillets, wheel pants and their fairings, the tail cone, and propeller spinner, the entire airplane was formed of flat sheet metal. In essence, the fuselage was really a cone and a can. As can be seen in the photographs, the fuselage jig was made up of 4" x 6" wooden beams to which the formers were clamped.

Most ingenious was the main fuselage ring (bulkhead #2) located just ahead of the front cockpit at the main wing spar and landing gear juncture — one of the few non-aluminum structural assemblies in the airplane. It was built-up welded #4130 sheet steel and carried the spar fittings as well as attachment points for the diagonal wing bracing strut, the upper landing wires, and lower flying wires. This assembly was heat-treated.

The entire engine installation, forward of the stainless steel firewall, came off as a unit, simply by disconnecting four main bolts and the engine controls. This made the engine completely accessible for servicing when the cowlings were removed. A modification of the engine bearers made it possible to accept any one of the alternate Menasco in-line engines.

The landing gear was the same type as that used on the Gee Bee racers. The main wheels were 18"x8"x3" Goodyear Airwheels with mechanically operated heel brakes (both cockpits) and Cleveland Air Oil oleo shock absorbers. The brake system was actually a disc (several discs) arrangement, quite similar to the New

MEL THOMPSON

Fuselage bulkhead #2 being fabricated.

MEL THOMPSON

"Dapper" Dan Burnett enjoying the coziness of the fuselage.

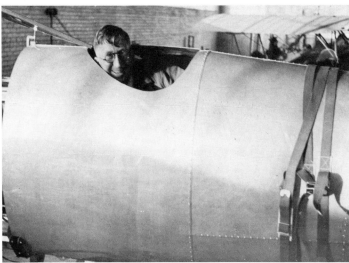

RYAN AERONAUTICAL CO.

Millard Boyd cutting out the first cockpit hole — by hand.

Departure bicycle brake system so long in use in this country. This writer has flown many hours in a 1936 Ryan ST (NC14985) with disc brakes and never had any serious problems with them as long as they were always kept in correct adjustment, etc. All wheel bearings were fitted with bronze bushings and were easily replaceable. A Goodyear eight inch streamlined tail wheel was mounted on a trombone type, rubber shock absorber. Later there was an oleo strut available as an option, and actually became standard on later models.

All of the landing gear fairings (pants) were Alclad dural. The first few STs used the softer aluminum at deep fairing sections because they were for the most part hand-formed. Production brought into use the more rigid and wear resistant Alclad in these areas.

Wings were constructed of solid spruce spars, 13 stamped aluminum alloy ribs, steel compression members and fabric covering. Ailerons and flaps were constructed with steel tube spars, aluminum alloy ribs and dural

First fuselage being assembled.

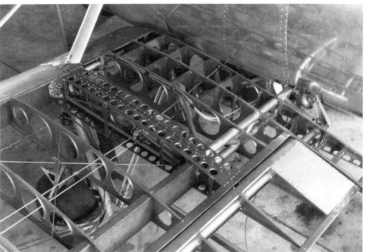

Stub-wing and wing assembly. Notice bicycle chain for flap actuation sprocket, right center of photo. S/n 101 or 102.

Right-hand stub-wing frame weldment assembly.

(Right) Serial number 101, during wing and landing gear assembly to fuselage.

First wing assembly.   RYAN AERONAUTICAL CO.

First wing partially assembled —(spars & ribs).

(Right) That unforgettable and beautiful landing gear fairing design and structure (later design).

(Below Right) Installation of clam-shell type wheel pants on prototype.

(Below) Landing gear assembly. Left side of left gear is shown.

Another view, showing right side of left gear.

Wing assembly department. "Dapper" Dan Burnett, shop foreman, lower right.

RYAN AERONAUTICAL CO.

leading edges. Both were, of course, fabric covered, as were the wings. Airfoil section was the NACA 2412, used throughout production. Leading edges of the wings were covered with 17ST aluminum sheet to a point well aft of the forward spar.

It appears that the early STs, up to s/n 117, NC14985, were designed with the bicycle chain and hand crank arrangement to move flaps. Twelve turns for takeoff, if the pilot so chose, and 24 turns for full down 45 degree flap for landing. Starting with s/n 118, the control was changed to a large vertical lever on the right hand side of the cockpit, which when operated would lower the flaps in three positions to full down, a maximum of 45 degrees. All later models had this flap lever.

The tail surfaces were constructed entirely of tubular aluminum alloy with stamped aluminum ribs, and the entire surfaces fabric covered.

ERICKSON PHOTO *via RYAN AERONAUTICAL CO.*

Serial number 101 showing wing with aileron and flap attached.

Ailerons in jig.   MEL THOMPSON

Good view of flap control bicycle chain and crank handle   MEL THOMPSON
in rear cockpit.

Elevators shown in construction jig.   MEL THOMPSON

Wing flaps in jig.   MEL THOMPSON

MEL THOMPSON

Tail wheel and strut assembly on aft fuselage.
Note bungee-cord dampners.

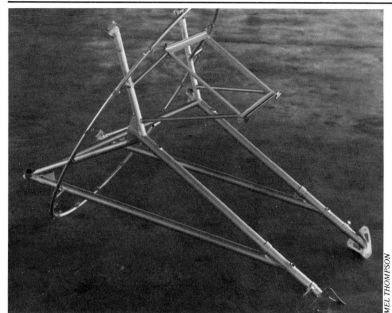

Engine mount assembly includes cowl aft ring and oil tank mount — early model.

Large experimental butt fairing. Ship could be s/n 109. Notice riveted front cockpit cover.

Later version of wing butt fillet. Notice also cockpit leather coaming.

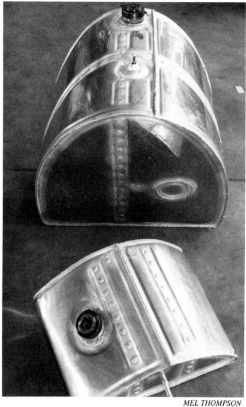

MEL THOMPSON

Fuel (top) and oil tanks. Rivets indicate location of baffles.

Government engineers supervised weighting with sandbags for the static load tests. No less than 715 pounds—approximately 200 pounds more than Department of Commerce requirements—were placed on a single wing rib. Loads exceeding seven and one half times the maximum "air strain" were piled on control surfaces without damage. The test airframe was loaded on its side and in the inverted position as well. Control surfaces were easily operated carrying the full load of sand bags. Static tests successfully completed, the ship was then ready for assembly and flight testing. It appears that the airframe used for these tests was s/n 101, X14223.

An optional and often-used feature, was an auxiliary fuel tank that could be placed in the front cockpit in place of the passenger seat. The tank had a capacity of 18 gallons, increasing range from 400 to 650 statute miles. This did not affect the total weight or balance of the airplane, thus had the approval of the Department of Commerce.

DON'T BE AN OSTRICH

... and hide your head in the sands of obsolete equipment. Students and sport pilots want modern ships to fly—ships of metal, responsive, fast, maneuverable; ships with in-line power, dual brakes, flaps and tab controls. If you can't supply such equipment someone else *can* for smart operators from coast to coast are standardizing on Ryan Sport Trainers.

The Ryan ST has *everything* student and sport flyers want. It's a money maker from the day you put it on the line. Our files are filled with such voluntary reports as: "has increased my business 100%". . ."it sells itself" . . ."brings new customers from competitors". . ."never knew a ship could have such an appeal to students." Better get our deal—today is none too soon. A few choice dealerships are available.

RYAN AERONAUTICAL COMPANY
LINDBERGH FIELD   SAN DIEGO, CALIF.

> **Sport Pilots: Fly A Champion**
>
> *Tex Rankin won the 1937 International Aerobatic Championship in a stock Ryan ST-A against a field of stunt specials. You'll be proud to own and thrilled to fly a Ryan. A dealer near you will be glad to demonstrate.*

Chapter Three

A Star is Born
Story of the Prototype

The crew that built the first ST, s/n 101. Test pilot John Fornasero in cockpit. RYAN AERONAUTICAL CO.

The prototype ST, s/n 101, licensed first as X14223, was completed early in June 1934, and thereafter was rolled out daily for engine runups and other adjustments. It was powered with the Menasco B-4 of 95 hp.

In the early morning of June 8, 1934, test pilot John Fornasero and the ST were ready for their first flight together. The airplane carried registration X14223, on the rudder only. Claude Ryan gave final instructions to Fornasero. John then just ran down the field a couple of times to test out the rudder and elevator controls. Next, he ran down the field and lifted off the ground about a foot or two to get the feel of it in the air. There was plenty of room for a short lift-off and landing. The next flight consisted of a gradual take-off and a long easy turn around the airport and a landing. Then he lifted off again and checked the lateral, longitudinal and directional stability. These take-offs were to the west-northwest. Eager and hopeful eyes remained glued to the pair as Fornasero continued to approach a stall and spin by pulling up slowly, kicking in a little rudder to check out spin entry conditions, etc. A 16mm film shown in later years revealed him rocking the wings gently from side to

side with ailerons, smoothly and slowly, and then with elevators, he pitched up and down a few times.

Soon he came in for a landing, made just as gently as he had the take-off. The small group of Ryan employees rushed out to hear Fornasero's report shortly after he landed. Sitting on the edge of the cockpit, displaying a broad grin, he gave his first approbation of their success. "She's perfectly balanced," he declared excitedly..."handles easily...the 'sweetest' airplane I've ever flown."

The airplane was equipped with the Story ground-adjustable propeller, which later proved insufficient, and was replaced with a wood propeller.

Later that day, he flew it again for more testing of controls and systems. This time he came in for a perfect three-point landing on the hard clay surface. This goes to show that because only tail wheel type (conventional) airplanes were available at that time, most pilots were very comfortable doing a three-point with such a narrow gear tread, which the ST had. Today's pilots lack that extensive experience and usually land Ryan STs, STMs, etc., on the main wheels, known as a "wheel landing." They even do this on grass strips. As a friend of mine once said, "you

Ryan test pilot John Fornasero in cockpit of prototype. First man to fly a Ryan ST.

SAN DIEGO AEROSPACE MUSEUM

need the education of the feet to do a three-point landing in a Ryan ST." How true, as it really is a rudder airplane when you are anywhere near the ground.

No doubt about it, Claude Ryan had come up with a winner. "Further tests will be made here immediately," Ryan said. "Then the plane will be flown to Mines Field in Los Angeles for final approval by the Department of Commerce."

According to Millard Boyd, Ryan engineer, two weeks later the airplane had passed all static and flight tests and on June 19, 1934, it was flown by John Fornasero up to Mines Field. The ship carried the "X" designation at this time. The Bureau of Aeronautics test pilot, L.J. Holoubek, asked Johnny to demonstrate it by putting it through a series of strenuous and exacting flight maneuvers to determine that construction or engineering

First take-off of prototype s/n 101.

RYAN AERONAUTICAL CO.

Showing off s/n 101 over Lindbergh Field, San Diego.

RYAN AERONAUTICAL CO.

changes would not be necessary. The inspectors would stand out on the field while the pilot landed it at 60 mph. The way they determined the speed was by having a space marked off on the field. Boyd continued by saying that he would stand at one end of the field while Holoubek stood at the other end. Johnny was to come in low and fly as low as he could between the both of them. Holoubek had a stop watch, and Boyd was to drop a handkerchief as soon as Johnny flew past. It was a bit crude but it worked. After all this was done with Fornasero at the controls, test pilot Holoubek would go through the same maneuvers all over again. They found that construction or engineering changes would not be necessary. It was the first airplane in months to receive unqualified government approval on its first test flights.

Claude Ryan flew the airplane back to San Diego and on June 21, 1934, ATC #541 was issued and the coveted "NC" license and approval was awarded to the Ryan ST. The X was removed from s/n 101, and NC was applied to the 14223, on the upper right and lower left wings. The word "Ryan" was painted on the upper left wing, and the slogan "The New Ryan" was applied to the vertical fin. The latter was a standard to be applied to all the production STs after that.

Serial number 101 was used almost daily as a demonstrator and then put into regular use as a trainer for Ryan school students. Meanwhile, an extensive advertising campaign was undertaken while the shops were tooling up for production.

Claude Ryan envisioned mass production right from the start, which would mean an assembly line technique, dictating definite design requirements to fit the necessary manufacturing methods. His original specifications and general arrangements, dated August 21, 1933, were turned over to the little engineering staff for redesign on a production basis.

New methods of production were perfected which included development of a recognized drop-hammer process. It promised to be an important step in their search for more economical semi-mass production methods.

At the very beginning of production, 27 men were producing one ship every second week. During that first year, Ryan had nearly tripled the size of the plant and, with inauguration of new production methods, had made it possible to increase production from 10 airplanes a month to 30 with but a slight increase in personnel.

Claude, however, was not satisfied with the airplane's performance. Design potential was just not being met with the 95 hp Menasco, and he was fighting increased costs and higher-than-anticipated production figures. He desperately wanted the $3500 market and with hopes of staying within this figure fading, the thought of adding more power or other refinements left no chance of being even close to the original price. A constant price rise eventually reached $6500 for the standard D-4 (125 hp) powered model ST-A.

It was not long before a buyer appeared and made it known that he would like to purchase the first Ryan ST off the production line. The second ST, s/n 102, NC14909, was nearing completion in the factory when a very unfortunate thing happened involving the prototype, s/n 101. On December 19, 1934, Sanford Baldwin, a 22 year old Ryan student from Framingham Center, Massachusetts (near Boston), came out to the field to fly NC14223, a routine flight just to build up time. It is thought that he had fainted and lost control after coming out of a loop which was entered initially by a "power dive." He was over the bay at the time, near and adjacent to the Marine base. After the loop, the airplane swayed from side to side as though the pilot were doing a "falling

Just after getting ATC approval and its "NC" registration. John Fornasero in cockpit. ERICKSON PHOTO VIA RYAN AERONAUTICAL CO.

Left to right: T. Claude Ryan, John Fornasero, Earl Prudden. Working on a radio gear for ST? Shot shows good detail of s/n 101. Notice dent in right wheel pant.   RYAN AERONAUTICAL CO.

leaf" maneuver. The ship was seen to dive straight down into the marshes. It struck the ground in a nose-down attitude. It actually crashed into the mud flats in back of the Marine base on Barnet Avenue, San Diego. A motor launch, carrying 25 sailors, put out from the naval training station, and sped to the scene. Sanford was killed and the airplane was a complete loss.

Friends of the pilot related later that he was subject to dizzy spells, and it was quite possible he had suffered a recurrence while flying that day. A few days before, Sanford was seen atop a ladder in the Ryan hangar affixing some Christmas decorations when someone noticed he complained of being dizzy. He came down the ladder to regain his composure.

According to eyewitness Ed Morrow, John Fornasero had told Baldwin, who apparently had a hang-over from the day before, it was okay to go up but not to "cut any capers." Morrow said the cowling came off and flew back and could have hit Baldwin on the way down. The accident occurred some months after the airplane was licensed and it had been flown many times by Ryan students up to this time.

Serial number 101 had a short life, but during that time it was flown not only by Fornasero and some Ryan students, but also by Claude Ryan himself. It should be noted that Howard Hughes flew serial number 101 on November 20, 1934, at the old United Airport at Burbank, California. Hughes' 20-minute demonstration flight could have been in consideration of a future purchase. In addition, this first Ryan ST was also used by National Air Race manager Cliff Henderson as the official scout plane, at Mines Field,

Los Angeles.

Undoubtedly the most important of the STs built, it was just about hand-built from scratch, and the ship in which many student pilots started their initial flight training.

S/N 101, X14223 tail section.   RYAN AERONAUTICAL CO.

Sanford Oscar Baldwin, Jr., in s/n 101, while a student at Ryan School.   EV CASSAGNERES COLLECTION

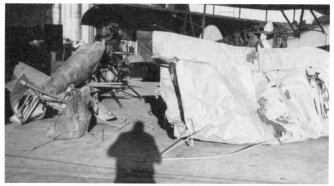

Remains of s/n 101 after accident which killed Sanford Baldwin.   MEL THOMPSON

Sanford Oscar Baldwin, Jr., killed in s/n 101.   LOUIS B. BRIASCO

EV CASSAGNERES COLLECTION

(Left) Serial number 101, X-14223 on rollout.

(Below) Serial number 101, a striking shot.

The NEW RYAN

RYAN AERONAUTICAL CO.

(Left) Serial number 101, 14223. Notice the "X" has been airbrushed out of the photo on the tail.

(Below) The prototype now with its new NC number next to another great classic, the new Douglas DC-2.

RYAN AERONAUTICAL CO.

RYAN AERONAUTICAL CO.

(Right) First flight of s/n 101. John Fornasero is pilot.

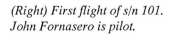

RYAN AERONAUTICAL CO.

Chapter Four

Production and Sales Begin

First two STs on the production line.

The second Ryan ST, now under construction, was s/n 102, NC14909. It would be used to carry on the program of cost, operational and production analysis. Claude Ryan flew both ships on several occasions and decided more power had to be installed. The Menasco B-4 engine was quite adequate for normal flying, but the airplane was mediocre in aerobatics, definitely not advanced enough for Claude. He felt that if the proper training of students was to be accomplished, a significant increase in performance was warranted.

The third (s/n 103, NC18910) and subsequent ST-As would have the 125 hp Menasco C-4 engine as standard (ATC #571). The ST with Menasco B-4 of 95 hp would be built on customer demand only. Eventually only five B-4 powered STs were ever built; s/n 101, NC14223; s/n 102, NC14909; s/n 104, NC14911; s/n 117, NC14985 and s/n 155, ZS-AKZ (South Africa). It is believed that the middle three (102, 104 & 117) were subsequently changed to the C-4 Menasco engine.

The first of several custom-built models was s/n 109, NC14953. It was listed as a model ST-B. Well known race driver/auto magnate Cliff Durant ordered it as a single-place sport plane with a permanently installed second fuel tank in the front cockpit, which was covered over with a special removable aluminum cover secured by Dzus fasteners.

The "New Ryan" was the sleekest looking airplane on the American market. It shared a sky filled, for the most part, with biplanes of wood and fabric. When it appeared, it marked the end of the biplane era and triggered the beginning of the sleek and streamlined monoplanes. Well-to-do sportsman pilots were quick to appreciate the racy good looks of this airplane. It was a mixture of old and new concepts. While wire-braced airplanes were definitely considered old for monoplanes, the lines of the ST gave it the high-performance look of the contemporary Granville Brothers' Gee Bee and Wedell-Williams racers and the new Boeing P-26 fighter of the era.

In the summer of 1936 it was realized that the widespread popularity of the ST, with the resultant heavy increase in factory orders, made it possible for the Ryan company to announce price reductions of $400 on the 95 hp ST and $300 on the 125 hp ST-A. The former prices of $4385 and $4685 respectively were then reduced to $3985 for the ST and $4385 for the ST-A; rather shocking when compared with late 1980s prices of over $100,000 for a beautifully restored and

Another view of the initial production line. NC14913 in the background.

(Above) Leonard Peterson, first customer, with NC14909 and T. Claude Ryan at time of delivery of first production ST to Seattle.

(Left) Very rare photo of Claude Ryan in cockpit of a Ryan ST during production years. He was making a test flight of first production ship (X14909) prior to delivery flight to first customer in Seattle, Washington, March 29, 1935.

Rare photo of s/n 102, showing an "X" on the underside of left wing. Also notice "chin" of nose cowl does not have cooling opeing for cyliner heads.

flying Ryan ST-A.

As a result of the reduction, it was announced by the Ryan School of Aeronautics that their famous "Delux" combination Course No. 5 (which heretofore included a new 95 hp ST together with complete CAA approved "transport training" at a combined cost of $4642) would then be available at a new low combination cost of $4242. The ST-A then became available on this same plan at the $4642 price which was formerly charged for the ST.

A significant production design change was undertaken on ST-A s/n 120, NC16031, and subsequent aircraft. On the earlier STs the wing flap had extended from the aileron inboard to within about six inches of the fuselage. As a production economy the flap span was reduced on s/n 120 and stopped at the

R. Cliff Durant in September 1935 with ST NC14953, "NX14953," s/n 109.

stub wing and outer panel joining line. This reduction in flap area had little effect upon landing characteristics of the later ST-As.

The ST-A had a good power-to-weight balance and Claude Ryan was pleased with its performance. Also pleased were some 85 or so immediate private customers, despite a constant price rise which eventually reached $6500 for a standard model. However, the quest for even more speed, power, and performance led to the ST-A Special. Ten of these versions were built under ATC #681, which allowed installation of the Menasco C-4S supercharged 150 hp engine. A slight improvement in high altitude performance was possible with this engine but for an airplane such as the ST, this feature was not a necessity nor in popular demand at the time.

One colorful individual who approached Claude Ryan was W. H. Irwin, who requested setting up a Ryan dealership-distributorship in his home state of Georgia. "I want to buy some of those airplanes, about 15 of them", he said. (Actually, he purchased only six.) Claude replied, "We will have to build them. We don't have that many on hand. If you could give us a 'good faith' deposit to help us finance production. . ." Irwin interrupted with: "I'll pay for them when you're ready to deliver." With that he reached into his pocket and pulled out $25,000 worth of Tel and Tel bonds and handed them to Ryan. "Maybe you can borrow on these," he said. Ryan, rather startled, asked, "Aren't you afraid to carry negotiable bonds around in your pocket?" Irwin replied, "I always keep a lot of negotiable stuff with me; I don't trust people much."

Then Ryan inquired, "But aren't you afraid you will get held up? Why do you trust us?" Irwin very slowly opened his jacket and exposed the biggest six-gun Ryan ever saw, and, looking straight at Claude, said, "I killed a man once." That's all Ryan had to hear. Ryan locked the bonds in the safe.

"I never got myself involved with those bonds where I couldn't produce them, because I remembered

that six-shooter," he recalled in later years.

Ryan did deliver the airplanes, by a six-plane formation ferry flight all the way to Georgia. However, he had underestimated the cost and just about broke even. (One of the STs in that group was NC14985, still flying, and formerly owned and flown by this author. The others included NC14914, NC14957, NC14983, NC14984, and NC16039, Tex Rankin's airplane which still exists in 1994.)

One of the best known STs was made so by aerobatic ace John G. "Tex" Rankin. He purchased s/n 128, NC16039 (through Irwin, mentioned above) in 1936 and by the spring of 1937 had mastered its aerobatic capabilities. On Memorial Day 1937, at the International Aerobatic Competition at St. Louis, he won the championship and held it until the unfortunate forced landing accident in a new Republic Seabee at Klamath Falls, Oregon, in which he was killed ten years later. The Ryan was well liked by Rankin, and it has always been closely linked with his winning of the trophy. However, in order to hold that title for a decade, he had to switch to the more maneuverable biplane types. For close-in, tight snappy maneuvers he changed to his more familiar red, white and blue Great Lakes Special.

Rankin had a flair for talking people into deals which were more to his own advantage than to that of the other fellow. He asked Claude Ryan if he could borrow an ST to tour the country doing airshows to drum up business for the company. He did not succeed in selling many airplanes and spent more time in the air than on the ground. Why he did not sell more, considering the seemingly impossible maneuvers he put the plane through, is hard to understand. This airplane was NC14914, s/n 107.

One day during that tour Rankin telephoned Ryan in San Diego and said, "You will never believe what happened to me. I was taking off to demonstrate the airplane at Detroit and, believe this or not, the rudder fell off." Then he attempted to calm Ryan by saying, "Now, don't get excited, the airplane's all right. I didn't crack up. But you know something, that airplane you fellows designed is so stable and so controllable, I didn't need a rudder. I flew it with ailerons and elevator and made a perfect landing." Rankin was so elated over the experience that he wanted to fly the plane just as it was across the country to demonstrate its safety. Ryan engineers made a quick design change to the inadequate rudder hinges, the cause of the problem.

Due to the obvious sleek lines and advanced design of the ST, several of them won movie contracts. One such movie was *Dive Bomber* starring Fred MacMurray and Errol Flynn, in which an ST-A was a British fighter. Its most notable cinema appearance was in the 1938 release, *Too Hot To Handle*, starring Myrna Loy, Walter Pidgeon and Clark Gable. Others were *Test Pilot*, again with Myrna Loy, Clark Gable and Spencer Tracy, and the 1941 epic, *Fighter Squadron*. In the latter picture, two STs were featured along with the Brown Racer and Travel Air "Mystery Ship" racer. Decked out in war camouflage, the little planes were used to represent the latest British fighters.

For those of us who lived during the radio "soap opera" serial era, memories of the adventures of "Howie Wing" are still vivid. Howie and his girlfriend cavorted from one situation to another chasing the bad guys in his

fast Ryan ST-A, NC17300. For ten cents and the box top from a breakfast cereal you could get a picture of Howie in his Ryan.

Serial number 128, NC16039 was often used in the movie flicks, one time with a "bump" cowl over the nose section to simulate a radial engine. However, sharp aviation buffs could immediately spot the difference when frontal photos would reveal the crankshaft and propeller a little high of the normal center of the radial engine.

FRED BARBER

NC14984 rear cockpit, October 1939.

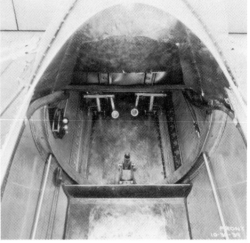

FRED BARBER

NC14984 front cockpit, October 1939.

UNDERWOOD COLLECTION

National Pacific Aircraft Show, April 1938, Pan Pacific, Los Angeles. Actual Hollywood-built model display of Tex Rankin's ST with manikins of Clark Gable and Myrna Loy. The life-size cardboard figures below are of Gable, Loy, and Tracy, lead actors in the newly released film, "Test Pilot." Rankin and the Ryan performed in the film.

*Line-up of new Ryans at distributor Howard Batt's facility at Clover Field, Santa
Monica, California, about 1936-37. DC-2s in background.*

Nice shot of "Tex" Rankin (front cockpit) WILLIAM WAGNER
with a student in NC16039.

NC16039 showing another view with C. E. GALLOWAY
"Bump" cowl used in movie. Note lack of spinner.

ST-A Special NX16039 when used in MITCH MAYBORN
*"Tex Rankin Airshows" flown by Putt Humphreys. Notice
long pipe along belly to carry "smoke" for show work.*

NC16039 with "Bump" cowl fitted for an PETE BOWERS
early flying movie.

DICK WOOD

Ryan ST-A Special while carrying personalized "Chichi Bu," ship had just landed in San Diego after flight from St. Louis (22 hours). Flown by Harry Marshall, March 9, 1939. This is s/n 188, NC18904.

EV CASSAGNERES

Christmas, 1941, crash of s/n 181 in Brazil. No one hurt on ground. Oscar Ferreira, Jr., pilot, lived. Notice military-type windshields.

RYAN AERONAUTICAL CO.

Another Ryan secretary, Orva Johnson, before flight with one of the Ryan School pilots.

RYAN AERONAUTICAL CO.

Ryan secretary E. Adelaide Smith, later to become Mrs. Earl Prudden.

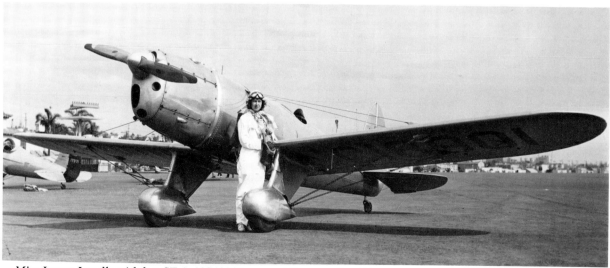

Miss Laura Ingalls with her ST-A, NC18901, upon delivery at San Diego.

TELEDYNE RYAN AERONAUTICAL

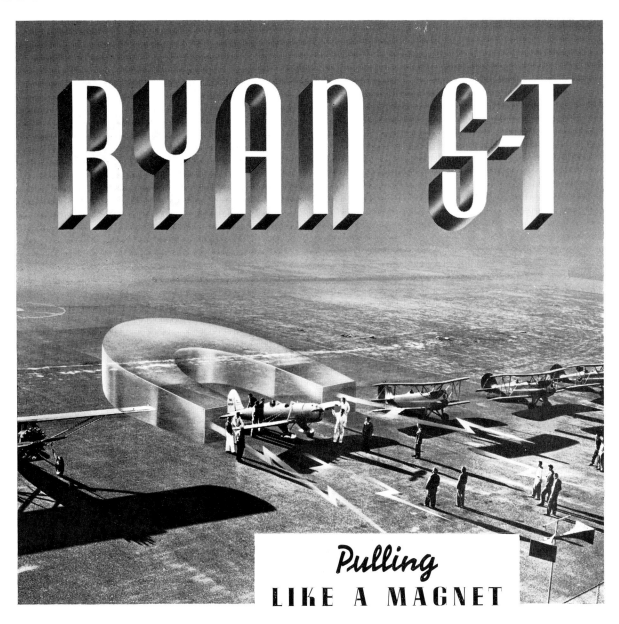

RYAN S-T

Pulling LIKE A MAGNET

Watch a Ryan S-T land at any airport.

As modern as the latest airline transport—fast, sleek and a delight to fly—this airplane has a universal appeal.

Without competition in its field since it was introduced, the new 1937 S-T Series now combines even greater operating and maintenance economy with its outstanding high performance.

The S-T has a cruising speed fully a third faster for comparable horsepower...modern metal construction of polished Alclad...quick acting flaps for slow, short landings...maximum visibility for pilot and passenger...and full equipment without extra charge. Write for complete information today.

To Distributors and Dealers : On the line, the universal appeal of the Ryan S-T is daily demonstrating its ability to actually pull in business for operators at higher than competitive prices. This is profitable business that speaks your language. Ryan has a new Distributor Franchise that is still available in certain territories. Write, or better, wire today for particulars.

RYAN AERONAUTICAL COMPANY • LINDBERGH FIELD • SAN DIEGO, CALIF.

BETTY LUND CARY   TELEDYNE RYAN AERONAUTICAL CO.   ROBERT LUPTON

(Top left) Betty Lund Cary and Brooks Huff on wing of Ryan ST-A, NC16041.

(Top middle) Barbara Kibbee, San Diego, Ryan School student, about spring 1940.

(Top right) "Bobby" Lupton next to ST-A, NC17349, "West Wind." A well dressed lady pilot of the day. 1937.

(Middle right) How's that for a public relations shot? A classic DC-2, a classic Ryan ST and a bevy of classic ladies!

(Bottom right) Women flight students. Left to right, Marjorie Towers, Adelaide Smith, Mary Dalton, Ruth Clark, Barbara Towne, and Barbara Kibbee.

EV CASSANGNERES

RYAN AERONAUTICAL CO.

(Right) Speed flyer Frank Hawks "trying on" a <u>new</u> Ryan.

(Below) Crash of NC17366, September 23, 1940.

ERICKSON PHOTO VIA RYAN AERONAUTICAL CO.

FRANK S. MASON, JR.

GENE MILIKEN VIA ELMER G. LEEHMAN

(Left) James Dods, killed in NC14952 in Hawaii.

(Bottom left) Diar Clark under hood, used for "instrument" or "blind" flying. 1937.

(Below) Serial number 355, NC9, at Tucson, Arizona, January, 1942.

ROBERT C. BAKER

MRS. DIAR CLARK

JOHN PAUL GREENWOOD

EV CASSAGNERES

WARREN SHIPP

HISTORICAL AVIATION ALBUM

(Top left) Impressive view of NC17368 over Virginia piloted by John Greenwood. Trim is red.

(Left) Rare photo of a sleek canopy design. Could be s/n 355, NC9. Further details unknown. Also possibly s/n 322, NC18923.

(Lower left) Last civil Ryan ST-A built, s/n 355, NC9.

(Bottom left) Peter Dana with friend and NC14910 in its final paint scheme. This is the transcontinental ship.

(Below) Peter Dana, as a captain for Northeast Airlines, about 1969.

NORTHEAST AIRLINES VIA BARBARA CIESIELSKI

Ryans in the Movies

WALTER M. JEFFERIES, JR.

WALTER M. JEFFERIES, JR.

WALTER M. JEFFERIES, JR.

WALTER M. JEFFERIES, JR.

(Top left) Shows professional movie cameras mounted on top of fuselage for aerial close-ups of pilot "in-action." This rare photo of s/n 128 reveals the letter "W" on the tail which stands for Warner Brothers Pictures.

(Middle left) This rare photo offers a nice view of s/n 128, NC16039, in "RAF" wartime camouflage paint scheme for movie "Dive Bomber," 1941.

(Top right) Two views of "bump" cowl used in s/n 128 and s/n 139 in movie scenes

WALTER M. JEFFERIES, JR.

(Left) On location in San Diego, California, for 1941 movie "Dive Bomber." Appears to be s/n 139, which has "bump" cowl and turn-over bar.

Here is s/n 139, NC17305, with "bump" cowl most likely in Paul Mantz hangar during service and repair, etc.

WALTER M. JEFFERIES, JR.

WALTER M. JEFFERIES, JR.

"RAF Fighter" on location in San Diego (North Island?), ready for battle — is actually s/n 139, NC17305.

WALTER M. JEFFERIES, JR.

Clearly shows s/n 139, NC17305 in RAF camouflage markings, for 1941 movie "Dive Bomber."

WALTER M. JEFFERIES, JR.

Shows s/n 139, NC17305, with "turtle-back" to simulate "RAF Fighter," a la Spitfire?

Chapter Five

Exported Ryans

First order of three Ryans to South Africa shown at Port Elizabeth Airport in 1938. Serial number
146, ZS-AKR, in the center.

J.W. TAYLOR

It was in 1936 that the first export models were delivered. Two ships went to Brazil in South America, s/n126 and 127, and registered there as PP-TMB and PP-TBQ respectively. ST-A s/n 132, NC16043, was shipped to Australia and initially registered in that country as VH-UZA, and later VH-BWQ.

Then in 1937 one each went to Australia (s/n 147) and Venezuela (s/n 165), as new airplanes from the Ryan company.

SOUTH AFRICA

Haller Aviation (Pty) Limited, a private flying school and general aviation firm, operated from Port Elizabeth and also had bases at East London and Grahamstown. Haller ordered six ST-As for training purposes in their flight school in 1937. During February,

D.H. Evans, rear cockpit and W. Healy in the front of s/n 169,
ZS-ALZ, at Port Elizabeth, South Africa, in July 1938.

JIM BASSETT

Pilot R. F. Haywood standing by one of the South Africa Ryans JIM BASSETT *at Port Elizabeth, 1938-39.*

March, and April, ST-As s/n 142, 145, 146 and the B-4 powered ST s/n 155 were delivered, followed in August by the shipment of ST-As s/n 168 and s/n 169. Serial number 168 had a canopy. At the same time, South Africa Flying Service (Pty) Limited, of Germiston, ordered an ST-A in order to keep up with their competition and introduce some modern equipment into their activities. Therefore, in May 1937, s/n 158, ZS-AKZ, was crated and shipped from San Diego.

When South Africa entered World War II, Haller was put onto a full time training basis at Port Elizabeth, and later moved to Wonderboom Airport at Pretoria, on January 1, 1940, where they operated as civilians, training pupil (student) pilots. About May 1940 they were again moved, this time to Randfontein where they continued to operate the Ryan, along with a variety of aircraft, including the prewar Gypsy Moths.

In July 1940 Haller was absorbed into the South African Air Force, and as of August 1940 Haller Aviation ceased to exist. At that time they were re-equipped with D.H. 82 Tiger Moth aircraft. The Ryans, along with other aircraft, were transferred to a pilots pool at Waterkloof where they were used by pilots in the South African Air Force (S.A.A.F.) while they awaited being posted to various units.

As these Ryans became due for major overhaul, or were damaged in accidents, they were removed from service and written off due to the non-availability of spare parts. As far as is known, none of them survived the war years, and none are on the South African Civil Aircraft Register at this writing.

MEXICAN AIR FORCE ORDER

Founded in November of 1915, the Mexican Military Aviation School (Escuela de Aviatiacion Military or E.M.A.) had seen many types of training aircraft in use throughout its history. In 1937, under the command of Lt. Col. P.A. Luis Farell Cubillas, a veteran flyer with extensive military action experience, the training aircraft consisted of six Consolidated-Fleet model 11A (Canadian Fleets), six Fleet 11-32s and a number of Mexican-built Azcarate E trainers known as the "Aviones Blancos" (White Birds), a few Vought Azcarate Corsairs and one Fairchild KR-34.

To upgrade to more modern equipment, the Mexican Ministry of War and Navy placed an order in September 1937 with the Ryan company for six ST-A Special (STM) trainers. All six of these airplanes were test flown in November 1937 by Paul "Pablo" Wilcox, Ryan test pilot.

The Ryans were delivered (in crates via train) on December 9th or 11th, 1937 to Mexico City at the military airfield at Balbuena. These airplanes were s/n 182 through 187, and were assigned Mexican serial numbers 1 through 6 respectively. They were used for advanced training. The Mexicans considered the Ryans as "nervous aircraft" that required an experienced pilot at the controls, so only students with 90 hours in the Fleets were allowed to fly the Ryans.

Of the six Ryans, four were lost in accidents in 1938 and one in 1939. Those were s/n 187, 185, 182, 183 and 186 in that order.

Serial number 184 continued to fly until about 1940, and was ordered sometime later not to be flown when the school was moved to Veracruz. Then the school was again moved, to Guadalajara Jalisco, where the cadets occupied the Hacienda Del Espiritu Santa, adjacent to the airfield. S/n 184 was placed in the courtyard of the Hacienda as a monument, and was a favorite place for the cadets to get their pictures taken with their girlfriends by the Ryan.

This Ryan remained there until after the war when it was bought by a retired captain pilot who took it to Ensenada, Baja, California, as his personal airplane. His name is unknown. He was killed in a motorcycle accident between Ensenada and Tijuana and the airplane was eventually purchased by an American and shipped to the USA.

RYAN AERONAUTICAL CO.

(Above) Production line of Mexican Air Force STMs.

(Right) Ryan STM s/n 184 originally from the Mexican Air Force, and the only one left. Shown somewhere over Florida. Presently carries registration NC17360.

(Below) Six STMs on the flight line in San Diego, waiting for shipment to the Mexican government.

EAA / JIM KOEPNICK

MEL THOMPSON

(Right) Mexican Air Force STM. Good view of wing tip insignia (red, in center, white and green).

(Below) Mexican Air Force and their newly aquired STMs. Pilots and supporting personnel.

(Lower left) Cadets of the Military Flying School, 1938. Tallest is Gustavo Melgarejo. Rare Photo.

(Lower right) Refueling one of the Mexican Air Force STMs, at Balbuena Airfield, Mexico City, 1938. Cadet Melgarejo in white overalls. Rare Photo.

(Bottom) Captain Gustavo Melgarejo by Mexican Air Force STM, 1938. Rare Photo.

RYAN AERONAUTICAL CO.

RYAN AERONAUTICAL CO.

SANTIAGO FLORES RUIZ   SANTIAGO FLORES RUIZ

SANTIAGO FLORES RUIZ

HONDURAS - GUATEMALA - ECUADOR - BOLIVIA - NICARAGUA

With the uncertain world affairs of 1938, the advent of a major war in 1939, and global war in 1941, the picture at Ryan changed, as it did with virtually all aircraft manufacturers. Assembly lines suddenly converted from peaceful civil aircraft to machines of war. Central American governments led the way in the purchase of military oriented STM (Sport Trainer Military) models. At first orders were impressive but small; six from Mexico, three from Honduras, 12 from Guatemala and one from the Defense Ministry of Ecuador in Washington, D. C. These were for military purposes, "fighter trainers" as they called them, and emerged from the Ryan plant as STM models. Most of these airplanes would be operating in the thinner air of the higher airfield elevations of Latin America. Thus, all were fitted with supercharged Menasco C-4S engines, of 150 hp. The Mexican and Honduran machines were flight-delivered.

Lt. James Harvey Gray flew an ST across the Andes Mountains from Santiago, Chile, to Mendoza, Argentina, at altitudes up to 17,000 ft., the first such flight of a plane in that class range. Gray later had this to say about his experience flying the Ryan on that trip: "I skimmed through the pass at 200 feet above the terrain. Mountain terrain is different, and that stretch was rougher than a cob. In the event of a forced landing, the railroad track was the only place no matter how high

you were. I was on a Panagra DC-3 once when it was rolled over on its back by the turbulence. The pilot completed a nice slow roll while I was picking the frijoles and coffee out of my hair."

Gray continued, "I also recall another STM experience in Bolivia. There was a German instructor down there at Cochabamba, a captain from the Luftwaffe. One of my friends told me the captain was spreading the word around that the Ryan was no good for operation at the flying school because of the low flying wires under the wings, his story being that when the plane sat down in the tall weeds there, it would flip over on its back. Of course, they did have a mowed landing strip, and the rest of the field was usable except for the weeds about three feet high.

"So, with this propaganda in mind, when I got there I landed in the weeds — just a dumb pilot who didn't know any better — taxied over to the mowed strip, and back to the line. Outside of having to duck about a half-ton of hay from the prop, it was a perfectly normal landing. Anyhow, nearly normal. I didn't mention that once I hit the weeds I had applied about 50% power to hold the tail down just in case. That took care of the only criticism the German had to offer."

The STM was basically the same as the STA-Special. All were two-place, although those delivered to Guatemala and Honduras had the front cockpit covered and an extra fuel tank installed, primarily for the ferry flight. The Honduras order of May 31, 1938, was the first time armament was installed on the Ryan ST aircraft. The specs called for machine gun mounting brackets and suitable synchronizing gears for the engine. The airplanes were delivered with the gun mounts installed but the guns themselves were fitted by the Honduran Air Force at a later date.

A similar set of specifications was received from Guatemala towards the end of the year. Their first six STMs, s/n 192 through 197, were delivered by and invoiced in July 1938. These were unarmed trainers. Not to be outdone by their neighbors to the south, a second order for an additional six STMs, s/n

RYAN AERONAUTICAL CO.

(Above) Appears to be one of the Honduras STMs showing machine gun mounting detail.

(Right) STMs ready for flight delivery to Honduras on flight line in San Diego.

RYAN AERONAUTICAL CO.

(Top) Guatemala STM, clearly showing their military paint scheme.

(Middle) Guatemala STM, single cockpit version. Notice American star-style insignia on underside of left wing.

(Bottom) Another Guatemala STM with only tail stripes and ship number 30 applied.

PETER C. BOISSEAU

PETER C. BOISSEAU

PETER C. BOISSEAU

300 through 305, was placed on December 15, 1938. This contract specified the mounting of two 7mm Colt machine guns on the fuselage, synchronized to fire through the propeller arc plus two free-firing .30- caliber Lewis guns, one installed on each wing. Suitable streamlined covers and firing devices were to be supplied also. In addition, the order called for similar gun mounts for installation on the six Ryans previously delivered. As with the Honduran STMs, Ryan provided the mounts and synchronizing systems, but the guns themselves were installed and boresighted by the Guatemalan Air Force.

One ST-A Special, s/n 199, was sold new on October 31, 1938. It was picked up at San Diego by its new owner, Mr. Gordon Barbour, of New York City. He flew it across the country and hangared it at Caldwell-Wright Airport, Caldwell, New Jersey. Barbour owned the Barvia Company, an import-export business, with offices in Paterson, New Jersey, New York City, and La Paz, Bolivia. At this time the airplane carried registration NC18905.

However, at the end of January Barbour went down to Bolivia, taking the Ryan with him. He had hoped to interest the Bolivian government in purchasing some Ryans for military training. This never materialized, and the airplane stayed in Bolivia until it was found on a duck farm in Cochabamba in the spring of 1980 by missionary pilot Eugene Hershey.

After a mountain of paper work Hershey purchased this airplane and shipped it to the United States, where it is being restored at this writing. Although the manufacturer's name plate is missing, there are tell-tale signs that it is, in fact, s/n 199. It was initially purchased with an 18 gallon front cockpit auxiliary fuel tank, a hand-wobble pump, front cockpit cover (with piano hinge), radio shielding, an Eclipse electric starter, instrument panel lights and switch.

NICARAGUA

In August 1938 s/n 141 (NC17307) was sold to Guardia Nacional (National Guard) in the Republic of Nicaragua at Managua.

The only history known is that it was lost in a forced landing in some lake in that country and never reclaimed. This possibly took place in September 1939. The Ryan could still be at the bottom of that lake.

CHINA ORDER

Getting back to the STs around the world, we find that an obscuring veil of secrecy fell over all military operations with the advent of war in Europe in 1939. Contracts and the movement of men and material became matters known only to high ranking government officials. "Name of purchasing government, type and quantity of aircraft not disclosed" was a standard news release. Ryan Aeronautical received such an order on November 15, 1939, from the Republic of China. The contract was the largest the company had received up to that time, in excess of $550,000. The order called for 48 STC-4 two place trainers and 2 STC-P4 single-place pursuit trainers. These designations were called out in the initial contract, but the eventual and official designation for all fifty planes was STM-2E. Power was specified as Menasco C-4S2, the "2" apparently referred to an uprating of power from 150 hp to 165 hp and actually spelled it out in the contract. There is no record of this version of the Menasco engine so it is therefore assumed it may never have been offered as a "new" model Menasco.

As standard equipment on the two "pursuit trainers", one .30-caliber fixed machine gun was installed inside the fuselage and synchronized to fire forward through the propeller arc. It is conjecture at this point, but it is possible that only the two single place pursuit trainers were eventually so armed. This same contract also granted manufacturing rights for the ST type airplane to be built by the Central Aircraft Manufacturing Company of Loiwing, China.

All negotiating contracts were handled through China Airmotive Company. This concern, incorporated in the District of Columbia, in 1932, was organized as selling and purchasing agent for the aeronautical

RYAN AERONAUTICAL CO.

(Above) Rare photo of Chinese STM-2E showing gun-sight and machine gun barrel in upper portion of engine area below oil tank. Notice short outside Longeron. Serial number 307.

(Right) Another rare photo of Chinese STM-2E clearly showing machine gun barrel just to the left of propeller spinner. Serial number 307.

RYAN AERONAUTICAL CO.

(Left) Extremely rare photo of China Ryan STM-2E, #42R, shown in camouflage, with landing gear pants and fairings removed. Kunming, China, about 1940. Possibly s/n 397.

(Below) Extremely rare photo of China Ryan STM-2E. Notice Chinese insignia on lower side of left wing.

SAN DIEGO AEROSPACE MUSEUM

SAN DIEGO AEROSPACE MUSEUM

trade in the Far East. They had been doing business with the governments of Nationalist China, Dutch East Indies, and Siam (Thailand). The partnership consisted of A. L. Patterson and N. F. Allman, U.S. citizens and Leslie A. Lewis, a British citizen. Contracts were usually made through Patterson, with Lewis representing the "seller", in this case Ryan Aeronautical. The group had a large warehouse in Shanghai until the Sino-Japanese War of 1937-38, when they were forced to relocate in Hong Kong.

Although these transactions were being handled through private sources at the time, the actual aircraft specifications and inspection during construction was being done by Chinese military representatives. The STM-2Es were completed and painted in unmarked overall silver, without insignia. They were crated, and the first shipment was dispatched in February 1940. The final shipment of Ryans arrived in the spring of 1941. They were STM-2Es, s/n 356 through 374, and 377 through 405, and STM-2Ps, s/n 375 and 376.

The situation in Asia was deteriorating fast as the Japanese continued their conquest of China. Upon shipment of the Ryans, China Airmotive was quick in routing them through Manila and then under a different flag on to Rangoon, India. It was here that Central Aviation Manufacturing Company accepted them and arranged transportation to Loiwing, in Hunan Province near the China-Burma border. Many of the STMs were assembled at Rangoon and flown into the interior by Chinese or other volunteer pilots. Most were laboriously trucked over mountainous dirt roads to Loiwing training bases.

Loiwing was a large operational base for China during the last months of her freedom from Japanese domination. It formed a complex of training, repair and dispatching areas and formed the seed from which the famous American Volunteer Group, the Flying Tigers, evolved. Located here also was Central Aviation's factory. As the STMs were assembled and flight tested, most of them were flown to Poashan, located halfway between Loiwing and Kunming, China, where the major portion of basic training was carried out. Other Ryans were sent to Chengtu, Ipin, and Kunming.

An interesting note to this author from well-known writer of "God is My Co-Pilot", Robert L. Scott, Jr., states the following regarding experiences he had while a pilot over there in the Air Transport Command during WW II: "In March and April or May 1942, when I did fly a C-47 across the Hump from Dinjan, Eastern Assay, India, to Kunming, Yunnan, China, with as I recall, two Ryan PT-16s (actually two of the STM-2Es) as part of cargo. They were in good condition and I recognized them very readily as I had flown the same trainers at Lindbergh Field, San Diego, in 1939, or 1940."

Enemy bombings were increasing in accuracy and intensity and it became impossible to schedule the manufacturing of the Ryan STs as intended. During one fateful day, the factory was nearly leveled by a bombing attack that left at least six STMs wrecked beyond repair — a few days earlier there were twenty of the Ryans lined up at Kunming ready for the day's training to begin. Due to a faulty alarm system at Kunming, the enemy bombers appeared and devastated the airfield. Fifteen of the Ryans were destroyed, the others severely damaged. By the summer of 1941, the Chinese were forced to resort to delaying tactics. The remaining flyable aircraft and related equipment was shifted to more remote areas.

When the Japanese invaded Hong Kong in December 1941, the China Airmotive Company suffered substantial damage and was taken over by the enemy. The stock of aircraft and supplies was confiscated and the private source for Ryan airplanes went with it. Leslie Lewis and his family spent the remainder of the war in a Japanese prison camp. During the last dying days of free China it would have been sheer luck if any of the STM-2Es reached the safety of India.

William Wagner of the Ryan company said that he was with Ryan at this time, and that they photographed virtually all other orders, but for some strange reason no photos were apparently ever taken of the China Ryans. At least none can be found in the Ryan files.

After exhaustive research by this writer, no records have ever been found to determine the full history of the China Ryans. Even photographs have been scarce or hard to come by. Final dispositions are sketchy at best.

Although the STM-2Es were "armed" airplanes, there are no known confirmed reports of how many were actually fitted with machine guns, or of any combat encounter with the enemy. Their history still remains wrapped in the intrigue and uncertainties of WW II lore.

In the meantime, and for more than six years, the civilian Ryan ST was selling well and had established itself in the sport aviation community in the U.S.

There was no part of the country that did not have at least one based there either as a rental at some fixed base operation or privately owned and flown by a sport-minded dapper young man about town. It was the "Corvette of private aviation." Most of them were owned by what today we would term the "jet set" or "Yuppie" crowd. To be "in" you flew a Ryan ST.

SAN DIEGO AEROSPACE MUSEUM

LES REISSNER, PHOTOGRAPHER

(Above) Another rare photo of Ryan STM-2E and apparently one of their pilots.

(Left) Only known STM-2E to exist. Taken outside of the Beijing Aviation Museum, about 1989. Has Menasco C4S-2 engine. Serial number 459. Airframe s/n unknown.

Already Enlisted for Hemisphere Defense

★ ★ ★

Back when "Hemisphere Defense" was a mere implication of the Monroe Doctrine, Ryan STM primary military trainers were doing yeoman's service in the air forces of Mexico, Guatemala and Honduras. As soon as "Hemisphere Defense" became a ringing challenge to the U.S.A. these modern metal low wing trainers were enlisted in the U. S. Army Air Corps. Constantly being supplied in increasing numbers Ryans play an ever more important role in the Army Cadet Training Program. Ryan Aeronautical Company, Lindbergh Field, San Diego, California.

CONTRACTORS TO THE U. S. ARMY AIR CORPS

As the favored primary military trainers, Ryan STMs fly the warplane markings of many progressive nations.

Chapter Six

Experimental Versions

Ryan serial number 180 shown on the ramp at Langley Field in Virginia. J.P. REEDER

Other than prototypes for other models, there were three ships which experienced some major changes to their airframes, for experimental purposes.

The first one was serial number 180, an ST-A Special, which was actually ordered new in 1938 for the National Advisory Committee for Aeronautics (NACA, now NASA). It was registered NACA-96.

It was delivered by air to Langley Field, in Hampton, Virginia, the NACA "proving grounds" for many exotic airplanes. Some of the experiments made

with the Ryan had to do with different aileron and flap configurations as can be seen in photographs. Some of these are shown in this chapter. Several experiments in elevator configurations were investigated, and then some steep approach techniques were tried. It was flown by many pilots on the NACA staff, and often used for familiarization fights and short transport trips such as to the Naval Operating Base in Norfolk, Virginia, just across the bay.

Closer view of aileron tests on serial number 180 at Langley Field. J. P. REEDER

One of a series of elevator tests for checking various chord lengths, serial number 180. NASA

(Left) May 1942 aileron tests show internally-balanced sealed ailerons in the presence of a balanced split flap on serial number 180, Langley Field.

(Below) Serial number 180, NACA 96. Internally-balanced sealed ailerons in the presence of a balanced split flap.

NASA

J. P. REEDER

J. P. REEDER

J. P. REEDER

RYAN STW

Another rare photo of serial number 338, NC18919 with a Warner engine. DICK WOOD

If this writer had a nickel for all the times he has run across people, often highly experienced Ryan pilots, who have been either confused or just not as aware of the inline versus radial engine types, ST and PT-22 series, he would be a millionaire today. Ninety-nine percent of the time they think back to when they flew or saw a Menasco powered ST and all the time, when they pulled a picture out of their billfold and it showed a Ryan PT-22, which was powered with the Kinner radial engine.

I wonder what would have happened to the history of these birds if Ryan had produced any number of these fine airplanes with the Warner in the original ST and STAs, etc.

Serial number 338, NC18919 on test flight. RYAN AERONAUTICAL CO

MEL THOMPSON

MEL THOMPSON

MEL THOMPSON

MEL THOMPSON

Pictures from top to bottom:

Serial number 108, NC14952 with landing lights installed on both wings. John Fornasero in cockpit.

Close view of fixed landing light on wing of Serial Number 108, NC14952. Dan Burnett checking wing dihedral.

Rare photo of serial number 109, 14953, with an "X". It was being test flown as an ST-B by test pilot John Fornasero before delivery to airplane's first owner, Cliff Durant, famous auto race driver.

Experimental ventral fin on an early ST.

Well, it just so happens that Ryan did do some experiments with just such an installation. Of all the Ryans built, these planes are least known, even to some historians. There were only two such airplanes so powered, and only for a short period of time.

It is unfortunate that they did not work out, as a Warner did look good on the nose of a Ryan ST, and was efficient. The timing was poor, due to the high demand for Warner radial engines for military training aircraft just before World War II.

There is some confusion as to the details of these two airplanes. The aircraft were serial number 337, NC18920 (or X18920), and serial number 338, NC18919 (or X18919). The confusion lies in the fact that serial number 337 had a higher registration than 338, and that they have been often referred to as PT-20 airplanes. In fact, if one looks at photographs of either aircraft with the Warner installation, it is plain to see the cockpit "flat type" cut-out is of the PT-16 configuration, with the longerons on the inside of the cockpit, rather than the outside as in the PT-20s.

MEL THOMPSON

Here is an early (1936) full-sliding canopy design supposedly for Canada.

To clear the air on all the numbers, that is the serial, registration, military serial numbers, etc., I feel it best to quote a letter from William Wagner, now retired, who was a long-time vice president of Ryan Aeronautical Company, and who was there at the time of this experimental work.

"On March 12, 1940, the Air Corps training detachment in San Diego accepted PT-20 (really PT-16, author) manufacturer's serial number 337, equipped with a Menasco C-4 engine. On November 20, 1940, the same Air Corps detachment accepted serial number 337 with modification to PT-20A accomplished by installation of the Kinner B-5 engine, PR-440-1, in place of the original Menasco C-4. Serial number 337 had Air Corps serial number 40-2401.

"Now we get into a fine discrepancy on s/n 338. The same acceptance form, the original of which I have, shows that this plane with Air Corps serial number 40-53 was delivered as a PT-20 on August 9, 1939. Going back to our PT-16 records I find that PT-16 with Air Corps Number 40-52 had manufacturer's serial number 320, while serial number 321 had Air Corps serial number 40-54. Serial numbers 320 and 321 were delivered in October 1939 and converted to PT-16A configuration in January 1941. The fact that Air Corps Serial number 40-53 was skipped and later used for No. 338 would lead me to believe, as is clear from the pictures, that this was an original PT-16 configuration, not a PT-20.

"On November 12, 1944, we were advised by a Charles A. Adolph of Macon, Georgia, that he had purchased serial number 338. On November 17, 1944, our service department advised Mr. Adolph, 'Checking our records we find that serial number 338 was an Army PT-20 and was scrapped by the Army in 1940.'

"I (Wagner) have come to the conclusion that 337 was a PT-20 while 338 was an older company-owned airplane of PT-16 configuration to which the serial number 338 had somehow been applied in March 1940, even though the airplane had obviously been built in August 1939."

However, as can be clearly seen in the photographs of both 18919 and 18920, there is no outside longeron visible. This author feels they were both of the PT-16 configuration.

In conclusion, it appears that s/n 338, NX18919 was issued its license on May 29, 1939, with a Warner SCA-50 radial engine of 160 hp (derated to 2050 rpm and 145 hp by a throttle stop), and that serial number 337, NX18920, was licensed June 21, 1939, with the 125 Warner installed.

They sure were pretty with the smooth plain cowl around that Warner, but as to how they flew there are no records available. Final disposition of either one is unknown.

Well known Jimmy Doolittle with Claude Ryan, standing next to one of the Warner powered ships.

Chapter Seven
Ryan ST Series Enters the Military

Ryan XPT-16 at rollout from San Diego plant.

By 1939, the American military began a buildup of men and machines. In June of that year, the Ryan Aeronautical Company received a contract totaling $96,275 for the Ryan YPT-16 trainer. This was the military designation for the civil ST-A-1 or STA-1.

To enter the fast-growing domestic military market, Ryan developed the airplane for evaluation in the 1939 U.S. Army Air Corps primary trainer competition. The Army tested it as the XPT-16, s/n 306. Its performance won a 15-plane service evaluation order, these to be designated YPT-16s. The Ryan ST-As had not been built in strict accordance with military requirements. In the redesign for the YPT-16s, the basic and familiar ST airframe underwent its first external appearance change. The cockpit openings were cut larger, down to meet the channel stiffeners. Addition of a turnover mast at the front cockpit windshield, a Bendix hand-cranked direct-drive inertia engine starter, toe brakes and parking brake completed the redesign and met the immediate military specifications. This was the first low-wing trainer to convince the Army to break away from their 30-year precedent of biplanes being used for initial instruction of aviation cadets.

Serial number 306 rolled off the assembly line as an ST-A and was assigned registration number

NC18907, which was painted in the usual places on the wings and tail. It was test flown on February 3, 1939, by Bob Kerlinger, and put into service as a trainer in the Ryan School on Lindbergh Field.

When this order came in for a PT-16 to be used for evaluation by the Air Corps, s/n 306 was pulled off the line, painted in the military stars and stripes, and designated as the XPT-16. Kerlinger then flew it to Wright Field, Dayton, Ohio. At this time it was powered with the Menasco C-4. With all tests passed, 306 was redesignated YPT-16, and 15 additional airplanes were ordered. The delivery of the 15 YPT-16s (s/n 307 through 321) under contract P05607, Spec. R-703-9, placed low-wing primary trainers on the Air Corps inventory. Needless to say they were given a fair and rough trial through everyday military-type flying. The powerplants did not hold up, however, under these daily demands. Up to that time, these were to be the only Menasco powered airplanes used in the military service.

Due to the poor service of the Menasco, the Air Corps was more or less forced to order 14 of the YPT-16s modified to accept an air-cooled radial engine. Ryan began experimenting immediately with several radials in the 150 to 165 hp range, but the Air Corps, for logistic considerations, had pretty well put their

DICK WOOD

Ryan YPT-16s in main Ryan factory at San Diego after a rough day of flight training. Typical scene repeated every night. Note small "classrooms" in rear of building.

Ryan YPT-16 flight line, at San Diego.

RYAN AERONAUTICAL CO.

Ryan YPT-16, Menasco powered, showing its ship No. 33.   BUD BODDING

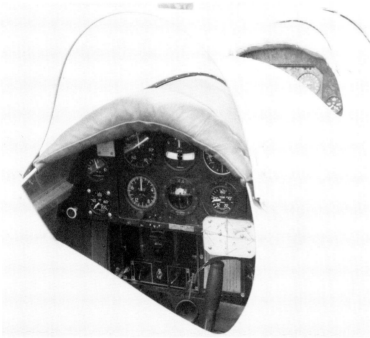

RYAN AERONAUTICAL CO.

Ryan YPT-16 rear cockpit, radio equipped. Notice lower right panel in white, old A-N navigation system layout.

approval on the five cylinder 132 hp Kinner R-440-1 (civil B-5 model). The modification program was completed by Ryan between January and April, 1941, and the airplanes redesignated PT-16A. This was done in accordance with Ryan Aeronautical Company's specification number 1199, dated August 31, 1940, and contract number W535-ac-16204, dated September 27, 1940. On January 7, 1941, 306 went through a modification to make it a PT-16A also, with a change to the Kinner R-440-1 (B-5). The fate of 306 is not known, but it is believed to have been assigned to some training detachment in the Air Corps.

It will be noted that during the manufacture of the PT-16s, s/n 312 was constructed and assigned civil registration NC18922. It was first assigned to the Ryan school, and carried their number "3" on the tail. This same airplane was used as a "PT-16 Army demonstrator" while based at the school during the war years and was finally sold in June of 1945, as a civilian ST-A to the Earl Henry Flying Service in Blackwell, Oklahoma. That airplane still exists, and is on display at the U.S. Air Force Museum, Dayton, Ohio.

Experience with the YPT-16s and their subsequent modifications had demonstrated the need for further extensive airframe changes to be incorporated on the next model.

PT-20

An official order (W535-ac-13316), dated October 1939, was received for an additional 30 Menasco powered STM models, carrying the designation PT-20. This was at a unit price of $6453 with the contract requesting the first airplane to be delivered in 60 days.

The new changes included cockpit load-carrying longerons moved from the inside to the outside of the fuselage, as can be seen clearly in the accompanying photographs. This allowed for greater access by the military aviator wearing a seat-pack parachute, which certainly can be cumbersome, not only during entry or egress, but in any emergency situation where a pilot had to leave the airplane in flight. This is probably the most noticeable difference from the PT-16 and the civil STs. In the initial order they came through with the Menasco C-4 engine. They also had a parking brake and adjustable seats.

As a result of the Kinner working out so well in the YPT-16As, 29 of the 30 PT-20s were converted to the Kinner R-440-1 (B-5) between September 1940, and April 1941, and redesignated PT-20A, and immediately put into service.

The Ryan serial number block 323 through 354, and assigned Air Corps s/n 40-2387 through 40-2416 inclusive, were used for the PT-20 series, excluding

(Above) PT-20s and PT-16s on training flight line of Ryan School, San Diego.

(Left) PT-20 over San Diego. Instructor Paul Wilcox in front cockpit.

Two PT-20s were briefly evaluated with the Menasco D-4 engine installation and designated as the PT-20B models. They were s/n 324 and 332. Neither engine nor airframe faired any better, and on April 8, 1941, the Air Corps ordered them converted to Kinner-powered PT-20A variants. They were actually converted to the Kinner R-440-1 (B-5) on April 25, 1941, for 324 and March 26, 1941, for 332.

When a radial engine was first being considered, the company built up an experimental ST-A or ST-K, by assembling it with a PT-20 fuselage, tail, wings and landing gear, but with military type (frame) windshields, and installed a Kinner K-5 radial engine. The airplane was given s/n 406, and assigned registration NX18924, and was more or less a PT-20A prototype to test the suitablilty of the Kinner engine.

Some fairings and the tail cones and wheel pants were removed from all PT-16s and PT-20s in service, due to the daily rough military-type flying and "green" pilots.

Following the military (Air Corps) change to radial engines in the PT-16s and PT-20s, and completion of the Netherlands East Indies orders (covered later), the slate was wiped clean of Menasco-powered Ryan airplanes after approximately 314 of these types had been built. The final production of the low-wing open-cockpit trainer concept was Kinner powered, not counting the much later PT-25 Ryans.

It appears that no PT-16 Ryans exist other than the original s/n 312, NC18922, an ST-A. However, there are 3 PT-20s still around — s/n 329, N9652H (manufacturers plate only), s/n 341, N17348 all complete and original, and s/n 352, formerly N69094 and now N14984 (papers).

(Right) Brand new PT-20 at San Diego.

RYAN AERONAUTICAL CO. & NATIONAL AIR & SPACE MUSEUM

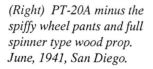

(Left) PT-20A with Kinner and full wheel pants, San Diego.

RYAN AERONAUTICAL CO.

(Right) PT-20A minus the spiffy wheel pants and full spinner type wood prop. June, 1941, San Diego.

PETER BOWERS

Chapter Eight

Ryan PT-21

PT-21s outside the factory awaiting delivery. Notice round fuselage numbers.

World War II was on the horizon, and the need to train military pilots was now critical, so the War Department put in an order for 200 Ryan primary trainers in September 1940. They were to be used exclusively for the expanding Army Air Forces (U.S. Army Air Corps) and naval pilot training program.

They were to be the most advanced refinement of the earlier ST (including PT-16 and PT-20) series trainers, in production since 1934. This would now become the Ryan model ST-3 (ST-3KR), which would eventually carry the military designations: PT-21, NR-1 (Navy) and PT-22.

Unfortunately, aesthetics are not top priority when the military orders hardware; the first and most important requirement is that it be functional and rugged. Beauty would only be a fringe benefit as the result of the first two. The PT series were not necessarily pretty (although beauty is always in the eyes of the beholder), nor did they have the appeal of the original STs.

Since the job at hand was paramount, and these new and fledgling pilots would eventually be flying high-powered military fighter and bomber aircraft, the trainer had to be less forgiving than the earlier ST series and more rugged. They had to be able to take the rough day-after-day military punishment with a minimum of maintenance and downtime. Not only did the PT airplane represent something similar in feel to a fighter of the era, but they looked a little like it too.

According to an interview with Claude Ryan many years ago, he said that in order to stay in business, he had to go along with the military way of designing airplanes. He really wanted to take the basic ST airframe and beef it up for the military, perhaps even spreading the landing gear out for a wider tread, etc., but the military took charge and came up with the design of the PT-21 and -22, and Ryan went along with it in order to survive. He was not in favor of the design they finalized, but went into production anyway, of course. Although the basic configuration is the same as the STs, there is no one component or part that is interchangeable with the ST.

Serial number 1000, in flight over Coronado, with Point Loma and entrance to San Diego Harbor in background.

RYAN AERONAUTICAL CO.

It was almost a complete new structure.

The initial design concept was to make the landing gear wider and more rugged in construction. This was because of the student pilots' habit of making rough landings as they developed the necessary feel of flying an airplane without the advantage of being able to actually see the main wheels, such as in a Cub; that alone eliminated the beautiful full-panted landing gear of the ST. Cockpits were made wider and more efficiently arranged to accommodate a pilot with a military seat-pack parachute. The longerons were again, as in the earlier PT-20, put on the outside of the fuselage.

Because the Menasco did not stand up to the rough military flying in the PT-16s and PT-20s, the Kinner radial engine was employed in the initial design. For a finer feel of flight controls, the ailerons and elevators were balanced. Because the original ST clamshell fairings at the bottom of the rudder would cause problems at times, the new design had the lower rudder area faired in with fabric, which apparently worked out quite well.

The military's usual equipment list included the fire extinguisher, map case, adjustable cockpit bucket seats, baggage compartment outside (just aft of the rear cockpit), large hanging rudder pedals with toe brakes, a hefty flap handle, complete set of dual instruments and controls for instructor (front cockpit) and student (rear cockpit), and fighter-type handles on the control sticks.

The prototype PT-21 was serial number 1000, and carried civilian registration number NX18925. It was never in the military. It was used strictly as a test airplane at the Ryan factory at San Diego, where it went through several design changes and configurations. The airplane made its maiden flight on October 9, 1940. Due to its experimental status, it was never issued an ATC number. This airplane was powered with the Kinner B-54 engine rated at 125 hp at 1925 rpm.

One of the modifications tried on the airplane was a nicely designed full and sliding canopy for both cockpits. This was actually proposed to accommodate the Canadian military who expressed an interest in using the Ryans in their training program for the war effort. The canopy was never produced (other than that initial one) and eventually removed from NX18925.

The next modification was the installation of a Kinner R-55 (160 hp) with a narrow "bump" type cowl, sometimes referred to as a speed ring. Speed was apparently not the criteria, but cooling was. Cooling was found minimally improved, so the cowl was removed.

Edo floats were also tried (about April 1941), but it is not known how well they worked out. This was most likely ordered with the Dutch pilots and their training scenario in mind.

RYAN AERONAUTICAL CO.

Serial number 1000 with a "Speedring" bump cowl over the Kinner.

RYAN AERONAUTICAL CO.

Another view of serial number 1000 with the bump cowl.

RYAN AERONAUTICAL CO.

Serial number 1000 with Lycoming IO-435 (175 hp) installed. Note radio antennas.

RYAN AERONAUTICAL CO.

(Above) Serial number 1000 showing the experimental Canadian-required canopy. Canada was considering purchasing these Ryans for their pilot training program.

(Left) Serial number 1000 on its beaching gear or wheels. Notice ventral fin below rear fuselage and removal of fuselage tail cone fairing. Floats are EDO model 1965s.

(Below) Serial number 1000 just off the water at San Diego.

RYAN AERONAUTICAL CO.

Serial number 406, prototype PT-20A cockpits.   EV CASSAGNERES COLLECTION

Then a flat engine was installed in NX18925, a Lycoming 0-435-1 of 185 hp, the same engine as used in the PT-25.

It is not known what ever became of old s/n 1000, but pure speculation is that it could have ended up in the scrap heap at the factory, or parted out for use in other PT-series airplanes. Actually, it could still be in existence stashed away in a barn someplace around the country. Airplanes have a way of living like that.

The second prototype was s/n 1001, NX18926, built to study the production standards and apply for the ATC number 749. The ATC was issued on February 16, 1942, long after the PTs were in production. This one also never became a military airplane and stayed civilian all its life. It was designated officially as a Ryan ST-3KR, and was powered with the Kinner R-55 engine of 160 hp. It was used at the San Diego plant as well as at Wright Field, in Dayton, Ohio, for testing. The airplane is still in existence and flying in California as of this writing (1994). Interestingly, it still carries registration number NX18926, but now has a Kinner R-56 of 160 hp.

One hundred Ryan PT-21 aircraft were built and were given manufacturing serial numbers 1002 through 1180, Army Air Corps serial numbers 41-1881 through 41-1980. (See Chronology)

Production and historical information on the PT-22, NR-1 series is not covered in this book, but can be found in other publications on Ryan history.

Prototype PT-20A serial number 406, NX18924, at San Diego.   RYAN AERONAUTICAL CO.

(Right) One-of-a-kind modification for exhibition work: PT-22 biplane, serial number 1644, N246R. Cliff Winters, in the cockpit. Shortly after this photo was taken he lost his life and this airplane was destroyed.

PETER M. BOWERS

(Left) PT-21 at Wright Field, Ohio.

U.S. AIR FORCE

(Right) PT-21 departing from Lindbergh Field, San Diego, June 1941.

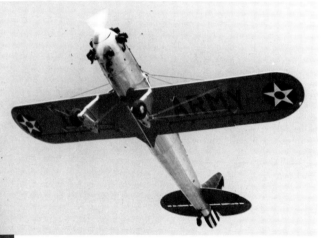

PETER M. BOWERS

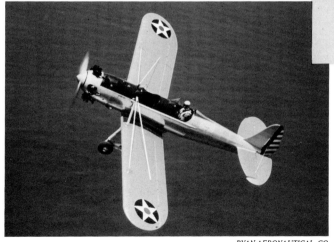

RYAN AERONAUTICAL, CO.

(Left) PT-21 Serial number 1037, 41-1916 over the Blue Pacific.

RYAN AERONAUTICAL CO.

Serial number 1001 shown with "NC" registration.

RYAN AERONAUTICAL CO.

Serial number 1001 somewhere over Southern California. Shown with its "NC" registration.

RYAN AERONAUTICAL CO.

NR-1, serial number 4197, on test flight over San Diego.

RYAN AERONAUTICAL CO.

NR-1s on flight line at the naval air station in Jacksonville, Florida. August, 1942.

(Below) NR-1 production line at San Diego.

RYAN AERONAUTICAL CO.

Chapter Nine

Ryans to the Netherlands East Indies

Final assembly line of STM-2s for the Netherlands East Indies. RO-30 in foreground is serial number 427, which was lost in the war.

RYAN AERONAUTICAL CO.

While the United States military services were squaring away the STs into PTs for their particular needs, Ryan received a substantial order from the Netherlands East Indies.

To understand the Netherlands decision to purchase these Ryan airplanes built in the United States, we must dig into the history of their military situation with regard to the threat of Japan.

It was in the late 1930s when Japanese expansionist intentions became clearer. Defense authorities in the Netherlands East Indies realized that war with Japan would ultimately be unavoidable. For many years, they realized that Holland could never come to the aid of her colonies, but would have to rely on her British or American allies for help.

The air defense of the East Indies, an immense area as large as Europe, posed many problems. The Royal Netherlands Indies Army (K.N.I.L.) had an Air Division, which was created in 1915, but this was only a modest force and up to 1935, was compelled to rely

on the bare minimums of pilots and aircraft. Its strength, including reserves and training types, never exceeded sixty to seventy aircraft. The maximum number of pilots serving with the Air Division was 23. The Army's principal task at the time was to maintain internal order, although it was also charged with the defense of the naval bases at Surabaja and Tandjong Prior, as well as the oil fields of Trakan and Balikpapan. The main job of defending the archipeligo in the event of war was the responsibility of the Navy.

The East Indies defense staff decided that large numbers of modern aircraft were necessary to counter the threat emanating from Japan. The best method of defending this vast territory was attack. The need, therefore, was for a fleet of bombers to be dispatched on short notice, i.e. ready and tested aircraft. If they placed the contract with the Fokker aircraft factory in Holland, time would be lost in designing, testing and constructing new aircraft. Therefore, they chose the Martin B-10 twin-engined bomber to be supplied "off

STM-2s for the Netherlands East Indies on the production line. RO-45, serial number 442, lower left of photo.

RYAN AERONAUTICAL CO.

the shelf."

For the training program, prior to 1940, more than 35 (possibly 45) Koolhoven FK-51 biplane trainers (later employed on observation and liaison duties) and 12 twin-engined Lockheed 12s for training bomber crews were ordered.

In March, 1939, on the occasion of its 25th birthday, the Air Division was renamed Military Aviation of the Royal Netherlands Indies Army (M.L.-K.N.I.L.) and was given a more independent status.

The tension in the Pacific through ever-more demanding Japanese claims on oil and rubber exports intensified, so the basic Ryan ST design played a very important part in the training of pilots to meet this new onslaught. The little silver trainers were to be used for primary, basic, advanced, and instrument flying, combined. Student aviators would go directly from these ships into the Koolhoven FK-51 or right into multi-engine equipment.

In a letter dated June 20, 1940, the N.E.I. Army requested purchase of 40 STM-2 aircraft. These STM-2 airframes were basically the same as the PT-20 and STA Special, ATC #681. This first order was placed before the system of Purchase Negotiation Requests came into force. (Ryan contract numbers are not known.) The first 64 Ryans were exported under Export License No. 2906, for a total of $782,868 issued before August 21, 1940.

The STM-2 was primarily designed for military training. It made its appearance with numerous new refinements in design and construction, all of which were made to provide greater comfort for the pilot,

increase efficiency in giving flight instruction and simplify and facilitate maintenance.

Many of the improvements were the direct result of the extensive service testing they (PT-16 and PT-20) had received during previous months at Wright Field, Dayton, Ohio, and at the Air Corps civilian training detachment at the Ryan School of Aeronautics, where a fleet of the STs and STAs had been in operation.

The principal change in external appearance was the placing of the upper longerons around the cockpits on the outside of the fuselage skin, instead of internally as was the previous practice. By making this change in longeron location, and by increasing the size of the cockpit cut-outs, the cockpit was made considerably larger, providing much easier entrance and exit (egress) for both student and instructor. The length inside the cockpits was also increased and instrument panels were set farther forward.

Efficiency of the airplane for training purposes had been improved by making the parachute-type seats adjustable to accommodate different pilot physical sizes, and by providing toe-operated brakes in both cockpits, as was the practice in military aircraft of the time. Positions of both seats were adjustable vertically and longitudinally. A parking brake, operated from the rear cockpit, was another added feature.

Wing walks were installed on both wing roots, instead of only on the left side as in the civilian model. The elevator tabs were now operated by a crank-type control with an indicator installed in both cockpits, replacing the "drag wire" (or hand held open cable)

Serial number 409, STM-2 over Southern California, for the Netherlands East Indies Army. RYAN AERONAUTICAL CO.

previously used. This made for easier and more sensitive adjustment.

The tail wheel was made steerable through 45 degrees on each side, then became full swiveling. The rudder and tail wheel were so rigged that should the latter be damaged, operation of the rudder would remain positive.

Other important changes included the installation, forward of the front cockpit, of a nose-over post attached to the main steel bulkhead (No. 2); new-type throttle controls combining the spark and mixture controls which were previously on the instrument panel; hand-holds on the wing tips to facilitate handling of the airplane on the ground and in the hangar; longer, military-type sticks; reinforced nose cowling; the installation of Dzus fasteners for the removal of the inspection sections of the engine cowling; and improved-type front cockpit flap control.

Along with the Ryan company refinements were improvements by the Menasco company. Provision was made for the installation of either the Menasco C-4 in-line 125 hp engine, or the supercharged C-4S of 150 hp. Steel cylinders were provided for the engine instead of the cast iron type previously installed. New cam follower guides and redesigned rocker arm assemblies, together with other minor changes, assured longer service between overhauls and reduced powerplant maintenance.

The wire-braced wings had spruce spars, aluminum alloy ribs and fabric covering (linen). The landing gear carried the ever-popular and aesthetically appealing fully-faired-in wheel pants, like their civilian counterparts.

That first group of airplanes were s/n 407 through 446 (RO-10 to RO-49). A second batch of 20 airplanes, s/n 495 through 514 (RO-50 to RO-69), were built and shipped during the month of February 1941, for a total of 60 aircraft up to that point.

The actual order was placed by the Netherlands East Indies Government. The Ryans were to be operated in Java by the Netherlands East Indies Air Arm, named (in Dutch) "Wapen der Militaire Luchtvaart van het Koninkiijk (Royal) Nederlands Indisch Leger," or "ML" for short, actually the N.E.I. Army. The Navy versions (STM-S2, which we will get into later) were to be operated by the Netherlands Naval Air Service, named (in Dutch) "Marine Luchtvaart Dienst," or "MLD" for short.

The first of the STM-2s were ordered to be equipped with Menasco C-4S "Pirate" supercharged 150 hp engines. They ordered the Army ships (s/n 407 thr 446) first, then lent four of them (RO-20,s/n 417; RO-28, s/n 425; RO-30,s/n 427; RO-43, s/n 440) to the Navy, on November 29, 1940. The Navy returned them to the Army on February 11, 1941.

The first group of STM-2s were shipped to the Pilots and Observers School (Army Primary Flying School) at the Kalidjati Air Base to the north of Bandung in Western Java. These ships replaced the Koolhoven FK-51s as basic trainers. Kalidjati had been the first air base of the M.L. — K.N.I.L., but in 1931, it had been closed because of a poor financial situation.

From about July 1, 1939, Kiladjati was to be the base for the Pilots School as the proximity of Bandung city to Andir Air Base resulted in too many complaints because of the noise produced by student aircraft. The school was stationed there from July, 1936, until December 5, 1941. On that last day the school was temporarily closed.

While these Ryans were operated at Kalidjati, they were seen in their all-silver color. Several or all of the six fighter squadrons had one Ryan each to enable each squadron leader to test his pilots if he doubted their flight capabilities.

Japanese military might was slowly moving into the South Pacific area and by mid-year of 1941 threatened to engulf all nations as far down-under as Australia. It was an extremely precarious period and military operations were being conducted under unorthodox conditions and unbelievable handicaps.

On January 31, 1942, some new classes of pupils were taken in at Kalidjati. Just a few days later, the Kalidjati Airbase was badly needed as an operational base, so the school was sent to the new Tasikmalaja Airfield that had been completed in January. As was expected, the situation would not permit quiet circumstances for the flight school, so on January 10, 1942, it was decided to evacuate the students and instructors to Melbourne, Australia.

After Holland went to war with Germany, the movements of all merchant ships were observed carefully. The Navy had actually ordered 48 STM-2s and STM-S2s. The first 12 naval Ryans were shipped from Los Angeles on November 18, 1940, on the SS Hoegh Silver Dawn and put ashore in Surabaja Harbor on January 3, 1941. An additional eight left on December 7, 1940, on the MS Java, with four more on MS Klipfontein on December 21, 1940.

These aircraft were actually built in the following sequence: 18 in November 1940, 12 in December 1940, and 18 in January 1941. They were serial numbers 447 through 494 (S-11 to S-58) for a total of 48.

Both land and sea versions of these Ryans went to the Naval Air Service (MLD), and were test flown on January 17, 1941 (presumably, unpacking and reassembling lasted two weeks). Most of the STM-S2 seaplane versions operated at Morokembangan, Surabaja (known as Soerabaja in Dutch), a naval air base. They used the Ryans to train future Netherlands pilots of the Do-24 flying boat and PBY Catalinas. American instructors stationed there talked of it as "Little Pensacola." The first two American instructors that arrived were Mr. Reed and a Mr. Eddy. Others were John Russel and Killiam Hardy. These instructor pilots spent one year there to train Dutch as well as Chinese and Javanese aviators.

Although training was the main duty of the Ryans, when the war got hot in the area, they were constantly being dispersed and used in other roles. The airplanes were pressed into service as reconnaissance aircraft and to supply remote outposts or patrol ships. It was not unusual for the pilots to strap a five-gallon fuel tank in the front cockpit and go out on a long coastal patrol. When the fuel became low the pilot would land at a convenient clearing or inlet, refuel the ship and resume his flight. During air raids the Ryans would be hidden under palm leaves and the seaplanes flown to flooded rice paddies which were often used as auxiliary airfields. Several of the Ryan seaplanes were sent to Borneo to perform harbor patrol duties.

There have been popular but erroneous reports that the Dutch Ryans were armed or field modified to carry a machine gun under the engine cowl. There is no conclusive evidence or proof or even reliable verbal reports that this feature was ever undertaken either by the Ryan company or the Netherlands Air Force. Some of the pilots were so confident in the STM's maneuverability that in all sincerity, they wanted to arm them, but this was never done.

The naval STM-2 Ryans later were based at Madioen (Madiun) in eastern Java. This was known as the Maospati Airfield, near Madiun. They were sent there at the beginning of January 1942, for safety. The 50-mile ferry flight to Maospati Airfield was not without incident, when a few of the students managed to run out of fuel because of poor navigation techniques. They made forced landings, as a result, in "sewahs" (rice paddies). However, none of the pilots received any injuries in spite of several turnovers.

There are a number of reports involving the agile Ryans serving with the Dutch colonial military services. Several were caught or chased by Japanese aircraft while on training or reconnaissance flights; some

STM-S2, serial number 471, over Java.   MINISTERIE VAN DEFENSIE MARINE (HOLLAND)
via H.J. BROEKHUIZEN

STM-2, serial number 487, in flight over San Diego. Ship built for the Netherlands East Indies Navy.

RYAN AERONAUTICAL CO.

managed to get back to their base safely, while others were shot down.

One bizarre flight took place and would have to be classified as sheer heroism. With so many Japanese aircraft constantly flying over the Surabaja Naval Air Base by late summer of 1942, the Dutch position in the East Indies became untenable. Most of the remaining Ryan airplanes were disassembled and put aboard ships bound for the safety of Australia. A few days before the final evacuation of Java, a native Javanese aviator, whose wife had been killed in a Japanese bombing attack, took a Ryan up to revenge his loss. Knowing an enemy attack was imminent, he managed to get airborne in time to find the incoming fighters and bombers and coerced one of the airplanes to "chase me." When the situation was just right, the Javanese deliberately pulled up into or possibly dove into his pursuer. The two entangled airplanes plummeted into the sea.

Some seaplane version Ryans (STM-S2) were lost during student-pilot solo-training flights. They were unarmed seaplanes, and, of course, vulnerable to Japanese attack. They had to depend entirely on their maneuverability in order to escape any on-slaught. Many times the little ships came back home with bullet holes throughout the structure, and even some parts shot away.

One case involved U.S. Navy Lt. Earl Lee, a flight instructor, when he had an experience while flying over Surabaja Bay. He had a student in the rear cockpit and they were making touch-and-go landings in the bay. Just as they settled into the water, a geyser shot up directly in the plane's path. Lee immediately took control and gave the Ryan full power. The geyser was from an attacking Japanese airplane, possibly a Zero, Betty or Babs. (Surabaja had never been attacked by a Japanese carrier. Actually, Surabaja was being attacked by the 23rd Naval Air Flotilla, operating from Kendair Air Base.) Lee and his student were able to fly just above the water, but did get hit nevertheless, and had to ditch.

Sometime shortly thereafter, Lee was up with another student and had another "experience." Flying at an altitude of 7000 feet, they were attacked by a Japanese Zero fighter. With the engine in the Ryan at full power, they played cat-and-mouse in and out of the clouds, diving and spiraling toward the bay. Finally, just above the water, the Zero made a good

Rare photo of serial number 510 after being captured by the Japanese in Java.   RICHARD M. BUESCHEL

pass, hit the Ryan repeatedly, and killed the student. A second Zero joined in, but after two more passes, gave up the fight. This took about 25 minutes and the little STM-S2 was still flying. Lee figured his floats were most likely hit by the Japanese bullets and would not support him on the water. He elected to land in a rice paddy — which he did, successfully.

During another attack on Surabaja the training went on normally. The aviators were given orders to fly at a very high altitude in order to report Japanese airplanes approaching Surabaja. At times the Ryans engaged in dogfights with the Zeros. The Ryan showed such maneuverability that it did a fair job of staying out of the firing range of the Japanese airplane. One Ryan had an aileron shot off and still the pilot was able to set the plane down on the water safely.

Naturally, when airplanes of the war are discussed, the stories flow like water, and the Netherlands Ryans are no exception. With the passing of time the stories change their slant, so people need to be extremely cautious as to what they take "for gospel truth". One such incident involved a Netherlands aviator who wanted to protect his family against a Japanese air raid. He put his wife and seven-year-old child into the front cockpit of a Ryan and flew from Surabaja to a "Kampong" village.

On March 1, 1942, all remaining seaplanes of the Netherlands Naval Aviation Department were flown from Surabaja to Lake Gengkong near Modjokerto and sunk. Among them were Fokker T-4s, C-11Ws, and possibly a few of the Ryans. Although documentation of the final disposition of many of the Ryans is just about non-existent, some rumors have surfaced to suggest that the Japanese had captured about 15 complete Ryan STM-2s (Army), of which ten were in flying condition and five needed minor repair. There is no data indicating at which

airport the incident took place, but it could possibly have been at either Kalidjati or Tasikmalaja.

Two dutchmen, Theordorus Wesselink and C. R. Patist, respected Netherlands aviation historians, claim that Kalidjati was captured by the Japanese on March 1, 1942. They say that the Ryans on the field, now in Japanese hands, eventually flew with the Japanese rising sun on the fuselage and wings. They were used as trainers for aerobatics and formation flying. One of the trainers was observed over Malang by a Dutch pilot, Lt. H. F. C. Holts, who had been a prisoner near an airfield near Batavia. He declared that he had seen how the Japanese used an entire fleet of captured Ryans, and at one time two of the Ryans had a mid-air collision due to bad airmanship. It is assumed these Ryans were from the M.L. (Military Luchtvaart), as the Naval Ryans had already gone to Australia.

RYAN STM-S2 SEAPLANE VERSION

The STM-S2 was exactly the same airplane as the land-plane trainer with the exception of a larger front spar in the stub wing and the replacement of the landing gear with seaplane floats, which were the Edo model 1965.

The lift truss was completed with a single pair of streamline wires between the two floats instead of the two counter wires as used on the landplane. The flying wires were of stainless steel on the seaplane, and the interior was protected against corrosion by metal primer (probably zinc chromate). Water control of the airplane was provided for by water rudders which could be retracted as well as steered from the cockpits.

(Left) *STM-S2, serial number 447, over the Pacific Ocean near San Diego.*

(Below) *STM-S2, serial number 447, first one built, shown after test flight in San Diego Harbor.*

RYAN AERONAUTICAL CO.

RYAN AERONAUTICAL CO.

RYAN STM-2 & STM-S2

SHIPMENTS INFORMATION

SOURCE - Ministerie Van Def Marine, The Hague, Netherlands. Letter July 11, 1967.

Contracts with Ryan Aeronautical Company, San Diego, California, pre-World War II.

Last contract June 25, 1940	12 STM-S2 (S-11 to S-22) s/n 447 - 458
Supplementary contract	12 sets of floats
Second contract July 8, 1940	12 STM-S2 (S-23 to S-34) s/n 459 - 470
Third contract Aug. 15, 1940 (time of delivery 180 days)	12 STM-2 (S-35 to S-46) s/n 471 - 482
Third contract (time of delivery 210 days)	12 STM-S2 (S-47 to S-48) s/n 483 - 484

STM-S2	S-11 to S-22, s/n 447 to 458	Left L.A. SS Hoegh Silver Dawn, November 18, 1940
STM-2	S-23 to S-30, s/n 459 to 466	Left L.A. MS Java, December 7, 1940
STM-2	S-31 to S-34, s/n 467 to 470	Left L.A. MS Klipfontein, December 21, 1940
STM-S2	S-11 to S-17, s/n 447 to 453	Date of shipment - October, 1940
STM-2	S-18 to S-30, s/n 454 to 466	Date of shipment - November, 1940
STM-2	S-31 to S-42, s/n 467 to 478	Date of shipment - December, 1940
STM-2	S-43 to S-58, s/n 479 to 494	Date of shipment - January, 1941

March 1, 1941, 20 aircraft at Morokrembangan; 11 flying school, 9 maintenance.
February 1942, 33 shipped to Australia for evacuated flying school.
Later handed over to RAAF when school went to USA.

Original log book information on serial numbers 457 and 463

RYAN STM-S2 s/n 457 Aboard Hoegh Silver Dawn, S-21 contract 6-25-40, Taken over November 1940, Shipped November 18, 1940, Arrived Java January 3, 1941, Known flights February 26, 1941. March 8 through 14, 1941, Photo taken on May or June 9th

RYAN STM-2 s/n 463 Aboard MS Java S-27 contract July 8,1940, Taken over November 1940, Shipped December 7, 1940, Arrived Java January 22, 1941, Known flight March 18-25 & May 9-15, 1941, Photo taken on May 9.
Note: Before July 7, 1941 tail rudder painted orange After July 7, 1941 tail rudder painted gray.

STM-2, serial number 467, in RAAF (Royal Australian Air Force) colors, somewhere in Australia, about summer, 1942.

PETER M. BOWERS

STM-2, S-15, serial number 451, landing at Surabaja, Netherlands East Indies.

MINISTERIE VAN DEFENSIE MARINE (HOLLAND) via H. J. BROEKHUIZEN

STM-2, in RAAF color scheme. Serial number is unknown.

COMMONWEALTH DEPARTMENT OF INFORMATION (AUSTRALIA)

Chapter Ten

Ryan YPT-25

YPT-25, serial number 42-8703, Wright Field, Ohio.

PETER M. BOWERS

World War II was well underway in 1942 when the United States Army and other government authorities made a request to the Ryan Aeronautical Company. They asked the company to undertake studies toward the conversion of the PT-22, then in production, to non-strategic materials. Economic experts decided that to maintain the necessary output of combat aircraft, such types as trainers and transports would have to be built of wood or molded products so as to conserve on aluminum and steel. The result was the Ryan Model ST-4, later designated PT-25 and YPT-25. The airplane was built almost entirely of plastic-bonded wood.

Aluminum alloys and all strategic material were almost entirely eliminated, with the exception of the engine cowling, which represented less than two percent of the total weight of the airframe.

This airplane turned out to be the last in the "ST" series to be built by the Ryan company. The design was the first and only in the series that could be flown solo from either the front or rear seat, and it was sometimes jokingly referred to as the "Plastic Trainer." It bore some resemblance to the other Ryans (trainers, not the SC) except for the snub nose and tapered wing. It was also similar in general appearance and

configuration to the Timm PT-220-C, constructed partly with "Aero-mold," and the St. Louis model PT-LM-4, NX25500, both of which were built in 1942. The Howard DGA-125 was another very similar design.

Performance was greatly improved over other Ryan trainers, and the cockpits were much roomier and more comfortable. No forgings, castings or extrusions of any description were called for in the manufacture of the PT-25.

This airplane was built to the Air Corps contract number AD-21204, Specification 714-2. The initial contract was accepted on June 5, 1943, and on June 1 and July 4, 1943, five airplanes were delivered, at the factory. Actual serial numbers were (AF) 42-8703 to 42-8707.

The ship was to be supplied to the United States Army Air Corps to be used for elementary training, and was equipped for night as well as for instrument or "blind" (as it was called then) flying.

They were all test flown at San Diego, by Joe Rust in September, 1942, and then delivered by WASP (Women Airforce Service Pilots) pilots to their assigned bases. Serial number 8703 went to Salinas, Kansas, and was seen there on September 2, 1943. Serial number 8705 was seen at Cimmaron Field,

Excellent structural view of first PT-25.   EV CASSAGNERES COLLECTION & RYAN AERONAUTICAL CO.

and was light and responsive on the controls.

A perforated center-section air brake (apparently similar to that of the D. H. Moth Minor and the earlier Ryan SC) enabled the approach glide to be steepened for small-field operations. Stall characteristics were said to be ideal for a primary trainer in that the positive stall reaction prepared the student for advancement to basic and high-speed operational types.

An interesting sidenote is that Charles A. Lindbergh, when visiting the Ryan plant during the PT-25 production, was given the opportunity to fly the airplane for a few minutes. This could have been about April, 1942.

By the time Ryan had conducted the initial devel-

September 13, 1944. There is no historical data available as far as can be determined to indicate the fate of the other 3 PT-25s. Nor have any records been found of the airplanes in service, at their respective bases.

The PT-25 was a two-place tandem open cockpit single engine monoplane. It was powered by a six-cylinder, horizontally opposed air-cooled Lycoming O-435-1 engine of 185 hp. As its earlier brother, the ST, the "dash 25" had attractive lines and excellent handling in the air as well as on the ground. Test pilot Rust said he performed practically every known military and aerobatic maneuver and the airplane handled it with ease and perfection. He said it possessed the right degree of stability in all three axes,

RYAN AERONAUTICAL CO.

All PT-25s shown with "Instrument Hoods" in place, San Diego, California.

Clarles A. Lindbergh (left), Donald Hall (center), "Dapper" Dan Burnett (right), April, 1942.   RYAN AERONAUTICAL LIBRARY

opment work and produced a service test quantity of these airplanes, the war was well underway and the aluminum scarcity had eased. As a result, further production of the wood trainers was not undertaken.

Final disposition of the PT-25 airplanes have never been determined fully and is still being researched. One of them, s/n 42-8705, was known to exist in Dallas, Texas, as late as August, 1947. See photograph below.

YPT-25, serial number 42-8705, Dallas, Texas, August, 1947.   PETER M. BOWERS

RYAN ST-4 YPT-25

SPECIFICATIONS

Engine	Lycoming 0-435-1 185 hp
Wing Span	32'-10 1/2"
Length	24'-3"
Height	6'-7 3/4"
Empty Weight	1,250 lbs.
Gross Weight	1,800 lbs.
Service Ceiling	20,300 feet
Range (statute miles)	378 statute miles
High Speed (sea level)	149 mph
Cruising Speed	134 mph @ 75% power
Landing Speed	50 mph
Rate of Climb	1,590 fpm
Wing Area	161.2 sq. ft.
Wing Loading	11.1 lb./sq. ft.
Power Loading	9.7 lbs per hp
Fuel Capacity	27 U. S. gal.
Oil Capacity	3 U. S. gal.

RYAN ST-4 YPT-25

CHRONOLOGY

Ryan s/n	U. S. Gov't s/n	Eng. & HP	Disposition
?	42-8703	Lyc. 185	?
?	42-8704	Lyc. 185	?
?	42-8705	Lyc. 185	?
?	42-8706	Lyc. 185	Dallas, TX Aug. '47
?	42-8707	Lyc. 185	?

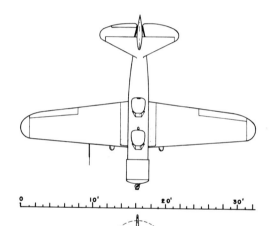

(Right) Ryan YPT-25 three view.

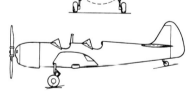

RYAN AERONAUTICAL CO.

(Below) "Pretty shot."

RYAN AERONAUTICAL CO.

Chapter Eleven

Where Are They Now?

Whenever this writer has found himself in the company of aircraft historians, pilots, Ryan buffs, Ryan owners, or just plain aviation enthusiasts, such as at the Oshkosh EAA Convention, some of the most difficult questions posed to me have been — how many Ryans are still in existence, where are they and how many are in flying condition?

For over 30 years I have attempted to update a Master List of all existing Ryans (including the earlier M-1, B-1 Brougham, and SC). The list would show the current owner's name and address, the current FAA assigned registration number, and the present status — in storage, flying, being restored, being repaired, for sale, etc.

In many cases today it is difficult to determine what is actually represented under all the paint of an existing Ryan. What is original? What is made up from parts? Does the existing airplane carry the "N" number of one of the long-gone original airplanes that was lost in an accident, for instance.

When an original Ryan became inactive, its NC number became available to be applied to any other aircraft, so many of these numbers were applied to later Pipers, Cessnas, or whatever. Twenty years ago there was little attention paid to "N" numbers. With this new interest in keeping an old airplane with its original NC number, owners are now going back and attempting to pick up the original number again, which might be appropriate for the time period for the individual Ryan.

When an inactive Ryan is reentered on the FAA listing and if the old NC number has been reapplied and no particular number is requested, the FAA will arbitrarily assign one. The present owner of s/n 111 tried to re-register it and ended up with N86555, a "modern" number.

To add to the confusion, many of the Ryans were built originally for export or for military use, and never had an NC number assigned to them in the first place. After World War II some of these airplanes made their way back into the United States or were found in some barn, and the owners applied for a registration number. Often many of them were built up from parts, so

Jim Dewey (left) and T. Claude Ryan.
May 7, 1972. Serial Number 184, NC17360.

TELEDYNE — RYAN AERONAUTICAL CO.

they really did not represent an actual original serial number.

In such cases, the owners would start a search for the papers of a former original Ryan that had been destroyed or lost in an accident, but the papers still existed. High prices are paid for such paperwork, which keeps authentic numbers painted on the airplane but also makes it easier to sort of prove that it was an "originally manufactured" Ryan for civil use, regardless if the existing hardware was an STM from some foreign country or one of the "PT" models used by the United States military training forces.

Some very interesting stories have evolved due to all of the above, and I am sure further stories are out there in the "woodwork" waiting to be told. It's therefore most difficult today to tell what's out there and if it's an original or reproduction or replica.

Another question arises as to what could still be out there that we don't even know about that has not been found yet. Considering all the Ryans built—for instance, out of that large group of ships built for China, and the many STM-2s built for the Netherlands East Indies, there just *HAVE* to be some airframes out there in some open field, barn, shed, garage, hangar loft or out behind the hangar in some remote parts of the world. I can't imagine that some of them are not left. There are just too many unaccounted-for.

This writer has had some first-hand experiences that are worth relating. One has to do with the 1950s or 1960s, when I recall seeing in a gas station in East Derby, Connecticut, the complete fuselage shell of Laura Ingall's airplane. Years later I tried to find it and traced it to a little riverfront village, but a search and knock on every door turned up nothing. I still wonder every time I drive by that area.

Not too many years ago I listened to a reliable friend and restorer of many fine antique airplanes relate the story of one Ryan ST that apparently was landed on a frozen lake (late fall?) in Maine, taxied up onto solid ground, and put into a barn or garage of some sort and left there. My friend said that the fellow who knew exactly where it was died before he was able to go with him to take a look at it. This story was heard about 1970 or 1975. So there it sits waiting for someone to find it.

Another is told by a present owner who spent a couple of years tracing a Ryan to a remote Montana ranch, only to be told by the irate land owner that the airplane sat out behind his barn for years, and he got sick of looking at it and having people driving onto his property to ask about buying or seeing it or taking a picture of it. So two weeks ago, he told my friend, if he had been there at that time he would have gladly given it to him but that he decided to just bulldoze it into the ground and get rid of it. When my friend asked if he could dig it up with a pick and shovel to try to find the nameplate and serial number, the

Original serial number 110, N14954, Boeing Field, 1957, while owned by Mira Slovak.   PETER M. BOWERS

Rebuilt serial number 112, NC14956 being flown over New Jersey by Steve Pitcairn, 1988.   HOWARD LEVY

Serial number 114, Evergreen Field, Vancouver, Washington, August 1969.   LLOYD N. PHILLIPS

owner said to get off his property before he shot him. To this day, we have no idea what serial number that airplane could have been, and I am sure the name plate is under that dirt someplace.

One ST-A had been flying out west in Nevada, and either ran out of gas or had a mechanical problem and the pilot decided to land on a road. In the rollout he did some damage, and asked the nearest land- owner if he could put it into his barn temporarily until he could get back to take care of the problem and continue on his way. So there it sat for over 30 years. The pilot never did come back (like the Montana one). However, one of our Ryan buffs learned of the existence of this airplane, and spent many years dickering with the owner of the barn and finally was able to buy it from him and is now restoring the airplane.

In Memphis, Tennessee, for instance, I know there were three Ryans (ST-As) in that area that have never been accounted for and could still exist somewhere near there. There are many others around the country of which the final disposition has never been determined.

What about what does exist out there? Probably two people who have more hardware than any other Ryan owner

Serial number 115 at Gillispie Field, San Diego, California.   LARRY PETERSON

(Left) The author's children, Kirsten (left) and Bryan (right) in ST, serial number 117, May 1975.

EV CASSAGNERES

Serial number 117, NC14985, in Tropical Turquoise color scheme, New Haven, Connecticut, August 1962.   EV CASSAGNERES

Menasco D4-87, 134 hp engine installed in serial number 117, NC14985.   EV CASSAGNERES

are Fred L. Barber in Georgia and Bill Rose in Illinois. Barber, a former Eastern Airlines 727 captain, has spent years scouring both this country and Australia for parts and has most of them stored in his basement and attic.

Bill Rose, on the other hand, has one original Dutch STM-S2 flying (on wheels), and another one being restored to its original configuration on Edo floats, and an STM built up from parts, now in flying condition.

Rose has enough Menasco engines and parts and Ryan airframe parts to build up another eight Ryans eventually. If it were not for people like this, it's no telling what would ever have happened to it all.

Dorr C. Carpenter of Virginia has been responsible for finding, buying and restoring several Ryans over a period of 20 years, some from as far away as Australia.

One ST-A was found in Bolivia a few years ago by a DC-3 captain, and is now in the process of restoration. The airplane had been missing for many, many years until the DC-3 pilot just "happened" to see its nose in a break in a fence as he drove along a street in Bolivia. The story of his acquiring it and all the trouble he went through with the Bolivian and U. S. Governments could fill a book and is one of the most interesting Ryan stories out there.

Another Ryan made its way from the Netherlands East Indies during World War II, to Australia, then Norway, and the Philippines, and finally to the United States, where it is today. Another of the NEI Ryans went from Australia to Hong Kong, and finally to the United States.

One original ST-A was lost for many years until found by this writer in the basement of a Chicago apartment building. Today it exists and can been seen on display in the San Diego Aerospace Museum (California). It is actually serial number 166, NC-17361.

Due to the scarcity of the Menasco engines, as so few were originally built, many present day owners have experimented with modern engines. Some planes have been powered with a Lycoming flat engine, one has a Ranger, and a couple in Australia have been outfitted with the popular Gypsy Major inverted, in-line, four-cylinder engine.

Another ST-A was aerodynamically modified with extended span ailerons to give it a faster roll-rate for air show work.

Unfortunately, paint schemes have just about gone out of sight too. The original all silver scheme that graced the airplane when leaving the factory is a bit rare today. However, considering that some of the existing Ryans are based near either the Atlantic or Pacific oceans or the Gulf coast, with the ever-present problem of salt water corrosion, it is no wonder the owners choose to paint their airplanes. It's hard work to keep the high polish on these beautiful fuselages.

Airplanes are bought and sold almost daily, accidents happen, and sometimes airplanes and their whereabouts are kept secret for some reason, or hidden away by fanatics, and so distort the records, which is most unfortunate.

I am sure that some of the above has taken place since this writing. Such is the life of these wonderful, classic old airplanes. Times change. Our society changes, and therefore these airplanes are at the mercy of our aviation society, and the changing of our times and values, and our individual financial situation.

Let us who are older hope and pray that our future generations will learn to appreciate these fine machines, enough to put in the tremendous effort needed to keep existing Ryans flying, so they too can experience the fun and exhilaration many of us have enjoyed for so many years.

Often I also get asked about the engine problem, the problem that Menasco engines are virtually not available because so few were built, compared to many other early aircraft engines.

Additionally, due to my being the only supplier in the world of prints of the original manufacturer's drawings of the ST (not PT-22) ST-A airplane, the problem again arises as to what powerplant to suggest in case a purchaser of a complete set of these drawings wishes to build up a replica Ryan ST.

So — as of this writing (1994), the only 4 cylinder, inverted, in-line, air-cooled engine, with approximately the same weight, dimensions and horsepower (150), is the Spanish built Casa Tigre G4B, and the Walter LOM engine, M 332, of 140 hp, being built brand new, FAA approved and sold in the U.S. and Canada.

(Right) Serial number 118 at Ottumwa, Iowa, September 2, 1962.

PAUL STEVENS

(Left) Serial number 127 in Mogy-Mirim, Brazil, being towed by a "Kombi" (VW bus) to be put in a shop to be restored. Summer 1966.

EV CASSAGNERES

(Right) Serial number 128 in April 1990, just after restoration at Northern California.

REMO GALEAZZI

(Left) Serial number 148 in single-cockpit configuration.

ROGER BESECKER

(Left) Serial number 166, NC17361, at San Diego Aerospace Museum in the markings of the prototype NC14223. Notice incomplete logo on fin and single cockpit which original did not have. Also lack of lower rudder clam-shells.

TELEDYNE — RYAN AERONAUTICAL CO.

Serial number 151, N42X (former NC17348).

ROGER BESECKER

Serial number 154, N633X (former NC17351), at Caldwell, New Jersey, 1967.

ROGER BESECKER

Serial number 156 shown at the Pilot's Store in Nut Tree, California, 1990.

ED POWER, JR.

Serial number 184, NC17360, original Mexico STM, shown as completely restored. Formerly N7828C.

JIM DEWEY

Serial number 195, STM from Guatemala, carrying original NC17349, serial number 152.

DORR C. CARPENTER

Serial number 198, NC18902, after restoration, Rockford, Illinois, August 4, 1967.

JOE O'ROURKE

Serial number 302, Guatemala STM, carrying N11D, Ottumwa, Iowa, September 2, 1962.

PAUL STEVENS

Serial number 312, NC18922, a PT-16, at Air Force Museum, Dayton, Ohio, July 12, 1987.

RICK FARRELL

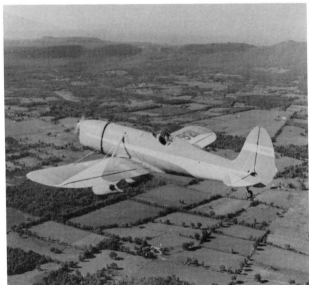

VIRGINIA FIORE via WARREN SHIPP

Serial umber 339, NC18921 over New York State. Pilot is Virginia Fiore.

TED J. KOSTON

Bill Dodd (left), and Ev Cassagneres just before flight in serial number 302, N11D. Harvard, Illinois, June 9, 1968.

Chapter Twelve

Let's Fly a Ryan ST

The author all ready to go fly the Ryan ST, NC14985.

EV CASSAGNERES

Just walking out to the flight line toward a Ryan ST is a thrill in itself. It gets the adrenalin going pretty quickly. It's like no other airplane.

When I built paper and wood models in the 1930s and 1940s, of the Ryan ST, Fairchild F-24s, Stinson Reliants, Waco cabins, real classics, I had not the slightest idea that I would ever fly any of these jewels. After I learned to fly in a J-3 and then years later after much "Airknocker" Aeronca, Luscombes, Cessna 120 and 140 time, an Aeronca C-3 here and an Ercoupe there, finally getting my hands and feet on the controls of many of the above mentioned classics, I thought I was just about on top of the world as an aviator.

Climbing into, or rather "putting on", like a suit of clothes a Ryan ST was and still is something else. If you are a very large person, don't expect to put on one of these jewels unless you find an oversize shoehorn. That cockpit is tight for a 1930s type open cockpit airplane. If you are blessed with average shoulders, they almost touch the sides of the cockpit, just right, so that when you roll left or right, into a turn, for instance,

you and the airplane go together. You really become part of the machine. For the average guy, it's a beautiful fit. No sloppiness like a wide cockpit Waco UPF-7.

Without a doubt, if a man or lady aviatrix loves to fly an airplane that one can wear like a finely tailored suit of clothes, and one that takes a "finger" touch to fly like nothing else he has ever mastered, then the old "New Ryan" ST is the airplane you have been waiting for.

For you lady pilots, you will never need a mirror, just lean out of the cockpit and stare into the fuselage to powder that oil grimed extremity. That old heavy gage alloy skin takes a polish that blinds you. A pilot will starve himself, wear himself out, and break his budget buying polish and using it. Take it from me, it's worth every mosquito bite for one hour of real airplane flying. Like one aviator writer put it many years ago, "whatever they call it, it just grins." No wonder; it's a proud airplane from a rather pedigreed and "spirited" family.

I can assure you that pilots with only tricycle gear experience will definitely not feel at home in this thoroughbred machine. Nor should they be allowed to even attempt to fly one, without much prior tail wheel time, perhaps in Luscombes, Stearmans, or other squirrelly experimentals.

One begins by climbing up onto the left wing center section (same as a horse). You proceed to swing your right leg over and into the rear solo seat or cockpit, then squeeze your left leg over and slide down into the seat with a p~ffitt. You're in up to your shoulders and practically become, as one pilot put it, "a part of the ship."

Strap yourself in and look over the controls. Stick and rudder pedals are in the usual places with throttle lever on the left wall. With stick back in the lap and brakes set (heel type), and after no more than two compression strokes (or blade pulls) on the wood propeller, a shot or two of prime, throttle cracked 1/4 inch, together with the mag switch on "both," you call "contact" to the man outside. The purr starts and you're in gear for a flight into the wild blue yonder, with goggles down and chinstrap snug.

If you have a lot of time in tail wheel airplanes then the long nose and blindness up front will not seem too strange or inconvenient. While taxiing out, the usual "S" turns will be necessary in order to see where you're going, and to get to where you want to go. Remember to keep that stick well back in your lap, and don't hesitate to use the proper downwind stick technique if winds tend to be a bit strong in any particular direction.

After the proper mag check and engine run-up, and checking of full control movements, flaps and fuel selector, and trim tabs as required, you're ready to aviate.

Goggles down, get lined up on the runway, and start feeding in gradual opening of the throttle to full power, finding that a minimum of rudder correction is necessary while at the same time correcting for torque effect with some rudder. Immediately it will become apparent that you had better know what a rudder is for, and, as a friend of mine once remarked, "you better have the education of the feet" in this airplane. I have found that by wearing either light tennis or "topsider" sneaks, you will have the best footwear on for that sensitive feel of the rudder. Be sure to place the ball of the foot right on the rudder cross tube, heels clear of the brake pads. Just forget about brakes alltogether. Actually you hardly need them even for taxiing.

As you roll down the runway, keep ahead of the Ryan directionally, let the tail come up on its own by keeping the stick basically in neutral or slightly forward. Concentrate on direction and soon you will be in the air and lift off at about 65-70 mph which is a good climb-out speed.

After reaching a desired altitude for becoming a bit more intimately familiar with the airplane, trim up for straight and level, and see how she handles hands off.

With an RPM of about 1950, depending on which Menasco you have, she should true out at about 105 to 120 mph. My report here is with a Menasco D4-87 engine of 134 hp, in Ryan ST s/n 117. You can use these figures sort of as a 'mean', depending on whether you're flying an ST-A, STM, STM-2 or STA Special.

In the stall mode you will find the airplane breaks pretty clean, and may have some tendency to drop a wing, which can be immediately picked up with the rudder.

What about aerobatics in a Ryan? You won't find a "snappier" airplane for a 1930s design. It really is a delight in that department. With the NACA 2412 airfoil, incorporating that nice curve on the bottom, it does excellent outside maneuvers and inverted flight. The airplane is stressed for a positive and negative "G" factor of 10 and it takes a lot of pull to exceed even 6, according to one pilot who uses an STM for aerobatic show work.

For loops I like about 120 mph in a shallow dive, with engine half throttled. Pulling up into the loop, advance the throttle fully until the ship has passed over the top and started down the other side, at which point the throttle is retarded, to prevent building excessive speed in the dive.

For snap rolls 90 to 95 is plenty. Any more speed induces high stick loads and undue strain on the airframe. A smooth, gradual use of back stick when entering the roll produces a much smoother roll than violently jerking it back, and overly increasing strain. For a roll and a half (snap) use about 110 - 115, carefully, to enter the roll smoothly.

A well executed slow roll can be done at varying speeds and is not a maneuver which exerts undue strain on the airplane. Enter a slow roll at 120 and full throttle. I sometimes get 140 mph when doing a very slow roll as excess speed is necessary to carry through the last half of the roll due to the engine not functioning. Pull the nose quite high while inverted. Use quite a good bit of forward stick on the last half of the roll out. This will prevent an excessive amount of whipping.

A nice one-and-a-half turn vertical snap roll can be executed at 140 mph. Pull up as in the first half of a loop, starting the snap roll when a vertical angle of about 70 degrees has been reached. Recovery is made in the full inverted position and after the pull out which is like the last half of a loop. You should be heading 180 degrees from the direction in which you first entered the maneuver.

True immelmans require about 150 mph and use considerable forward stick when rolling out to prevent excessive slipping. When doing such maneuvers as loops, immelmans and vertical rolls, trim the tabs such that the ship is quite tail heavy during the dive prior to execution of the maneuver. This will relieve the high pressure necessary to pull the stick back to enter the maneuver. For slow rolls, trim the ship a bit nose heavy before rolling over. This will partially relieve the forward stick pressure necessary to hold the nose well up when inverted.

An excessive amount of speed is unnecessary in any of these standard aerobatic maneuvers if they are to be done correctly and smoothly.

Spins are a bit tight with a fast rate of descent. Falling leaves are a delight, from either the driver's seat or the spectators view. In fact, I have never found any other airplane that can do a falling leaf any better. This is a maneuver not seen much these days. Basically, a falling leaf is an entry to a spin with an immediate recovery. In other words, bring it up to a power-off stall, at the stall, kick either right or left rudder, and immediately the opposite rudder, and just continue that sequence of rudder action, one right after another, down hill all the way, left, right, left, right, left, right, until you have had enough and satisfied your jollies. Believe me, you will feel quite elated when you have mastered this beautiful and rare maneuver.

One maneuver which evolved from just playing around a bit one day, goes like this: From cruise configuration and airspeed, about 110, cut the power to idle slowly, and at the same time come back on the stick, pulling up as though you were entering a steep power-off stall; continue to bring the nose up until about 55 degrees to horizontal. Just before the stall, while there is still some air pressure on the rudder, kick left rudder. From here on, you will be in for quite a ride. The tail will immediately swing around 180 degrees, and you and the airplane will hang almost motionless, partly inverted, heading in the opposite direction, at which time you will complete the maneuver as you would from the last quarter of an inside loop.

One time many years ago I had a 100,000 miles airline stewardess-skydiver in the front cockpit when I did this. She screamed at the standstill point, her hand went up in the air, but exclaimed after we landed, "It was the best airplane ride I've ever had," and she was serious.

Now that we have had all this fun way up in the air, we have to get the thing down on the ground in one piece — yes — the landing. The final maneuver that separates the men from the boys, as they say.

Try to remember that there are only two landing techniques to be used with this old high-performance airplane; full stall three-point, or DC-3 style "wheel" landings. Basically the type of landing surface will help determine what technique you may wish to use. If it is a hard surface runway, the wheel landing works quite well. On grass, however, the three-point attitude is fine and fun, with wheel landings possible if the surface is smooth enough and in good condition.

However, pilots with extensive experience in tail wheel aircraft, in all conditions, and current in these types, should be able to handle a three-point landing on hard surfaces. When I was flying the Ryan on a regular basis, and under all sorts of wind conditions and runways, I felt comfortable with most situations. One time stands out in my memory when it appeared all the chips were against me: the oil tank, which is located just above the engine, decided to split open, along the bottom seam, sending hot oil running down the top of the fuselage to the windshields. This happened about two miles from the airport, which only had hard-surface runways available. I was at about 1500 feet. On top of all that, I had a passenger in the front seat, with an assortment of very expensive camera equipment hanging all over him and draped around his supposedly new ski jacket. What a mess it was. What to do but get her down in one piece as soon as possible.

The only runway within reach under the conditions was the east-west one, which gave me a direct 90 degree, 15-20 mph cross wind from the left. Talk about sweating this one out would be the understatement of the year. My technique, which worked, was to come in without flaps, slow it up in a rather flat approach (I had 3800 ft to work with), and with the engine shut down (I thought it was blowing itself to pieces), left wing a bit low, and touch on the left wheel only, ever so gently, riding it out with the rudder, gradually letting the right wheel down to the surface. Believe me — riding it out trying to keep her straight, and, of course, doing absolutely nothing as far as brakes are concerned, I let the tail wheel come down with extreme caution, using finger tip control. Eventually it came to a stop. I just sat there trembling, while the line crew came out to push the airplane off the runway.

Fortunately, I learned to fly just after WW II, by feel, sound, smell and natural senses. Those of us who became pilots in that era have an edge when flying these classics today. Flying the Ryan is a challenge with its personality and uniqueness, but the nostalgia is priceless.

Several years ago I received a letter from former Ryan company test pilot Paul Wilcox, in which he commented on teaching fledgling student pilots how to land an ST. "We always taught 3-point landings on either hard surface or grass. Of course it is easier to land on wheels and then let her settle slow and easy but we were not looking for the easy way. Later on if the student wanted to go the easy route that was fine but we wanted to be sure they could handle it, now, at this time, the most difficult manner, and then we could be certain they would be prepared for most anything after that. Modern methods take all the fun and uncertainties out of it."

Without flaps the ST lands very normally with a somewhat flat approach. I found that a good approach speed was about 70-75 mph with a normal 500 fpm rate of descent. It will feel light after touching the ground and will require continued control attention, especially with a crosswind and even more so after the tail is down. With flaps fully down a very comfortable approach with the tail a little below thrust line on the flair will round out to a smooth and easy landing, without sudden changes, and leave the ST sitting solidly on the ground.

The use of brakes on the rollout to keep the airplane straight, I know, is somewhat debatable. However, I was checked out by a highly-experienced pilot by the name of Al Wheeler, who for years flew Ryans and other exotic classics of the 1930s and '40s. He taught me to never touch the brakes on the rollout — unless I had severe cross-winds and/or gusts, as a "last" resort to save the airplane. Too many people have gone over on their backs ignoring this advice. I found that as long as I adhered to his advice, I have never had a problem, to this day. He believed that the excessive use of brakes to keep an airplane straight on landing rollout was not the mark of good airmanship. Brakes are only there to stop the machine at the flight line before engine shut-down or for the run-up and mag check before take-off. My experience has proven him right.

What about slipping? I have found that a left slip on final approach, with or without flaps (and I know not everyone will agree with this) is delightful. One does not right slip due to the Menasco's straight exhaust stacks being on the starboard side, as the cold air with throttle retarded for approach could cause valve damage or warping I am told. When I am on final, I usually put the goggles down, slip my left shoulder under the left cockpit coaming, and stick my head out the left side for better visibility straight ahead, and to slow the airplane down a bit. This is where the sense of feel and sound becomes quite critical. Yes, I know it leaves the right side blind, so I usually take one final look on that side before entering the slip just to be certain there is not some obstruction in the flight path or on the runway.

It's extremely gratifying to make the flare from this slip and roll out straight and touch down ever so gently. I don't think any of you old-timers out there will disagree. However, keep up your air-speed, and feel substantial wind pressure on the top side of the elevators. Whenever they get light you may be closer to the stall than you think. This is one reason I never trim for landing, I trim in cruise flight and leave it alone after that.

One time I discussed this with Charles Lindbergh and asked if he ever flew that way, and he said that he did, unless it was a heavier type airplane such as a twin or heavy fighter. He felt it was a good technique to develop, due to its honest feel that your muscles are already used to. I started this by practicing at high altitude, where the air was thinner and there was room for error, in case things got out of hand or created a

surprise, I had time and space to correct without hitting something.

If you think you're well coordinated, then try this — it's the ultimate in cockpit gymnastics. In the early ST, not ST-A, STA Special or STMs, the flap mechanism did not consist of a simple push-button lever, such as the later models did. Rather, it was a small hand crank located in the lower right corner of the cockpit near the pilot's right ankle (a crank similar to a trim crank overhead in cabin aircraft) with an ordinary Diamond 1/8-inch-pitch bicycle chain. If you were to look down between your ankles while sitting in the rear cockpit, you could plainly see this chain making its way across from left to right or vice-versa over a couple of rollers.

Normal operation consisted of 12 turns of the crank handle for take-off, if you needed it (approximately 15 degrees of flap), and 32 turns for "full down" landing configuration (55 degrees of flap).

The gymnastics start when you're on the down wind leg preparing for a landing. You throttle back to about 1500 rpm, turn into the base leg and immediately take your left hand from the throttle (located on the left wall) and your right hand from the stick, placing your left hand on the stick where the right one was and putting your right hand on the flap crank handle. At this point, as you start cranking, your head will partly disappear into the cockpit.

Therefore, it is recommended that cranking cease every few turns so you can pop your head up to check relative position to the end of the runway, etc., and to make throttle adjustments as necessary. Now return inside for more cranking and continue this routine until full flap down position is attained.

Personally, I liked these gymnastics. They made me work, think and develop more technique in control. I was flying the airplane instead of it flying me. Things like this keep a pilot polished, so to speak. It's sort of like the difference in driving a modern power-everything car versus a 1929 type 34 Bugatti. Man is master of his machine.

You've made it down with ease and safety, but remember that this airplane is not finished flying until it sits on the line again and the mag switch says "off".

And there you have it — a flying machine with enough zip, grace and beauty to make you want to stay up all day. Wonder what the Red Baron would do if he had this sweetheart strapped to his back. Even if he couldn't shoot "em down", he'd still frighten them away with just the blaze of light as he flashed by; with that highly polished fuselage, he could probably blind them into oblivion.

Please understand that the numbers I have used in this pilot report are for the 1936 Ryan ST I flew for so many years, and may differ between the ST-A, STA Special and STM models and also who is flying. We all seem to fly differently, and have various techniques.

Chapter Thirteen

The Menasco Story

A brightly painted blue engine, upside down, with four cylinders, in-line, simple looking, sleek, interesting, allowing for some of the nicest cowling designs ever to grace the front end of an airplane — aerodynamically clean, beautiful and efficient — yes, that's the Menasco engine. In order to learn how this engine got its start we have to first look at the man whose name it bears.

Albert Sidney Menasco was born on March 17, 1897, in Los Angeles, California. Al had a bit of a rough start in life. At the age of 5, a neighborhood chum, fooling around with a handgun, carelessly let it fire, hitting Al in the stomach. It was about the same time that President McKinley was also shot in the stomach. McKinley developed peritonitis and died, but Menasco lived, even after a three hour ride, by a horse-drawn ambulance, to the local hospital. Not long after that, Mrs. Menasco, Al's mother, died. His father, hard working man that he was, found that he could not take care of Al and his sister, so had to put them into an orphanage in Los Angeles.

Al Menasco (left) and T. Claude Ryan standing by prototype ST, s/n 101, NC14223.   TELEDYNE RYAN AERONAUTICAL

Some years later Al's father married again, this time to a German girl who was highly educated and was also an accomplished concert cellist, then performing with the Philharmonic Orchestra. She had a son, by another marriage. His name was Ferde Grofé. He was an accomplished musician and composer. His best known work is the "Grand Canyon Suite."

Soon Al was living with his dad again, and his stepmother. They decided he needed some discipline and a good education, so enrolled him in a German Grammar School in Los Angeles. Al did not take to this strict discipline and occasionally skipped school. At the age of 11 he decided to run away altogether to find out what it was like "out there." He was soon caught and sent to Juvenile Hall in Los Angeles. Because Al behaved himself there, he was soon released and went to live with an older brother, Milton, an artist. This all happened in 1908-09. Things were tough then and jobs not easy to find, but Al managed to find a job as a movie extra for a while.

Then he found himself back in school, this time the Manual Arts High School in Los Angeles. It was while at this school that he met Cliff Henderson, and

Lincoln Beachey

AVIATION HERITAGE

they became long time friends. Henderson went on to become manager of the Cleveland and Los Angeles National Air Races. The two of them joined the local Aero Club and began to build model airplanes and gliders. They used their bicycles as wind tunnels to test their creations.

Then about 1910, Al learned of an air meet out at Dominguez, about half way to Long Beach on the old Red Car Line. It was held on a plateau where the Dominguez oil field now exists. The event caught his fancy and he went there the first day, and actually got to see some of the world's greatest aviators of the day, with names like Orville and Wilbur Wright, Glenn Curtiss, Santos Dumont from Brazil, Louis Blériot, Hubert Latham, Louis Paulhan. He was, as he said, captivated by the scene, but had to go back to school.

In 1911 the same event took place and again Al rode his bicycle out there, having skipped school for most of the ten days the meet lasted. It was at this meet that Al met Lincoln Beachey.

But it was at the 1912 meet that Al decided to, as he put it, "toss the school books out the window." At that time he was living at 16th and Union Avenue. He had a local neighborhood friend, Farnum Fish, who liked building and flying model airplanes, as Al did. Farney, as he was called, did not care much for school, and was a

Farnum Fish with a passenger at San Diego Air Meet, 1911.

AVIATION HERITAGE

problem, so the family sent him to the Wright School in Dayton, Ohio. At that 1912 meet, Farney came back as a full fledged flyer and Al said, "I kissed everything good-bye and attached myself to him." Al took care of his airplane, under the watchful eye of one of Wright's best mechanics, a Mr. Hazard. Al wiped off the airplane, oiled the chain to the two propellers and for this he was promised a ride.

Farney was asked to take a photographer aloft but was not aware of the low fuel in his tanks, and soon Farney and the photographer landed in a cactus patch, so ending Al's first chance at his first airplane ride.

After the 1912 meet, Al lost interest in aviation for some time. He became a mechanic at a truck factory in Los Angeles. These trucks had either Wisconsin engines or Continental engines. Both of those companies are still in business.

To quote Al: "My interest in engines was always paramount to all else. After the truck factory I indulged in some weekend motorcycle racing and became interested in racing automobiles. We had built a few prototype cars at the truck factory. I had the misfortune to get badly cracked up in 1914 and after I came out of that I was laid up for the best part of a year. I opened a shop on 812 West Jefferson Street in Los Angeles, at Jefferson and University, around the corner from University of Southern California. I painted the sign myself and it said 'Auto Repairing.'"

At the age of 17, Al sat around for a week or so until people with White Steamers would come in to get them repaired. He knew nothing about steam but managed to get the work done to the customer's satisfaction.

He got into racing with his automobile experience and it was while involved in that activity at the 1915 World's Fair at San Francisco that his attention was again drawn to aviation.

At this fair he met Art Smith, called, "the Boy Aviator," at the age of 21, from Fort Wayne, Indiana. Smith was the first to use a stationary engine which he converted with carburetor and oiling changes to operate inverted. Up to that time most of the barnstorming aviators were using Gnome or LeRhone rotary engines.

Smith eventually asked Al to build him a car similar to the one Al had. After the car was finished, Al was back in Los Angeles and sweeping out his shop and wondering where his next customer was coming from, when he received a letter from Smith. The letter offered Al a job in San Francisco, to build twelve cars and three airplanes and then join him in a tour of the Orient.

That was the beginning of a long-time association with Art Smith. They started to build the cars and planes in a shop in San Francisco but never finished them because soon it was time to board a ship bound for Japan, which they did, leaving on March 4th on the Chiyo Maru, a 22,000 ton Japanese ship.

Al spent much of the trip in the engine room, where they had a machine shop, machining many parts that he did not have time to do before leaving. The steering gear, hubs and axles for the cars and parts for the airplanes were all semifinished — incidentally, they had rack and pinion steering which is so highly touted today for sports cars. He did most of the finished machine work in the engine room of that ship.

Art Smith, 1913.

When they arrived in Japan, everything was semifinished. They had a big team of racing car drivers, including himself, and an organization of 23 members assembled in Japan. It took six weeks in Tokyo before they had three cars and one airplane ready for the first show at Aoyama Parade Grounds in Tokyo. He estimated that five or six million residents of Tokyo, at least, saw Art Smith flying over the area in that recently completed airplane. From then on, he was taken into the hearts of the Japanese.

Al and Art Smith also toured Korea, Manchuria, China, Formosa and the Philippines. They charged 5000 yen ($2500) for these air shows, which included two flights.

Smith took time out to give Al some very expensive flying lessons, cancelling about five dates to do this. This was at Niigata on the west coast of Japan. They used the home stretch of a mile race track there for the take-offs and landings, and then simulated landings on a nearby beach until Al had about 180 minutes of dual, which Smith felt was sufficient.

It was interesting to note that Al actually learned to do a loop before he ever learned to take-off and land. Anyway, their last show was in Shanghai, where they had a good field which enabled Al to make his first solo flight. Now he was considered a full-fledged aviator.

In November of 1915, Al and his friend Art Smith returned to the United States, where Smith eventually ended up as a test pilot at Langley Field, Virginia, and Al joined the Canadian Royal Flying Corps in Vancouver. He, too, ended up at Langley, as the man in charge of engine testing and instruction for the Signal Corps, as an aeronautical engineer with a civil service salary of $1800 a year.

As part of his work he made some corrections to the Hispano-Suiza engines which were then being built as the choice for a fighter program, which led him to join the builders — the Wright-Martin Company, the licensee in the United States and the company which eventually became the Curtiss-Wright Company. This concern built the Wright J-5 "Whirlwind" engine that was used in Lindbergh's Spirit of St. Louis.

After WW I was over, Al decided to go back to his home state of California, where he took a job as a machinist in a shop on West Pico Street for 60 cents an hour. He graduated from that job to selling machine tools and then started his own shop building air compressors. One of his early friends in auto racing was Karl Weber, who invented a glass grinding machine. Al joined Weber's company, the Weber Showcase Company. At that time the auto makers in Detroit were starting to build closed-in cars, and they (Al and his friend) could hardly build the glass machines fast enough, which put them in the chips again.

Langley Field in Virginia.

This DH-4 had been modified by Bellanca. Note wide Bellanca struts that were typical of Bellanca aircraft designs.   AVIATION HERITAGE

Meanwhile, his friend, Art Smith, had gotten into the air mail business as a pilot, while scattering most of his money from the Japan trips around Texas in oil well drilling. He also purchased 250 war surplus French Salmson engines from the United States Government, which had received the engines from France as part payment of reparations. The engine was known as the Liberty of France — a very advanced engine for its time, a nine-cylinder, water-cooled type of 230 hp.

Smith had plans to start an aircraft factory while he flew the mail, to build a sky-writing airplane so he could corner the sky-writing business. He had improved the war surplus deHavilland mail airplanes with several of his devices. And it was still the U.S. Airmail Service, not yet a private carrier.

Then the government asked for bids to replace the old deHavillands. The Curtiss and Douglas companies responded with two prototypes for evaluation. Curtiss's entry was a new model called the Carrier Pigeon, a biplane. It was an ungainly looking airplane by comparison and had a very high cowling that lessened forward visibility.

Smith was a friend of Curtiss and wanted to see the Pigeon get a fair trial. He did not just want to fly it around the field, but suggested he take it on his regular night run to Chicago under actual weather conditions. He showed much interest in that kind of flying at that time, and helped to develop various aids.

Then one day he flew the Pigeon on his run to Chicago and encountered bad weather for the return trip.

Al happened to be in New York at the time and was planning to meet Art in Washington the following day to visit the patent office. Ten inches of snow fell on New York that night. Art proceeded east and got as far as Bryan, Ohio, and decided to land at the emergency field there to fill his tanks so he would have enough fuel to circle over Cleveland if necessary. As he broke out of the clouds at Bryan, he circled a farm to get his bearings and did not see a tree, standing lone in the middle of a field, and struck it. Art Smith died as a result of the accident.

After the funeral at Ft. Wayne, Al offered to help Art's mother and father settle the estate. They found the principal assets were the 250 Salmsons in a warehouse at Dayton. Al was unsuccessful in trying to sell off all the engines to airplane manufacturers around the country so he shipped them all to his place in California.

Curtiss Carrier Pigeon.   AVIATION HERITAGE

Back home he started to convert them to American standards with the hopes of making enough money to take care of Mrs. Smith and Art's father, who was failing rapidly. That was a mistake, he said. They increased the horsepower to 260 by making a few improvements, but the engine started throwing parts, such as valves, valve springs and other pieces.

Just about this time the government established an Aeronautics Bureau through the Department of Commerce to create some regulations for the exploding industry. This was as a result of the successful flight to Paris by Charles A. Lindbergh.

Now it would be necessary to license aircraft properly and to set specifications for safety, among which were tests to prove airworthiness. Engines were required to pass certain tests to obtain an airworthiness certificate. Al felt the whole process or concept was proper and well done, but here he was stuck with the Salmsons unless he could get them certified. In order to accomplish this, they had to operate an engine at full throttle for 50 hours at the Bureau of Standards in Washington, D.C., within a range of temperatures and fuel consumption figures and other safety factors.

They made five trips to Washington and in their last attempt they ran the engine for 49 hours and 27 minutes before the last piece of the French engine blew (which was the crankcase), as they had replaced just about everything else by then.

By that time Al had assembled a good crew in his little shop, and said, "I'm back in the engine business, but I am going to build my own engines."

That was the start of the Menasco Manufacturing Company. They called it Menasco Motors. Jack Northrop, then a young man, was responsible for Al's decision to design and build an inverted type engine. Northrop explained that all previous engines were not built for the utmost aerodynamic efficiency, but to obtain the best power - weight ratio. Of 140 different types of aircraft engines then being produced, 90 percent were radials, of large frontal area.

Northrop stated that the inverted engine of small frontal area, with the crankshaft above gives a higher center of thrust and a lower center of gravity, plus more propeller clearance, which in turn allows for a shorter landing gear — a better aerodynamic situation all around.

Jack Northrop was interested at that time in building up a small prototype flying wing and this type of engine fit well into his plan. His design also included a retractable landing gear and other innovations.

Menasco had the most complete machine shop within the aviation industry then. Lockheed, Douglas, and Ryan and others were primarily aircraft builders, but lacked much in the way of metal-working machine tools.

So Menasco was able to execute the more difficult machined parts for them. Menasco built the first retractable landing gear for Northrop, of Jack's design. They called it a "piece of jewelry" at that time. They practically hand-tooled the whole job. According to Al Menasco, that was the first retractable landing gear built in the industry.

Menasco eventually grew into air racing. They were quite successful during that era and won four times as many races as all other engine companies combined. But they never built a racing engine. They were all stock, approved-type engines. After five failures with the French engine, Al made up his mind that when he built his own engine and put his name on it, there would be no failures at the Bureau of Standards 50-hour tests.

Keith Ryder and Miss San Francisco II.

Folkerts SK "Jupiter" after winning the 1937 Thompson Trophy Race.

No engine was submitted by Menasco for testing thereafter that could not run for 100 hours at 125% full throttle. Al did not even bother to go to Washington himself to attend the tests. They got seven Approved Type Certificates in a row — no other manufacturer had ever submitted to seven successive tests successfully. Their philosophy was to give the customer more than he asked for.

There is an interesting anecdote with regard to the second retractable landing gear Menasco built. It begins with a group of San Francisco flyers and sportsmen when they decided to build an airplane to compete in the National Air Races in Cleveland. They backed a young designer by the name of Keith Ryder, who produced an outstanding airplane — all metal, cantilever low wing, using Menasco's first supercharged engine and a retractable landing gear.

It was in 1930 that Menasco had first appeared at the National Air Races in Chicago. Now it was 1931, and this San Francisco group became so enthused when they saw their entry develop that they decided to build two of these airplanes. Menasco arrived at Cleveland and created quite an impression. These airplanes looked like the modern fighter of the day and were beautiful to just look at. They were in the small cubic inch class with their largest engine of only 544 cubic inches.

Anyway, there were 50,000 people in the grandstand at the start of the race. Airplanes were lined up abreast, known as a race horse start. If the wind was from the wrong direction, they took off opposite to the counter-clockwise direction of the course, circling a scattering pylon before entering the first lap on the proper course.

Al Menasco was in the grandstand as a guest of some prominent people, rather than his usual place at the starting line.

The flag dropped and all of the airplanes started rolling. Right in front, on the inside pole, came their airplane, "Miss San Francisco." That plane hopped off the ground and was in the air level with the eye in the grandstand in no time, while the others were still lumbering along down there on the field, and as it passed the grandstand, the wheels disappeared, the landing gear came up and went clean out of sight. No one had ever seen that happen except to a bird.

The crowd went wild, as the "Miss San Francisco" was down around that scattering pylon and back on the 10-mile course and out of sight before some of the other airplanes were barely airborne. Supposedly that was the first sight of the retractable landing gear to this big audience at the National Air Races.

It was a great show, the Olympics of the air, and put on by Al Menasco's old friend, Cliff Henderson, who had the genius of P.T. Barnum, according to Menasco. Henderson alternated the show between Los Angeles and Cleveland for the 12 years of its popularity, shortened at the end to four days.

Menasco engines dominated most events and finally in 1937, they succeeded in the ultimate victory of winning the Greve and Thompson Trophy races, the unlimited competition against engines as high as 1800 cubic inches displacement with their model C-6S4 engine, made the fastest time in the last lap of any American machine in the history of the event. The airplane was the Folkerts SK-3 "Jupiter." A young boy, Rudy Kling was the embryo pilot and it is believed he only had about 300 hours.

N. A. NABEL, JR.

Prototype s/n 101 with original Menasco B-4 engine. Photo shows Story ground-adjustable metal prop and original support structure for oil tank.

HISTORICAL AVIATION ALBUM *via EV CASSAGNERES*

Prototype s/n 101 with Menasco B-4 engine. Notice wood prop that replaced original Story metal prop, and change of oil tank support frame.

RYAN AERONAUTICAL CO.

Menasco C-4, 125 hp installation.

RYAN AERONAUTICAL CO.

Menasco C-4, 125 hp engine installation. Notice hand-crank for starter, upper left of photo.

EV CASSAGNERES

Menasco D4-87 134 hp engine installed in serial number 117, NC-14985.

EV CASSAGNERES

Menasco D4-87 134 hp engine installed in serial number 117, NC-14985.

ERICKSON PHOTO via RYAN AERONAUTICAL CO.

(Above) Menasco C-4, 125 hp engine before installation in aircraft.

(Right) Menasco C-4S, 150 hp installation in an ST-A Special.

RYAN AERONAUTICAL CO.

ORIGIN OF THE INVERTED ENGINE

Al Menasco said that inverted engines were not invented by him, but that the Europeans had inverted several engines and the Army Air Corps, under the command of Col. Dargue, was planning a South American good will tour in Loening amphibians and had ordered the Allison Machine Shop in Indianapolis, Indiana, to invert some Liberty engines. This was done so the pilot could see out over the engine and also to get proper clearance for the props. Thus started the Allison Engine Company, now known as Allison Gas Turbine Engine Manufacturers, still located in Indianapolis.

While Jack Northrop was working on that first flying wing and discussing the engine situation with Menasco, he wrote to both the Cirrus and deHavilland companies in England asking if they had considered an inverted design of their engines. No they had not, so Al decided to invert one of the Cirrus engines until he could produce one of his own models in the 90-95 hp range.

The Cirrus inversion served its purpose to expedite various ground tests with the Northrop Flying Wing until the first Menasco A-4 (90 hp) was finished and installed for flight tests. It was issued ATC #50. Bore was 4.5 inches, stroke 5.125 inches, displacement 316 cubic inches, compression ratio 5.5 to 1 and dry weight 265 pounds. That was early 1930.

Only five of the A-4 engines were ever produced before they tooled up for the 95 hp B-4 engine. The first one is on display in the Dallas, Texas, office of Menasco, Inc. The first production B-4 is on display at the National Air and Space Museum in Washington, D.C.

The success of the B-4 forced the business to move from Al's garage to a small factory on McKinley Avenue in Los Angeles, where it is today.

Menasco pioneered high pressure super-charging in aircraft engines, using manifold pressures double those of other engines. This, together with the inverted design's small frontal area, and large propellers are usually cited as the reasons behind Menasco's ability to get higher performance from an engine with a small displacement.

The company also made all parts in house, including the gears. His only competition in later years was Fairchild, and Sherman Fairchild became a lifelong friend. Menasco engines were never intended for racing but because of their ruggedness, power, reliability, and inverted configuration, the race pilots of the day found them perfect for their airplanes. The fact that they used ball bearings (wherever possible) instead of bronze bearings, gave his engine an edge for racing. Al learned this friction saving trick from the German engine designer Maybach.

The question as to how Al Menasco came up with the "Pirate," etc., names for his engines is quite interesting. He had always considered himself as a "free soul," under no restraints and able to do what he wanted — just like a pirate. Thus he decided to name his engines "Pirate," "Buccaneer" (super-charged), "Swashbuckler," "Freebooter," and "Corsair."

When Bill Boeing was on the Menasco board, he carried the company during the Depression. Things were not too good for Menasco in 1937, and the company was still making very few engines but had taken to making small counter-top washing machines, jacks, security valves, etc.

It was in 1938 that Al had a disagreement with the board of directors as to what direction the company would take; he left, but still remained the largest shareholder.

In the meantime the Air Force asked the company to build landing gears, largely because of their complete machine shop and skilled workers. The contract brought with it unlimited financing. During World War II the business boomed and Menasco became the largest manufacturer of landing gears and remains so today, even making gears for the Space Shuttle.

After leaving the company Al opened a Ford auto dealership in Culver City, California, which lasted until the start of World War II, when he received a commission as a major in the Army Air Forces' Material Command.

He was stationed in Detroit for much of WW II, assigned to the production of large military aircraft manufactured and assembled by the nation's major automakers as part of the war effort.

Al returned to Los Angeles in 1945, and again opened a Ford dealership. Among his best customers were actors, producers, directors from the movie industry. Clark Gable was one of them, and visited Al's ranch on several occasions.

In the middle 1950s Al Menasco decided to get out of the auto business and into the wine business, and purchased a ranch and vineyard in the beautiful Napa Valley, north of San Francisco. He lived there with his wife, Julie, right up to his death, at the age of 91, on November 14, 1988.

The Menasco company exists today as a wholly owned subsidiary of Colt Industries and is still the major manufacturer of large commercial and military aircraft landing gears.

DORR C. CARPENTER

Serial number 482, VH-CXR, with Gypsy Major, 135 hp.

Serial number 465 at Moorabin, Victoria, JOHN HOPTON - AUSTRALIA
*Australia, 1968. Shows Lycoming O-320, 150 hp
installation. Notice original Menasco nose fairing.*

Serial number 465 at Moorabin, JOHN HOPTON - AUSTRALIA
*Victoria, Australia, September or October 1968.
Shows Lycoming O-320, 150 hp installation.*

Chapter Fourteen

Chronology and Specifications

MENASCO AIRCRAFT ENGINES

MODEL B-2 MENASCO/SALMSON

Actually a French Salmson Z-9, a nine-cylinder air-cooled radial with a normal output of 250 hp at 1500 rpm, and a maximum output of 290 hp at 1750 rpm.

MODEL A-4 "PIRATE"
ATC #50

Developed in early 1930 as an inverted, four-cylinder, in-line air-cooled engine.
Approved rating of 90 hp at 1925 rpm.

MODEL B-4 "PIRATE"
ATC #65

Developed as an inverted, four cylinder, in-line, air-cooled engine. Approved rating of 95 hp at 2000 rpm.
The principal difference between the A-4 and the B-4 was in the arrangement of the accessories at the rear of the crankcase.
A memo dated April 7, 1936, covered approval of a battery ignition system. Another memo dated December 17, 1937, specified dual ignition, either Scintilla PN-4D or Bendix-Scintilla SF-4 R-1 magnetos or a Mallory battery ignition.

MODEL C-4 "PIRATE"
ATC #67

This engine received its ATC on January 14, 1931. It was again a further development of the A-4 and B-4 designs. It was rated at 125 hp at 2175 rpm.
ATC #67 was revised September 2, 1931, and again December 15, 1933, for specifying fuel of 80 octane rating. A memo dated April 7, 1936, covered approval of battery ignition systems. A specification dated December 17, 1937, called for fuel of 73 minimum octane rating, and dual ignition, with Scintilla PN-4D-F2, Bosch FU4, 888, JF4-ARS-13, or Bendix-Scintilla SF-4R-1 magnetos or Mallory battery ignition.

MODEL C-4S "PIRATE"
ATC #134

Issued this ATC number on November 21, 1934, the engine was rated 150 hp at 2260 rpm. It was approved for operation on 73-octane fuel. The supercharger gear ratio is 9.6 to 1.
Revised specification dated September 25, 1937 included a maximum (except take-off) rating as above with manifold pressure 32.3 inches hg. and one minute takeoff at 34.7 inches Hg. pressure. Dual ignition was either Scintilla PN-4D-F2, Bosch JF4-ARS-13 or Edison Splitdorf C magnetos. Specification dated November 16, 1937, added Bendix-Scintilla SF-4R-1 magnetos.
Approval to manufacture C-4S expired February 13, 1947.

MODEL B-6 "BUCCANEER"
ATC #68

Issued this ATC number on January 14, 1931, the engine was rated 160 hp at 1975 rpm. It was a 6 cylinder, inverted, in-line, air-cooled engine. About 90 percent of the parts of this engine are interchangeable with the B-4.
The bore was 4.5 inches stroke 5.125 inches. Displacement 489 cu. in., compression ratio of 5.5 to 1.

MODEL A-6 "BUCCANEER"
ATC #69

Issued this ATC number on January 14, 1931, the engine was rated 140 hp at 1925 rpm. It differs from the B-6 only in the system of carburetion. The mixture is supplied by a Stromberg NA-R5 2-inch carburetor of the up-draft type, mounted at the rear of the engine.

MODEL C-6S4 "SUPER BUCCANEER"
ATC #197

Issued this ATC number on July 12, 1938, the engine was rated 260 hp at 2300 rpm at 7500 feet altitude.

Similar to the C-6S with same bore and stroke.

MODEL C-6S "BUCCANEER"
NO ATC

The engine was rated 315 hp at 2600 rpm. Bore 4.75 inches, stroke 5.125 inches, displacement 544.5 cu in, compression ratio 5.8 to 1.

The engine was developed especially for racing airplanes.

The centrifugal supercharger is driven through a gear train having a ratio of 10.4 to 1.

This engine is identical to the B-6S except for the use of cylinders and pistons which are interchangeable with those of the "Pirate" C-4 and C-4S.

MODEL M-50
ATC #191

Issued this ATC number on February 8, 1938, the engine was rated 50 hp at 2500 rpm. The bore was 3.5 inch stroke 3.75 inches, displacement 144.4 cu in, compression ratio 5.25 to 1.

The engine was a 4 cylinder, horizontally opposed. It had a single ignition using a Bendix-Scintilla SF4L magneto. The engine is air-cooled.

MODEL 2-544 "UNITWIN POWER"
NO ATC

The engine was jointly developed in 1939 with the Lockheed Aircraft Corp. and Menasco Mfg. Corp.

It consisted of two Menasco C-6S4 (Super Buccaneer) engines placed side by side and geared to a single constant-speed propeller through a gear box and overriding clutches.

The advantages in such a twin-engine installation lie in retaining the reliability of twin engines without added complications and head resistance associated with the use of wing nacelles.

The engine provided 580 hp at 2400 rpm or 600 hp at 2500 rpm at 6800 feet altitude. Gear ratio (prop shaft) 1.5 to 1. Weight with all accessories was 1366 lbs.

MODEL D-4 "PIRATE"
ATC #67

In 1940, the D-4 appeared as an improved version of the C-4. It incorporated many refinements such as a new head design with 70 percent increase in cooling area due to improved finning, and fully enclosed rocker boxes, allowing oil lubrication of the rocker arms through the push rod enclosures.

Rocker boxes were scavenged through an additional line incorporated into the main scavenge pump. Spark plugs are centrally located. Pistons are forged. Connecting rods are of steel. New type oil pump with high capacity. New type manifolds and Stromberg up draft NA-R5 carburetor are used.

MODEL D4-83

This engine was in consideration but none are known to be in existence.

MODEL D4-87 "SUPER PIRATE"
ATC #67

This was a later model of the C-4 and was designed exclusively for the Canadian government to be used in some of their training aircraft at the outbreak of WW II. About 400 to 500 of these engines were built and shipped to Canada. None was ever sold in the United States (other than by Pacific Airmotive). Rumor suggests that the Canadian training plane got too heavy with this engine so the airplane was fitted with some other engine. It is also thought that the Menasco would be used in the Canadian Tiger Moth, but did not work out due to the opposite rotation from the Gypsy which messed up their rigging standards.

This engine was rated at 134 hp at 2260 rpm with the use of a Stromberg downdraft carburetor with model NAR-4D (1 7/16 in. venturi) and Bendix-Scintilla SF4R-9 magnetos. Maximum permissible cylinder head temperature 550° F, barrel 300° F, oil inlet 200° F.

Supercharging equipment for the C-4S will fit on the D4-87 but the C-4S accessory case will not.

Approval for models D-4 and D4-87 production expired on February 13, 1947. Engines manufactured after this date are not eligible for use in certified aircraft.

The D-4 or D4-87 engine would be designated a D-4B when equipped with a supercharger.

MODEL D-4B "SUPER PIRATE"
ATC #134

Same as the D-4 or D4-87 but equipped with a supercharger. The ATC # expired March 25, 1943.

NOTE - In 1939, Menasco purchased the remaining stock of engines and parts at the liquidation sale of the assets of the A.C.E. Corp. (American Cirrus Engines) of Marysville, Michigan, and thereafter they provided service to all users of American Cirrus engines.

The Menasco company acquired the remaining stock of "Gypsy" engines, parts from the Wright Aeronautical Corporation and revision of July 27, 1935, to ATC # 40 which had expired March 26, 1934, made eligible (for assy under this ATC #) the engine with serial numbers 51000 to 51050.

License to manufacture Menasco designs was purchased by Phillips & Powis Aircraft, Ltd., of Reading Aerodrome, Woodley, England.

No drawings are known to be in existence. Pacific Airmotive destroyed theirs some years ago, but Menasco furnished blueprints to deHavilland of Toronto, Canada, and to Phillips & Powis of Reading, England.

Some of the old engines have been used in northern United States and Canada on snow-sleds and air-boats.

MENASCO MANUFACTURING COMPANY AIRCRAFT ENGINES PRODUCTION SERIAL NUMBERS

B-4	162 through 187
C-4	170 through 500
C-4S	212 through 634-A3
D-4	
D-4B	7001, 7003-7031
D4-87	4301 through 4412

The above serial numbers were gleaned from name plates found on existing engines.

No known official Menasco company serial number list has ever been located.

MENASCO ENGINES

The Menasco Manufacturing Company, Los Angeles, California.

B-4 "Pirate"

Type	Air cooled, in-line, inverted
Bore	4 1/2"
Stroke	5 1/8"
Displacement	326 cu in
Compression Ratio	5.5 to 1
H.P. (Dept. of Comm. Rating)	95 @ 2000 rpm
A.T.C.	No. 65
Number of Cylinders	4
Ignition	2 Scintilla or Robt. Bosch magnetos
Carburetor	Stromberg NAR 3
Fuel Consumption	54 lbs/bbp/hr
Oil Consumption	.006 lbs/bbp/hr
Crankshaft Prop Hub End No. 10 S.A.E. Spline	
Dry Weight	285 lbs

MENASCO ENGINES

C-4 "Pirate"

Type	Air cooled, in-line, inverted
Bore	4 3/4"
Stroke	5 1/8"
Displacement	363 cu in
Compression Ratio	5.5 to 1
A.T.C.	No. 67
Number of Cylinders	4
Ignition	2 Scintilla or Robt. Bosch magnetos
Carburetor	Stromberg NA-R4D
Fuel Consumption	50 lbs/bbp/hr
Oil Consumption	.010 lbs/bbp/hr
Crankshaft Prop Hub End No. 10 S.A.E. Spline	
Dry Weight	290 lbs
H.P.	125 @ 2175 rpm

D-4 "Pirate"

Type	Air cooled, in-line, inverted
Bore	4 3/4"
Stroke	5 1/8"
Displacement	363 cu in
Compression Ratio	5.5 to 1
A.T.C.	No. 67
Number of Cylinders	4
Ignition	2 Scintilla SF4-R9 magnetos
Carburetor	Stromberg NAR-4D
Fuel Consumption	0.37 lbs/bbp/hr
Oil Consumption	0.010 lbs/bbp/hr
Dry Weight	305 lbs
H.P.	125 @ 2175 rpm

MENASCO ENGINES

C4-S "Pirate"

Type	Air cooled, in-line, inverted
Bore	4 3/4"
Stroke	5 1/8"
Displacement	363 cu in
Compression Ratio	5.5 to 1
H.P. (rated)	150 @ 2260 rpm @ 3000 ft @ 33" Hg.
A.T.C.	No. 134
Number of Cylinders	4
Ignition	2 Scintilla or Robt. Bosch mags
Carburetor	Stromberg NA-R5
Fuel Consumption	
@75% pwr 2050 rpm 9 1/2 gal/hour	
Oil Consumption	.025 lbs/bbp/hr
Crankshaft Prop Hub End No. 10 S.A.E. Spline	
Dry Weight	310 lbs
Supercharger Ratio (to crank speed)	9.6 to 1

MENASCO ENGINES

D-4B "Super Pirate"
(equipped with supercharger)

Type	Air cooled, in-line, inverted
Bore	4 3/4"
Stroke	5 1/8"
Displacement	363 cu in
Compression Ratio	5.7 to 1
H.P. (rated)	155 @ 2260 rpm @ 3000 ft
A.T.C.	"Non Assigned"
Number of Cylinders	4
Ignition	Bendix-Scintilla SF4R-9
Carburetor	Stromberg NA-R5 updraft
Fuel Consumption	0.48 lbs
Oil Consumption	0.020 lbs
Crankshaft Prop Hub End	?
Dry Weight	320 lbs
H.P.	125 @ 2175 rpm

D4-87 "Super Pirate"

Type	Air cooled, in-line, inverted
Bore	4 3/4"
Stroke	5 1/8"
Displacement	363 cu in.
Compression Ratio	6 to 1
H.P. (rated)	134 @ 2260 rpm
A.T.C.	No. 67
Number of Cylinders	4
Ignition	Bendix-Scintilla SF4R-9
Carburetor	Stromberg downdraft NAR-4D
Fuel Consumption	Same as D-4
Oil Consumption	Same as D-4

MENASCO MANUFACTURING COMPANY (1943)

HEAD OFFICE - Burbank, California
ESTABLISHED - 1926
PRESIDENT - Al Menasco

VICE PRES. - Bob Insley, O.E. Mohler, J.E. Royall
TREASURER - E.C. Carlson
SECRETARY - Robert R. Miller

During 1941, production was concentrated mainly on the 125 hp D-4 engine. Also that year they did an increasing amount of manufacturing of components — hydraulic shock absorber struts, for aircraft manufactured on the West Coast (Douglas, Boeing, North American).

Due to the lack of records, and the secrecy of World War II, it is only assumed that the last Menasco engine model was the C-4S2, apparently an up-rated version of the 150 hp C-4S to 165 hp by the designation "2". This designation was actually spelled out in the contract for the China Ryan STC-4 and STC-P4 airplanes in November 1939.

KINNER AIRCRAFT ENGINE

B-5, B-5R Series 2, & B-54

ATC	No. 51
Model	B-5, B-5R Series 2 or B-54
Rated hp	125 C.A.A. Rating
Rated rpm	1925 C.A.A. Rating
Type of Engine	Air-cooled radial
Number of cylinders	5
Bore	4 5/8"
Stroke	5 1/4"
Displacement	441 cu in
Compression ratio	5.25 to 1
Ignition	Two Bendix-Scintilla magnetos
Carburetor	Stromberg or Holley NA-R5A 419

KINNER R-440-1

BASICALLY SAME AS THE ABOVE

For PT-16A, PT-20A, and PT-21 airplanes
132 hp at 1975 R.P.M. at sea level
R-440-1 military designation via Technical Orders.
T.O. 01-100GC-1
T.O. 01-100GB-1

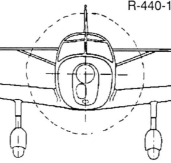

Chapter Fifteen

Ryan ST, ST-A, ST-A Special, STM, STM-2 Production Chronology

MODEL	POWER	REMARKS	PRODUCTION
ST	95 hp	Civilian	5
ST-A	125 hp	Civilian	73
ST-A Special	150 hp	Civilian	11
ST-B	125 hp	ST-A single cockpit	1
ST-W	125 & 160 hp	Warner eng. experimental	2
* STM	150 hp	Military export	22
PT-16	125 hp	U.S. Government	14
** PT-20	125 hp	U.S. Government	30
STM-2	150 hp	NEI Army	60
STM-2	150 hp	NEI Navy	48
STM-2E	150 hp	China	50
			316

* Export versions to -	Guatemala	12
	Honduras	3
	Ecuador	1
	Mexico	6
		22

** Includes s/n 406.

Note - Figures are based on actual original airframes produced and sold and accounted for. It does not include s/ns 1000 or 1001.

APPLICABLE INTERNATIONAL CIVIL AIRCRAFT REGISTRATION MARKINGS

Australia	VH	Bolivia	CP	Brazil	PT or PP	Canada	CF
Ecuador	HC	Guatemala	TG	Honduras	XH	Hong Kong	VR
Mexico	XA or XB	Netherlands	PK	New Zealand	ZK	Norway	N or LN
Philippine Republic	PI	South Africa	ZS	United States	N, X or		
Venezuela	YV				NC or NX		

RYAN ST CHRONOLOGY

S/N	REG NO.	MODEL	ENG./HP	REMARKS
100				Re; Boyd - Not used because number did not sound good.
101	X-14223	ST	B-4 95	Prototype
102	NC-14909	ST	B-4 95	First production ship
103	NC-14910	ST-A	C-4 125	Peter Dana airplane
104	NC-14911	ST	B-4 95	
105	NC-14912	ST-A	C-4 125	
106	NC-14913	ST-A	C-4 125	
107	NC-14914	ST-A	C-4 125	
108	NC-14952	ST-A	C-4 125	Went to Hawaii
109	NC-14953	ST-B	C-4 125	
110	NC-14954	ST-A	C-4 125	
111	NC-14955	ST-A	C-4 125	
112	NC-14956	ST-A	C-4 125	
113	NC-14957	ST-A	C-4 125	
114	NC-14982	ST-A	C-4 125	
115	NC-14983	ST-A	C-4 125	
116	NC-14984	ST-A	C-4 125	
117	NC-14985	ST	B-4 95	
118	NC-14986	ST-A	C-4 125	
119	NC-14987	ST-A	C-4 125	
120	NC-16031	ST-A	C-4 125	

S/N	REG. #	MODEL	ENG./HP	REMARKS
121	NC-16032	ST-A Sp	C-4S 150	
122	NC-16033	ST-A	C-4 125	
123	NC-16034	ST-A	C-4 125	
124	NC-16035	ST-A	C-4 125	
125	NC-16036	ST-A	C-4 125	
126	NC-16037	ST-A	C-4 125	Went to Brazil,16037 reassigned to s/n 178
127	NC-16038	ST-A	C-4 125	Went to Brazil
128	NC-16039	ST-A	C-4 125	Tex Rankin airplane
129	NC-16040	ST-A	C-4 125	
130	NC-16041	ST-A	C-4 125	Bettie Lund airplane
131	NC-16042	ST-A	C-4 125	
132	NC-16043	ST-A	C-4 125	
133	NC-16044	ST-A	C-4 125	
134	NC-17300	ST-A	C-4 125	
135	NC-17301	ST-A	C-4 125	
136	NC-17302	ST-A	C-4 125	
137	NC-17303	ST-A	C-4 125	
138	NC-17304	ST-A	C-4 125	
139	NC-17305	ST-A	C-4 125	
140	NC-17306	ST-A	C-4 125	
141	NC-17307	ST-A Sp	C-4S 150	
142	ZS-AIZ	ST-A	C-4 125	Went to S. Africa
143	NC-17343	ST-A	C-4 125	
144	NC-17344	ST-A	C-4 125	
145	ZS-AKP	ST-A	C-4 125	Went to S. Africa
146	ZS-AKR	ST-A	C-4 125	Went to S. Africa
147	ZS-ALY	ST-A	C-4 125	Went to S. Africa
148	NC-17345	ST-A	C-4 125	
149	NC-17346	ST-A	C-4 125	
150	NC-17347	ST-A	C-4 125	
151	NC-17348	ST-A	C-4 125	
152	NC-17349	ST-A	C-4 125	
153	NC-17350	ST-A	C-4 125	
154	NC-17351	ST-A	C-4 125	
155	ZS-AKU	ST	B-4 95	Went to S. Africa, last ST built
156	NC-17352	ST-A	C-4 125	
157	NC-17353	ST-A	C-4 125	
158	ZS-AKZ	ST-A	C-4 125	Went to S. Africa
159	NC-17354	ST-A	C-4 125	
160	NC-17355	ST-A	C-4 125	
161	NC-17356	ST-A	C-4 125	
162	HC-17357	ST-A	C-4 125	
163	NC-17358	ST-A	C-4 125	
164	NC-17359	ST-A Sp	C-4S 150	
165	YV-GTR3	ST-A	C-4 125	Went to Venezuela
166	NC-17361	ST-A	C-4 125	
167	NC-17362	ST-A	C-4 125	
168	NC-17363	ST-A	C-4 125	Went to S. Africa
169	ZS-ALZ	ST-A	C-4 125	Went to S. Africa
170	NC-17365	ST-A	C-4 125	
171	NC-17366	ST-A	C-4 125	
172	NC-17367	ST-A	C-4 125	
173	NC-17368	ST-A Sp	C-4S 150	
174	NC-17369	ST-A Sp	C-4S 150	
175	NC-17370	ST-A	C-4 125	
176	NC-17371	ST-A	C-4 125	
177	NC-17364	ST-A	C-4 125	
178	NC-16037	ST-A	C-4 125	
179	NC-18901	ST-A	C-4 125	Laura Ingalls' airplane
180	NACA-96	ST-A Sp	C-4S 150	For C.A.A. then N-180Y
181	NC-18903	ST-A Sp	C-4S 150	Went to Brazil
182	#1	ST-A Sp	C-4S 150	Mexican Air Force

S/N	REG. #	MODEL	ENG./HP	REMARKS
183	#2	ST-A Sp	C-4S 150	Mexican Air Force
184	#3	ST-A Sp	C-4S 150	Mexican Air Force
185	#4	ST-A Sp	C-4S 150	Mexican Air Force
186	#5	ST-A Sp	C-4S 150	Mexican Air Force
187	#6	ST-A Sp	C-4S 150	Mexican Air Force
188	NC-18904	ST-A Sp	C-4S 150	
189		ST-A Sp	C-4S 150	Honduran Air Force
190		ST-A Sp	C-4S 150	Honduran Air Force
191		ST-A Sp	C-4S 150	Honduran Air Force
192		ST-A Sp	C-4S 150	Guatemalan Air Force
193		ST-A Sp	C-4S 150	Guatemalan Air Force
194		ST-A Sp	C-4S 150	Guatemalan Air Force
195		ST-A Sp	C-4S 150	Guatemalan Air Force
196		ST-A Sp	C-4S 150	Guatemalan Air Force
197		ST-A Sp	C-4S 150	Guatemalan Air Force
198	NC-18902	ST-A	C-4 125	
199	NC-18905	ST-A Sp	C-4S 150	Went to Bolivia
200	NC-18906	ST-A Sp	C-4S 150	Went to Ecuador
201 to 214		Assigned for and to Ryan SC		
215 to 299		Reserved for SC but never used		
300		ST-A Sp	C-4S 150	Guatemalan Air Force
301		ST-A Sp	C-4S 150	Guatemalan Air Force
302		ST-A Sp	C-4S 150	Guatemalan Air Force
303		ST-A Sp	C-4S 150	Guatemalan Air Force
304		ST-A Sp	C-4S 150	Guatemalan Air Force
305		ST-A Sp	C-4S 150	Guatemalan Air Force
306	NC-18907	ST-A	C-4 125	XPT-16 #39-717
307	40-40	YPT-16	C-4 125	USAAC to YPT-16A
308	40-41	YPT-16	C-4 125	USAAC to YPT-16A
309	40-42	YPT-16	C-4 125	USAAC to YPT-16A
310	40-43	YPT-16	C-4 125	USAAC to YPT-16A
311	40-44	YPT-16	C-4 125	USAAC to YPT-16A
312	NC-18922	ST-A	C-4 125	
313	40-45	YPT-16	C-4 125	USAAC to YPT-16A
314	40-46	YPT-16	C-4 125	USAAC to YPT-16A
315	40-47	YPT-16	C-4 125	USAAC to YPT-16A
316	40-48	YPT-16	C-4 125	USAAC to YPT-16A
317	40-49	YPT-16	C-4 125	USAAC to YPT-16A
318	40-50	YPT-16	C-4 125	USAAC to YPT-16A
319	40-51	YPT-16	C-4 125	USAAC to YPT-16A
320	40-52	YPT-16	C-4 125	USAAC to YPT-16A
321	40-54	YPT-16	C-4 125	USAAC to YPT-16A
322	NC-18923	ST-A	C-4 125	
323	40-2387	PT-20	C-4 125	USAAC to PT-20A
324	40-2388	PT-20	C-4 125	USAAC to PT-20B
325	40-2389	PT-20	C-4 125	USAAC to PT-20A
326	40-2390	PT-20	C-4 125	USAAC to PT-20A
327	40-2391	PT-20	C-4 125	USAAC to PT-20A
328	40-2392	PT-20	C-4 125	USAAC to PT-20A
329	40-2393	PT-20	C-4 125	USAAC to PT-20A
330	40-2394	PT-20	C-4 125	USAAC to PT-20A
331	40-2395	PT-20	C-4 125	USAAC to PT-20A
332	40-2396	PT-20	C-4 125	USAAC to PT-20B
333	40-2397	PT-20	C-4 125	USAAC to PT-20A
334	40-2398	PT-20	C-4 125	USAAC to PT-20A
335	40-2399	PT-20	C-4 125	USAAC to PT-20A
336	40-2400	PT-20	C-4 125	USAAC to PT-20A
337	NX-18920	ST-W Warner S-50 125		Experimental
	40-2401	PT-20	Kinner B-5	
338	NX-18919	ST-W	Warner 165	Experimental
	40-53	YPT-16		
339	NC-18921	ST-A Sp	C-4S 150	

S/N	REG. #	MODEL	ENG./HP	REMARKS
340	40-2402	PT-20	C-4 125	USAAC to PT-20A
341	40-2403	PT-20	C-4 125	USAAC to PT-20A
342	40-2404	PT-20	C-4 125	USAAC crash 8-26-40
343	40-2405	PT-20	C-4 125	USAAC to PT-20A
344	40-2406	PT-20	C-4 125	USAAC to PT-20A
345	40-2407	PT-20	C-4 125	USAAC to PT-20A
346	40-2408	PT-20	C-4 125	USAAC to PT-20A
347	40-2409	PT-20	C-4 125	USAAC to PT-20A
348	40-2410	PT-20	C-4 125	USAAC to PT-20A
349	40-2411	PT-20	C-4 125	USAAC to PT-20A
350	40-2412	PT-20	C-4 125	USAAC to PT-20A
351	40-2413	PT-20	C-4 125	USAAC to PT-20A
352	40-2414	PT-20	C-4 125	USAAC to PT-20A
353	40-2415	PT-20	C-4 125	USAAC to PT-20A
354	40-2416	PT-20	C-4 125	USAAC to PT-20A
355	NC-9	ST-A	C-4 125	To C.A.A.

RYAN STM-2E & STM-2P for CHINA

S/N	MODEL	CHINESE S/N	REMARKS	S/N	MODEL	CHINESE S/N	REMARKS
356	STM-2E	1R		382	STM-2E	27R	
357	STM-2E	2R		383	STM-2E	28R	
358	STM-2E	3R		384	STM-2E	29R	
359	STM-2E	4R		385	STM-2E	30R	
360	STM-2E	5R		386	STM-2E	31R	
361	STM-2E	6R		387	STM-2E	32R	
362	STM-2E	7R		388	STM-2E	33R	
363	STM-2E	8R		389	STM-2E	34R	
364	STM-2E	9R		390	STM-2E	35R	
365	STM-2E	10R		391	STM-2E	36R	
366	STM-2E	11R		392	STM-2E	37R	
367	STM-2E	12R		393	STM-2E	38R	
368	STM-2E	13R		394	STM-2E	39R	
369	STM-2E	14R		395	STM-2E	40R	
370	STM-2E	15R		396	STM-2E	41R	
371	STM-2E	16R		397	STM-2E	42R	Photo on pg. 28 "Ryan Guide Book" (Authors Dorr Carpenter and Mitch Mayborn, Flying Enterprises Publications, Dallas, Texas 2nd Edition 1976)
372	STM-2E	17R					
373	STM-2E	18R					
374	STM-2E	19R		398	STM-2E	43R	
375	STM-2P*	20R	*Pursuit Trainer	399	STM-2E	44R	
376	STM-2P*	21R	*Pursuit Trainer	400	STM-2E	45R	
377	STM-2E	22R		401	STM-2E	46R	
378	STM-2E	23R		402	STM-2E	47R	
379	STM-2E	24R		403	STM-2E	48R	
380	STM-2E	25R		404	STM-2E	49R	
381	STM-2E	26R		405	STM-2E	50R	

Note: STM-2E also known as STM-E2, STC-4, STC-5
        STM-2P also known as STM-P2, STC-P4, STC-P5

406	PT-20 STK		NX-18924	Kinner K-5	Prototype Experimental

RYAN STM-2 & STM-S2 for NETHERLANDS EAST INDIES

S/N	MODEL	DUTCH #	AUSTR. #	MILITARY BRANCH	REMARKS
407	STM-2	RO-10		NEI Army	Captured
408	STM-2	RO-11		NEI Army	Lost in war
409	STM-2	RO-12		NEI Army	Lost in war
410	STM-2	RO-13		NEI Army	Lost in war
411	STM-2	RO-14		NEI Army	Lost in war
412	STM-2	RO-15		NEI Army	Lost in war

S/N	MODEL	DUTCH #	AUSTR. #	MILITARY BRANCH	REMARKS
413	STM-2	RO-16		NEI Army	Lost in war
414	STM-2	RO-17		NEI Army	Lost in war
415	STM-2	RO-18		NEI Army	Lost in war
416	STM-2	RO-19		NEI Army	Lost in war
417	STM-2	RO-20		NEI Army	Lost in war
418	STM-2	RO-21		NEI Army	Lost in war
419	STM-2	RO-22		NEI Army	Lost in war
420	STM-2	RO-23		NEI Army	Lost in war
421	STM-2	RO-24		NEI Army	Lost in war
422	STM-2	RO-25		NEI Army	Lost in war
423	STM-2	RO-26		NEI Army	Captured
424	STM-2	RO-27		NEI Army	Lost in war
425	STM-2	RO-28		NEI Army	Captured
426	STM-2	RO-29		NEI Army	Lost in war
427	STM-2	RO-30		NEI Army	Lost in war
428	STM-2	RO-31		NEI Army	Lost in war
429	STM-2	RO-32		NEI Army	Lost in war
430	STM-2	RO-33		NEI Army	Lost in war
431	STM-2	RO-34		NEI Army	Lost in war
432	STM-2	RO-35		NEI Army	Lost in war
433	STM-2	RO-36		NEI Army	Lost in war
434	STM-2	RO-37		NEI Army	Lost in war
435	STM-2	RO-38		NEI Army	Lost in war
436	STM-2	RO-39		NEI Army	Lost in war
437	STM-2	RO-40		NEI Army	Lost in war
438	STM-2	RO-41		NEI Army	Lost in war
439	STM-2	RO-42		NEI Army	Lost in war
440	STM-2	RO-43		NEI Army	Lost in war
441	STM-2	RO-44		NEI Army	Captured
442	STM-2	RO-45		NEI Army	Lost in war
443	STM-2	RO-46		NEI Army	Lost in war
444	STM-2	RO-47		NEI Army	Lost in war
445	STM-2	RO-48		NEI Army	Captured
446	STM-2	RO-49		NEI Army	Lost in war
447	STM-S2	S-11		NEI Navy	Lost in war
448	STM-S2	S-12		NEI Navy	Lost in war
449	STM-S2	S-13		NEI Navy	Lost in war
450	STM-S2	S-14	A50-7 A50-8 A50-10 A50-14 A50-16 A50-18 A50-19 A50-20	NEI Navy	To Australia
451	STM-S2	S-15		NEI Navy	Lost in war
452	STM-S2	S-16	(?)	NEI Navy	Aust.Hong Kng.Norway & US
453	STM-S2	S-17	A50-24	NEI Navy	To Australia
454	STM-S2	S-18	A50-27	NEI Navy	To Australia
455	STM-S2	S-19	A50-25	NEI Navy	To Australia
456	STM-S2	S-20		NEI Navy	Lost in war
457	STM-S2	S-21	A50-30	NEI Navy	To Australia & US
458	STM-S2	S-22	A50-17	NEI Navy	To Australia & US
459	STM-2	S-23	A50-11	NEI Navy	To Australia
460	STM-2	S-24	A50-15	NEI Navy	To Australia
461	STM-2	S-25	A50-33	NEI Navy	To Australia
462	STM-2	S-26	A50-21	NEI Navy	To Australia
463	STM-2	S-27	A50-12	NEI Navy	To Australia & US
464	STM-2	S-28	A50-4	NEI Navy	To Australia & US
465	STM-2	S-29	A50-22	NEI Navy	To Australia

S/N	MODEL	DUTCH #	AUSTR. #	MILITARY BRANCH	REMARKS
466	STM-2	S-30	A50-18	NEI Navy	To Australia
467	STM-2	S-31	A50-2	NEI Navy	To Australia
468	STM-2	S-32	A50-32	NEI Navy	Lost in war
469	STM-2	S-33	A50-34	NEI Navy	To Australia
470	STM-2	S-34		NEI Navy	Lost in war
471	STM-2	S-35	A50-23	NEI Navy	To Australia
472	STM-2	S-36		NEI Navy	Lost in war
473	STM-2	S-37	A50-1	NEI Navy	To Australia
474	STM-2	S-38	A50-19	NEI Navy	To Australia
475	STM-2	S-39	A50-9	NEI Navy	To Australia
476	STM-S2	S-40	A50-31	NEI Navy	To Australia & US
477	STM-2	S-41	A50-10	NEI Navy	To Australia
478	STM-2	S-42		NEI Navy	Lost in war
479	STM-2	S-43		NEI Navy	Lost in war
480	STM-2	S-44		NEI Navy	To Australia & US
481	STM-2	S-45	A50-32	NEI Navy	To Australia
482	STM-2	S-46	(?)	NEI Navy	To Australia
483	STM-2	S-47	A50-5	NEI Navy	To Australia
484	STM-2	S-48	A50-28	NEI Navy	To Australia
485	STM-2	S-49	A50-14	NEI Navy	To Australia
486	STM-2	S-50	A50-16	NEI Navy	To Australia
487	STM-2	S-51	A50-8	NEI Navy	To Australia
488	STM-2	S-52		NEI Navy	Lost in war
489	STM-2	S-53	A50-13	NEI Navy	To Australia, New Zealand
490	STM-2	S-54	A50-26	NEI Navy	To Australia & US
491	STM-2	S-55	A50-20	NEI Navy	To Australia
492	STM-2	S-56	A50-29	NEI Navy	To Australia
493	STM-2	S-57	A50-6	NEI Navy	To Australia
494	STM-2	S-58	A50-3	NEI Navy	To Australia & US
495	STM-2	RO-50		NEI Army	Lost in war
496	STM-2	RO-51		NEI Army	Lost in war
497	STM-2	RO-52		NEI Army	Lost in war
498	STM-2	RO-53		NEI Army	Lost in war
499	STM-2	RO-54		NEI Army	Lost in war
500	STM-2	RO-55		NEI Army	Lost in war
501	STM-2	RO-56		NEI Army	Lost in war
502	STM-2	RO-57		NEI Army	Lost in war
503	STM-2	RO-58		NEI Army	Lost in war
504	STM-2	RO-59		NEI Army	Lost in war
505	STM-2	RO-60		NEI Army	Lost in war
506	STM-2	RO-61		NEI Army	Lost in war
507	STM-2	RO-62		NEI Army	Lost in war
508	STM-2	RO-63		NEI Army	Lost in war
509	STM-2	RO-64		NEI Army	Lost in war
510	STM-2	RO-65		NEI Army	Captured
511	STM-2	RO-66		NEI Army	Lost in war
512	STM-2	RO-67		NEI Army	Lost in war
513	STM-2	RO-68		NEI Army	Lost in war
514	STM-2	RO-69		NEI Army	Lost in war

Note - All of the Netherlands East Indies Ryans were powered with Menasco C-4S 150 hp engines.

No further s/n's allocated up to 1000. Reason unknown. Perhaps uncertainty of World War II.

| 1000 | NX-18925 | ST-3,PT-21 | Kinner B-54 | | Second prototype ST-3KR (PT-21, PT-22, NR-1 series). |
| 1001 | NX-18926 NC-18926 N-18926 | ST-3,PT-22 | Kinner R-55 | | Third prototype ST-3KR (PT-21, PT-22, NR-1 series). Existing as N-18926 in 1976. Issued ATC #749 2/16/42 |

QUICK REFERENCE <u>*CIVIL MARKINGS*</u> *AUSTRALIA RYANS*

S/N	MODEL	NAVY S/N	RAAF S/N	Military Branch	AUST. CIVIL REG. #
450	STM-S2	S-14	A50-7(etc.)	NEI Navy	VH-AHF, VH-AHE ?
451	STM-S2	S-15		NEI Navy	
452	STM-S2	S-16	(?)	NEI Navy	VH-AGY, VR-HDL, LN-TVF
453	STM-S2	S-17	A50-24	NEI Navy	
454	STM-S2	S-18	A50-27	NEI Navy	VH-AGU, VH-WEB
455	STM-S2	S-19	A50-25	NEI Navy	
456	STM-S2	S-20		NEI Navy	
457	STM-S2	S-21	A50-30	NEI Navy	VH-BBJ, VH-BXN, VH-RUM
458	STM-S2	S-22	A50-17	NEI Navy	VH-AGV, VH-WFS
459	STM-2	S-23	A50-11	NEI Navy	VH-AGD
460	STM-2	S-24	A50-15	NEI Navy	
461	STM-2	S-25	A50-33	NEI Navy	
462	STM-2	S-26	A50-21	NEI Navy	
463	STM-2	S-27	A50-12	NEI Navy	
464	STM-2	S-28	A50-4	NEI Navy	VH-ARR, VH-BNG, VH-RAF
465	STM-2	S-29	A50-22	NEI Navy	VH-AGW
466	STM-2	S-30	A50-18	NEI Navy	VH-BBJ, VH-AGR
467	STM-2	S-31	A50-2	NEI Navy	VH-AHS, VH-RAE, VH-AGQ VH-ARS
468	STM-2	S-32	A50-32	NEI Navy	
469	STM-2	S-33	A50-34	NEI Navy	VH-AHD
470	STM-2	S-34		NEI Navy	
471	STM-2	S-35	A50-23	NEI Navy	VH-BWQ
472	STM-2	S-36		NEI Navy	
473	STM-2	S-37	A50-1	NEI Navy	VH-AGQ
474	STM-2	S-38	A50-19	NEI Navy	VH-AHE
475	STM-2	S-39	A50-9	NEI Navy	VH-AGR, VH-BBJ, VH-AGR
476	STM-S2	S-40	A50-31	NEI Navy	VH-AGZ
477	STM-2	S-41	A50-10	NEI Navy	
478	STM-2	S-42		NEI Navy	
479	STM-2	S-43		NEI Navy	
480	STM-2	S-44		NEI Navy	
481	STM-2	S-45	A50-32	NEI Navy	VH-AHA
482	STM-2	S-46	(?)	NEI Navy	VH-CXR
483	STM-2	S-47	A50-5	NEI Navy	VH-AGR
484	STM-2	S-48	A50-28	NEI Navy	
485	STM-2	S-49	A50-14	NEI Navy	
486	STM-2	S-50	A50-16	NEI Navy	
487	STM-2	S-51	A50-8	NEI Navy	
488	STM-2	S-52		NEI Navy	
489	STM-2	S-53	A50-13	NEI Navy	VH-AGS ZK-BEM
490	STM-2	S-54	A50-26	NEI Navy	VH-AGX, VH-RDH, VH-HDM
491	STM-2	S-55	A50-20	NEI Navy	VH-ADM ?
492	STM-2	S-56	A50-29	NEI Navy	VH-AHC
493	STM-2	S-57	A50-6	NEI Navy	VH-AGB, VH-ASB ?
494	STM-2	S-58	A50-3	NEI Navy	VH-AHG, VR-HDK (Philippines) PI-C324

QUICK REFERENCE <u>*CIVIL MARKINGS*</u> *SOUTH AFRICA RYANS*

S/N	MODEL	S. AFR. REG. #	SAAF #S/N	REMARKS
142	ST-A	ZS-AIZ		
145	ST-A	ZS-AKP	1446	
146	ST-A	ZS-AKR	1481	
147	ST-A	ZS-ALY		
155	ST	ZS-AKU	1482	
158	ST-A	ZS-AKZ	1506	
168	ST-A	ZS-ARY		Was U.S.A. NC-17363
169	ST-A	ZS-ALZ	1437	

Note - SAAF Indicates South African Air Force

CHRONOLOGY PT-21, PT-22, NR-1

S/N	A.A.F. *U.S. Navy Serial #	Model
1002	41-1881	PT-21
1003	41-1882	PT-21
1004	41-1883	PT-21
1005	41-1884	PT-21
1006	41-1885	PT-21
1007	41-1886	PT-21
1008	41-1887	PT-21
1009	41-1888	PT-21
1010	41-1889	PT-21
1011	41-1890	PT-21
1012	41-1891	PT-21
1013	41-1892	PT-21
1014	41-1893	PT-21
1015	41-1894	PT-21
1016	41-1895	PT-21
1017	41-1896	PT-21
1018	41-1897	PT-21
1019	41-1898	PT-21
1020	41-1899	PT-21
1021	41-1900	PT-21
1022	41-1901	PT-21
1023	41-1902	PT-21
1024	41-1903	PT-21
1025	41-1904	PT-21
1026	41-1905	PT-21
1027	41-1906	PT-21
1028	41-1907	PT-21
1029	41-1908	PT-21
1030	41-1909	PT-21
1031	41-1910	PT-21
1032	41-1911	PT-21
1033	41-1912	PT-21
1034	41-1913	PT-21
1035	41-1914	PT-21
1036	41-1915	PT-21
1037	41-1916	PT-21
1038	41-1917	PT-21
1039	41-1918	PT-21
1040	41-1919	PT-21
1041	41-1920	PT-21
1042	41-1921	PT-21
1043	41-1922	PT-21
1044	41-1923	PT-21
1045	41-1924	PT-21
1046	41-1925	PT-21
1047	41-1926	PT-21
1048	41-1927	PT-21
1049	41-1928	PT-21
1050	41-1929	PT-21
1051	41-1930	PT-21
1052	41-1931	PT-21
1053	41-1932	PT-21
1054	41-1933	PT-21
1055	41-1934	PT-21
1056	41-1935	PT-21
1057	41-1936	PT-21
1058	41-1937	PT-21
1059	41-1938	PT-21
1060	*4099	NR-1
1061	41-1939	PT-21
1062	41-1940	PT-21
1063	41-1941	PT-21
1064	41-1942	PT-21
1065	41-1943	PT-21
1066	41-1944	PT-21
1067	41-1945	PT-21
1068	41-1946	PT-21
1069	41-1947	PT-21
1070	41-1948	PT-21
1071	41-1949	PT-21
1072	41-1950	PT-21
1073	41-1951	PT-21
1074	41-1952	PT-21
1075	41-1953	PT-21
1076	41-1954	PT-21
1077	41-15173	to Ecuador
1078	41-15174	to Ecuador
1079	41-15175	to Ecuador
1080	41-15176	to Ecuador
1081	*4100	NR-1
1082	4101	NR-1
1083	4102	NR-1
1084	4103	NR-1
1085	4104	NR-1
1086	4105	NR-1
1087	4106	NR-1
1088	4107	NR-1
1089	4108	NR-1
1090	4109	NR-1
1091	4110	NR-1
1092	4111	NR-1
1093	4112	NR-1
1094	4113	NR-1
1095	4114	NR-1
1096	4115	NR-1
1097	4116	NR-1
1098	4117	NR-1
1099	4118	NR-1
1100	4119	NR-1
1101	4120	NR-1
1102	4121	NR-1
1103	4122	NR-1
1104	4123	NR-1
1105	4124	NR-1
1106	4125	NR-1
1107	4126	NR-1
1108	4127	NR-1
1109	4128	NR-1
1110	4129	NR-1
1111	4130	NR-1
1112	4131	NR-1
1113	4132	NR-1
1114	4133	NR-1
1115	4134	NR-1
1116	4135	NR-1
1117	4136	NR-1
1118	4137	NR-1
1119	4138	NR-1
1120	4139	NR-1
1121	4140	NR-1
1122	4141	NR-1
1123	4142	NR-1
1124	4143	NR-1
1125	4144	NR-1
1126	4145	NR-1
1127	4146	NR-1
1128	4147	NR-1
1129	4148	NR-1
1130	4149	NR-1
1131	4150	NR-1
1132	4151	NR-1
1133	4152	NR-1
1134	4153	NR-1
1135	4154	NR-1
1136	4155	NR-1
1137	4156	NR-1
1138	4157	NR-1
1139	4158	NR-1
1140	4159	NR-1
1141	4160	NR-1
1142	4161	NR-1
1143	4162	NR-1
1144	4163	NR-1
1145	4164	NR-1
1146	4165	NR-1
1147	4166	NR-1
1148	4167	NR-1
1149	4168	NR-1
1150	4169	NR-1
1151	4170	NR-1
1152	4171	NR-1
1153	4172	NR-1
1154	4173	NR-1
1155	41-1955	PT-21
1156	41-1956	PT-21
1157	41-1957	PT-21
1158	41-1958	PT-21
1159	41-1959	PT-21
1160	41-1960	PT-21
1161	41-1961	PT-21
1162	41-1962	PT-21
1163	41-1963	PT-21
1164	41-1964	PT-21
1165	41-1965	PT-21
1166	41-1966	PT-21
1167	41-1967	PT-21
1168	41-1968	PT-21
1169	41-1969	PT-21
1170	41-1970	PT-21
1171	41-1971	PT-21
1172	41-1972	PT-21
1173	41-1973	PT-21
1174	41-1974	PT-21
1175	41-1975	PT-21
1176	41-1976	PT-21
1177	41-1977	PT-21
1178	41-1978	PT-21
1179	41-1979	PT-21
1180	41-1980	PT-21
1181	4174	NR-1
1182	4175	NR-1
1183	4176	NR-1
1184	4177	NR-1
1185	4178	NR-1
1186	4179	NR-1
1187	4180	NR-1
1188	4181	NR-1
1189	4182	NR-1
1190	4183	NR-1
1191	4184	NR-1
1192	4185	NR-1
1193	4186	NR-1
1194	4187	NR-1
1195	4188	NR-1
1196	4189	NR-1
1197	4190	NR-1
1198	4191	NR-1
1199	4192	NR-1
1200	4193	NR-1
1201	4194	NR-1
1202	4195	NR-1
1203	4196	NR-1
1204	4197	NR-1
1205	4198	NR-1
1206	41-15177	PT-22 China
1207	41-15178	PT-22 China
1208	41-15179	PT-22 China
1209	41-15180	PT-22 China
1210	41-15181	PT-22 China
1211	41-15182	PT-22 China
1212	41-15183	PT-22 China
1213	41-15184	PT-22 China
1214	41-15185	PT-22 China
1215	41-15186	PT-22 China
1216	41-15187	PT-22 China
1217	41-15188	PT-22 China
1218	41-15189	PT-22 China
1219	41-15190	PT-22 China
1220	41-15191	PT-22 China
1221	41-15192	PT-22 China
1222	41-15193	PT-22 China
1223	41-15194	PT-22 China
1224	41-15195	PT-22 China
1225	41-15196	PT-22 China
1226	41-15197	PT-22 China
1227	41-15198	PT-22 China
1228	41-15199	PT-22 China
1229	41-15200	PT-22 China
1230	41-15201	PT-22 China
1231	41-15202	PT-22 China
1232	41-15203	PT-22 China
1233	41-15204	PT-22 China
1234	41-15205	PT-22 China
1235	41-15206	PT-22 China
1236	41-15207	PT-22 China
1237	41-15208	PT-22 China
1238	41-15209	PT-22 China
1239	41-15210	PT-22 China
1240	41-15211	PT-22 China
1241	41-15212	PT-22 China
1242	41-15213	PT-22 China
1243	41-15214	PT-22 China
1244	41-15215	PT-22 China
1245	41-15216	PT-22 China
1246	41-15217	PT-22
1247	41-15218	PT-22
1248	41-15219	PT-22
1249	41-15220	PT-22
1250	41-15221	PT-22
1251	41-15222	PT-22
1252	41-15223	PT-22
1253	41-15224	PT-22
1254	41-15225	PT-22
1255	41-15226	PT-22
1256	41-15227	PT-22
1257	41-15228	PT-22
1258	41-15229	PT-22
1259	41-15230	PT-22
1260	41-15231	PT-22
1261	41-15232	PT-22
1262	41-15233	PT-22
1263	41-15234	PT-22
1264	41-15235	PT-22
1265	41-15236	PT-22
1266	41-15237	PT-22
1267	41-15238	PT-22
1268	41-15239	PT-22
1269	41-15240	PT-22
1270	41-15241	PT-22
1271	41-15242	PT-22
1272	41-15243	PT-22
1273	41-15244	PT-22
1274	41-15245	PT-22
1275	41-15246	PT-22
1276	41-15247	PT-22
1277	41-15248	PT-22
1278	41-15249	PT-22
1279	41-15250	PT-22
1280	41-15251	PT-22
1281	41-15252	PT-22
1282	41-15253	PT-22
1283	41-15254	PT-22
1284	41-15255	PT-22
1285	41-15256	PT-22
1286	41-15257	PT-22
1287	41-15258	PT-22
1288	41-15259	PT-22
1289	41-15260	PT-22
1290	41-15261	PT-22
1291	41-15262	PT-22
1292	41-15263	PT-22
1293	41-15264	PT-22
1294	41-15265	PT-22
1295	41-15266	PT-22
1296	41-15267	PT-22
1297	41-15268	PT-22
1298	41-15269	PT-22
1299	41-15270	PT-22
1300	41-15271	PT-22
1301	41-15272	PT-22
1302	41-15273	PT-22
1303	41-15274	PT-22
1304	41-15275	PT-22
1305	41-15276	PT-22
1306	41-15277	PT-22
1307	41-15278	PT-22
1308	41-15279	PT-22
1309	41-15280	PT-22
1310	41-15281	PT-22
1311	41-15282	PT-22
1312	41-15283	PT-22
1313	41-15284	PT-22
1314	41-15285	PT-22
1315	41-15286	PT-22
1316	41-15287	PT-22
1317	41-15288	PT-22
1318	41-15289	PT-22
1319	41-15290	PT-22
1320	41-15291	PT-22
1321	41-15292	PT-22
1322	41-15293	PT-22
1323	41-15294	PT-22
1324	41-15295	PT-22
1325	41-15296	PT-22
1326	41-15297	PT-22
1327	41-15298	PT-22 China
1328	41-15299	PT-22 China
1329	41-15300	PT-22 China
1330	41-15301	PT-22 China
1331	41-15302	PT-22 China
1332	41-15303	PT-22 China
1333	41-15304	PT-22 China
1334	41-15305	PT-22 China
1335	41-15306	PT-22 China
1336	41-15307	PT-22 China
1337	41-15308	PT-22 China
1338	41-15309	PT-22 China
1339	41-15310	PT-22 China
1340	41-15311	PT-22 China
1341	41-15312	PT-22 China
1342	41-15313	PT-22 China
1343	41-15314	PT-22 China
1344	41-15315	PT-22 China
1345	41-15316	PT-22 China
1346	41-15317	PT-22 China
1347	41-15318	PT-22 China
1348	41-15319	PT-22 China
1349	41-15320	PT-22 China
1350	41-15321	PT-22 China
1351	41-15322	PT-22 China
1352	41-15323	PT-22 China
1353	41-15324	PT-22 China
1354	41-15325	PT-22 China
1355	41-15326	PT-22 China
1356	41-15327	PT-22 China
1357	41-15328	PT-22
1358	41-15329	PT-22
1359	41-15330	PT-22
1360	41-15331	PT-22
1361	41-15332	PT-22
1362	41-15333	PT-22
1363	41-15334	PT-22
1364	41-15335	PT-22
1365	41-15336	PT-22
1366	41-15337	PT-22
1367	41-15338	PT-22
1368	41-15339	PT-22
1369	41-15340	PT-22
1370	41-15341	PT-22
1371	41-15342	PT-22
1372	41-15343	PT-22
1373	41-15344	PT-22
1374	41-15345	PT-22
1375	41-15346	PT-22
1376	41-15347	PT-22
1377	41-15348	PT-22
1378	41-15349	PT-22
1379	41-15350	PT-22
1380	41-15351	PT-22
1381	41-15352	PT-22
1382	41-15353	PT-22
1383	41-15354	PT-22
1384	41-15355	PT-22
1385	41-15356	PT-22
1386	41-15357	PT-22
1387	41-15358	PT-22
1388	41-15359	PT-22
1389	41-15360	PT-22
1390	41-15361	PT-22
1391	41-15362	PT-22
1392	41-15363	PT-22
1393	41-15364	PT-22
1394	41-15365	PT-22
1395	41-15366	PT-22
1396	41-15367	PT-22
1397	41-15368	PT-22
1398	41-15369	PT-22
1399	41-15370	PT-22
1400	41-15371	PT-22
1401	41-15372	PT-22
1402	41-15373	PT-22
1403	41-15374	PT-22
1404	41-15375	PT-22
1405	41-15376	PT-22
1406	41-15377	PT-22
1407	41-15378	PT-22
1408	41-15379	PT-22
1409	41-15380	PT-22
1410	41-15381	PT-22
1411	41-15382	PT-22
1412	41-15383	PT-22
1413	41-15384	PT-22
1414	41-15385	PT-22
1415	41-15386	PT-22
1416	41-15387	PT-22
1417	41-15388	PT-22
1418	41-15389	PT-22
1419	41-15390	PT-22
1420	41-15391	PT-22
1421	41-15392	PT-22
1422	41-15393	PT-22
1423	41-15394	PT-22
1424	41-15395	PT-22
1425	41-15396	PT-22
1426	41-15397	PT-22
1427	41-15398	PT-22
1428	41-15399	PT-22
1429	41-15400	PT-22
1430	41-15401	PT-22
1431	41-15402	PT-22
1432	41-15403	PT-22
1433	41-15404	PT-22
1434	41-15405	PT-22
1435	41-15406	PT-22
1436	41-15407	PT-22

CHRONOLOGY PT-21, PT-22, NR-1

S/N	A.A.F. *U.S. Navy Serial #	Model	S/N	A.A.F. *U.S. Navy Serial #	Model	S/N	A.A.F. *U.S. Navy Serial #	Model	S/N	A.A.F. *U.S. Navy Serial #	Model	S/N	A.A.F. *U.S. Navy Serial #	Model
1437	41-15408	PT-22	1522	41-15493	PT-22	1607	41-15578	PT-22	1692	41-15663	PT-22	1777	42-57481	PT-22A
1438	41-15409	PT-22	1523	41-15494	PT-22	1608	41-15579	PT-22	1693	41-15664	PT-22	1778	42-57482	PT-22A
1439	41-15410	PT-22	1524	41-15495	PT-22	1609	41-15580	PT-22	1694	41-15665	PT-22	1779	42-57483	PT-22A
1440	41-15411	PT-22	1525	41-15496	PT-22	1610	41-15581	PT-22	1695	41-15666	PT-22	1780	42-57484	PT-22A
1441	41-15412	PT-22	1526	41-15497	PT-22	1611	41-15582	PT-22	1696	41-15667	PT-22	1781	42-57485	PT-22A
1442	41-15413	PT-22	1527	41-15498	PT-22	1612	41-15583	PT-22	1697	41-15668	PT-22	1782	42-57486	PT-22A
1443	41-15414	PT-22	1528	41-15499	PT-22	1613	41-15584	PT-22	1698	41-15669	PT-22	1783	42-57487	PT-22A
1444	41-15415	PT-22	1529	41-15500	PT-22	1614	41-15585	PT-22	1699	41-15670	PT-22	1784	42-57488	PT-22A
1445	41-15416	PT-22	1530	41-15501	PT-22	1615	41-15586	PT-22	1700	41-15671	PT-22	1785	42-57489	PT-22A
1446	41-15417	PT-22	1531	41-15502	PT-22	1616	41-15587	PT-22	1701	41-15672	PT-22	1786	42-57490	PT-22A
1447	41-15418	PT-22	1532	41-15503	PT-22	1617	41-15588	PT-22	1702	41-15673	PT-22	1787	42-57491	PT-22A
1448	41-15419	PT-22	1533	41-15504	PT-22	1618	41-15589	PT-22	1703	41-15674	PT-22	1788	42-57492	PT-22A
1449	41-15420	PT-22	1534	41-15505	PT-22	1619	41-15590	PT-22	1704	41-15675	PT-22	1789	42-57493	PT-22A
1450	41-15421	PT-22	1535	41-15506	PT-22	1620	41-15591	PT-22	1705	41-15676	PT-22	1790	42-57494	PT-22A
1451	41-15422	PT-22	1536	41-15507	PT-22	1621	41-15592	PT-22	1706	41-15677	PT-22	1791	42-57495	PT-22A
1452	41-15423	PT-22	1537	41-15508	PT-22	1622	41-15593	PT-22	1707	41-15678	PT-22	1792	42-57496	PT-22A
1453	41-15424	PT-22	1538	41-15509	PT-22	1623	41-15594	PT-22	1708	41-15679	PT-22	1793	42-57497	PT-22A
1454	41-15425	PT-22	1539	41-15510	PT-22	1624	41-15595	PT-22	1709	41-15680	PT-22	1794	42-57498	PT-22A
1455	41-15426	PT-22	1540	41-15511	PT-22	1625	41-15596	PT-22	1710	41-15681	PT-22	1795	42-57499	PT-22A
1456	41-15427	PT-22	1541	41-15512	PT-22	1626	41-15597	PT-22	1711	41-15682	PT-22	1796	42-57500	PT-22A
1457	41-15428	PT-22	1542	41-15513	PT-22	1627	41-15598	PT-22	1712	41-15683	PT-22	1797	42-57501	PT-22A
1458	41-15429	PT-22	1543	41-15514	PT-22	1628	41-15599	PT-22	1713	41-15684	PT-22	1798	42-57502	PT-22A
1459	41-15430	PT-22	1544	41-15515	PT-22	1629	41-15600	PT-22	1714	41-15685	PT-22	1799	42-57503	PT-22A
1460	41-15431	PT-22	1545	41-15516	PT-22	1630	41-15601	PT-22	1715	41-15686	PT-22	1800	41-20591	PT-22
1461	41-15432	PT-22	1546	41-15517	PT-22	1631	41-15602	PT-22	1716	41-15687	PT-22	1801	41-20592	PT-22
1462	41-15433	PT-22	1547	41-15518	PT-22	1632	41-15603	PT-22	1717	41-15688	PT-22	1802	41-20593	PT-22
1463	41-15434	PT-22	1548	41-15519	PT-22	1633	41-15604	PT-22	1718	41-15689	PT-22	1803	41-20594	PT-22
1464	41-15435	PT-22	1549	41-15520	PT-22	1634	41-15605	PT-22	1719	41-15690	PT-22	1804	41-20595	PT-22
1465	41-15436	PT-22	1550	41-15521	PT-22	1635	41-15606	PT-22	1720	41-15691	PT-22	1805	41-20596	PT-22
1466	41-15437	PT-22	1551	41-15522	PT-22	1636	41-15607	PT-22	1721	41-15692	PT-22	1806	41-20597	PT-22
1467	41-15438	PT-22	1552	41-15523	PT-22	1637	41-15608	PT-22	1722	41-15693	PT-22	1807	41-20598	PT-22
1468	41-15439	PT-22	1553	41-15524	PT-22	1638	41-15609	PT-22	1723	41-15694	PT-22	1808	41-20599	PT-22
1469	41-15440	PT-22	1554	41-15525	PT-22	1639	41-15610	PT-22	1724	41-15695	PT-22	1809	41-20600	PT-22
1470	41-15441	PT-22	1555	41-15526	PT-22	1640	41-15611	PT-22	1725	41-15696	PT-22	1810	41-20601	PT-22
1471	41-15442	PT-22	1556	41-15527	PT-22	1641	41-15612	PT-22	1726	41-15697	PT-22	1811	41-20602	PT-22
1472	41-15443	PT-22	1557	41-15528	PT-22	1642	41-15613	PT-22	1727	41-15698	PT-22	1812	41-20603	PT-22
1473	41-15444	PT-22	1558	41-15529	PT-22	1643	41-15614	PT-22	1728	41-15699	PT-22	1813	41-20604	PT-22
1474	41-15445	PT-22	1559	41-15530	PT-22	1644	41-15615	PT-22	1729	41-15700	PT-22	1814	41-20605	PT-22
1475	41-15446	PT-22	1560	41-15531	PT-22	1645	41-15616	PT-22	1730	41-15701	PT-22	1815	41-20606	PT-22
1476	41-15447	PT-22	1561	41-15532	PT-22	1646	41-15617	PT-22	1731	41-15702	PT-22	1816	41-20607	PT-22
1477	41-15448	PT-22	1562	41-15533	PT-22	1647	41-15618	PT-22	1732	41-15703	PT-22	1817	41-20608	PT-22
1478	41-15449	PT-22	1563	41-15534	PT-22	1648	41-15619	PT-22	1733	41-15704	PT-22	1818	41-20609	PT-22
1479	41-15450	PT-22	1564	41-15535	PT-22	1649	41-15620	PT-22	1734	41-15705	PT-22	1819	41-20610	PT-22
1480	41-15451	PT-22	1565	41-15536	PT-22	1650	41-15621	PT-22	1735	41-15706	PT-22	1820	41-20611	PT-22
1481	41-15452	PT-22	1566	41-15537	PT-22	1651	41-15622	PT-22	1736	41-15707	PT-22	1821	1-20612	PT-22
1482	41-15453	PT-22	1567	41-15538	PT-22	1652	41-15623	PT-22	1737	41-15708	PT-22	1822	41-20613	PT-22
1483	41-15454	PT-22	1568	41-15539	PT-22	1653	41-15624	PT-22	1738	41-15709	PT-22	1823	41-20614	PT-22
1484	41-15455	PT-22	1569	41-15540	PT-22	1654	41-15625	PT-22	1739	41-15710	PT-22	1824	41-20615	PT-22
1485	41-15456	PT-22	1570	41-15541	PT-22	1655	41-15626	PT-22	1740	41-15711	PT-22	1825	41-20616	PT-22
1486	41-15457	PT-22	1571	41-15542	PT-22	1656	41-15627	PT-22	1741	41-15712	PT-22	1826	41-20617	PT-22
1487	41-15458	PT-22	1572	41-15543	PT-22	1657	41-15628	PT-22	1742	41-15713	PT-22	1827	41-20618	PT-22
1488	41-15459	PT-22	1573	41-15544	PT-22	1658	41-15629	PT-22	1743	41-15714	PT-22	1828	41-20619	PT-22
1489	41-15460	PT-22	1574	41-15545	PT-22	1659	41-15630	PT-22	1744	41-15715	PT-22	1829	41-20620	PT-22
1490	41-15461	PT-22	1575	41-15546	PT-22	1660	41-15631	PT-22	1745	41-15716	PT-22	1830	41-20621	PT-22
1491	41-15462	PT-22	1576	41-15547	PT-22	1661	41-15632	PT-22	1746	41-15717	PT-22	1831	41-20622	PT-22
1492	41-15463	PT-22	1577	41-15248	PT-22	1662	41-15633	PT-22	1747	41-15718	PT-22	1832	41-20623	PT-22
1493	41-15464	PT-22	1578	41-15549	PT-22	1663	41-15634	PT-22	1748	41-15719	PT-22	1833	41-20624	PT-22
1494	41-15465	PT-22	1579	41-15550	PT-22	1664	41-15635	PT-22	1749	41-15720	PT-22	1834	41-20625	PT-22
1495	41-15466	PT-22	1580	41-15551	PT-22	1665	41-15636	PT-22	1750	41-15721	PT-22	1835	41-20626	PT-22
1496	41-15467	PT-22	1581	41-15552	PT-22	1666	41-15637	PT-22	1751	41-15722	PT-22	1836	41-20627	PT-22
1497	41-15468	PT-22	1582	41-15553	PT-22	1667	41-15638	PT-22	1752	41-15723	PT-22	1837	41-20628	PT-22
1498	41-15469	PT-22	1583	41-15554	PT-22	1668	41-15639	PT-22	1753	41-15724	PT-22	1838	41-20629	PT-22
1499	41-15470	PT-22	1584	41-15555	PT-22	1669	41-15640	PT-22	1754	41-15725	PT-22	1839	41-20630	PT-22
1500	41-15471	PT-22	1585	41-15556	PT-22	1670	41-15641	PT-22	1755	41-15726	PT-22	1840	41-20631	PT-22
1501	41-15472	PT-22	1586	41-15557	PT-22	1671	41-15642	PT-22	1756	41-15727	PT-22	1841	41-20632	PT-22
1502	41-15473	PT-22	1587	41-15558	PT-22	1672	41-15643	PT-22	1757	41-15728	PT-22	1842	41-20633	PT-22
1503	41-15474	PT-22	1588	41-15559	PT-22	1673	41-15644	PT-22	1758	41-15729	PT-22	1843	41-20634	PT-22
1504	41-15475	PT-22	1589	41-15560	PT-22	1674	41-15645	PT-22	1759	41-15730	PT-22	1844	41-20635	PT-22
1505	41-15476	PT-22	1590	41-15561	PT-22	1675	41-15646	PT-22	1760	41-15731	PT-22	1845	41-20636	PT-22
1506	41-15477	PT-22	1591	41-15562	PT-22	1676	41-15647	PT-22	1761	41-15732	PT-22	1846	41-20637	PT-22
1507	41-15478	PT-22	1592	41-15563	PT-22	1677	41-15648	PT-22	1762	41-15733	PT-22	1847	41-20638	PT-22
1508	41-15479	PT-22	1593	41-15564	PT-22	1678	41-15649	PT-22	1763	41-15734	PT-22	1848	41-20639	PT-22
1509	41-15480	PT-22	1594	41-15565	PT-22	1679	41-15650	PT-22	1764	41-15735	PT-22	1849	41-20640	PT-22
1510	41-15481	PT-22	1595	41-15566	PT-22	1680	41-15651	PT-22	1765	41-15736	PT-22	1850	41-20641	PT-22
1511	41-15482	PT-22	1596	41-15567	PT-22	1681	41-15652	PT-22	1766	41-15737	PT-22	1851	41-20642	PT-22
1512	41-15483	PT-22	1597	41-15568	PT-22	1682	41-15653	PT-22	1767	41-15738	PT-22	1852	41-20643	PT-22
1513	41-15484	PT-22	1598	41-15569	PT-22	1683	41-15654	PT-22	1768	41-15739	PT-22	1853	41-20644	PT-22
1514	41-15485	PT-22	1599	41-15570	PT-22	1684	41-15655	PT-22	1769	41-15740	PT-22	1854	41-20645	PT-22
1515	41-15486	PT-22	1600	41-15571	PT-22	1685	41-15656	PT-22	1770	41-15741	PT-22	1855	41-20646	PT-22
1516	41-15487	PT-22	1601	41-15572	PT-22	1686	41-15657	PT-22	1771	41-15742	PT-22	1856	41-20647	PT-22
1517	41-15488	PT-22	1602	41-15573	PT-22	1687	41-15658	PT-22	1772	41-15743	PT-22	1857	41-20648	PT-22
1518	41-15489	PT-22	1603	41-15574	PT-22	1688	41-15659	PT-22	1773	41-15744	PT-22	1858	41-20649	PT-22
1519	41-15490	PT-22	1604	41-15575	PT-22	1689	41-15660	PT-22	1774	41-15745	PT-22	1859	41-20650	PT-22
1520	41-15491	PT-22	1605	41-15576	PT-22	1690	41-15661	PT-22	1775	42-57479	PT-22A	1860	41-20651	PT-22
1521	41-15492	PT-22	1606	41-15577	PT-22	1691	41-15662	PT-22	1776	42-57480	PT-22A	1861	41-20652	PT-22

CHRONOLOGY PT-21, PT-22, NR-1

S/N	A.A.F. *U.S. Navy Serial #	Model
1862	41-20653	PT-22
1863	41-20654	PT-22
1864	41-20655	PT-22
1865	41-20656	PT-22
1866	41-20657	PT-22
1867	41-20658	PT-22
1868	41-20659	PT-22
1869	41-20660	PT-22
1870	41-20661	PT-22
1871	41-20662	PT-22
1872	41-20663	PT-22
1873	41-20664	PT-22
1874	41-20665	PT-22
1875	41-20666	PT-22
1876	41-20667	PT-22
1877	41-20668	PT-22
1878	41-20669	PT-22
1879	41-20670	PT-22
1880	41-20671	PT-22
1881	41-20672	PT-22
1882	41-20673	PT-22
1883	41-20674	PT-22
1884	41-20675	PT-22
1885	41-20676	PT-22
1886	41-20677	PT-22
1887	41-20678	PT-22
1888	41-20679	PT-22
1889	41-20680	PT-22
1890	41-20681	PT-22
1891	41-20682	PT-22
1892	41-20683	PT-22
1893	41-20684	PT-22
1894	41-20685	PT-22
1895	41-20686	PT-22
1896	41-20687	PT-22
1897	41-20688	PT-22
1898	41-20689	PT-22
1899	41-20690	PT-22
1900	41-20691	PT-22
1901	41-20692	PT-22
1902	41-20693	PT-22
1903	41-20694	PT-22
1904	41-20695	PT-22
1905	41-20696	PT-22
1906	41-20697	PT-22
1907	41-20698	PT-22
1908	41-20699	PT-22
1909	41-20700	PT-22
1910	41-20701	PT-22
1911	41-20702	PT-22
1912	41-20703	PT-22
1913	41-20704	PT-22
1914	41-20705	PT-22
1915	41-20706	PT-22
1916	41-20707	PT-22
1917	41-20708	PT-22
1918	41-20709	PT-22
1919	41-20710	PT-22
1920	41-20711	PT-22
1921	41-20712	PT-22
1922	41-20713	PT-22
1923	41-20714	PT-22
1924	41-20715	PT-22
1925	41-20716	PT-22
1926	41-20717	PT-22
1927	41-20718	PT-22
1928	41-20719	PT-22
1929	41-20720	PT-22
1930	41-20721	PT-22
1931	41-20722	PT-22
1932	41-20723	PT-22
1933	41-20724	PT-22
1934	41-20725	PT-22
1935	41-20726	PT-22
1936	41-20727	PT-22
1937	41-20728	PT-22
1938	41-20729	PT-22
1939	41-20730	PT-22
1940	41-20731	PT-22
1941	41-20732	PT-22
1942	41-20733	PT-22
1943	41-20734	PT-22
1944	41-20735	PT-22
1945	41-20736	PT-22
1946	41-20737	PT-22
1947	41-20738	PT-22
1948	41-20739	PT-22
1949	41-20740	PT-22
1950	41-20741	PT-22
1951	41-20742	PT-22
1952	41-20743	PT-22
1953	41-20744	PT-22
1954	41-20745	PT-22
1955	41-20746	PT-22
1956	41-20747	PT-22
1957	41-20748	PT-22
1958	41-20749	PT-22
1959	41-20750	PT-22
1960	41-20751	PT-22
1961	41-20752	PT-22
1962	41-20753	PT-22
1963	41-20754	PT-22
1964	41-20755	PT-22
1965	41-20756	PT-22
1966	41-20757	PT-22
1967	41-20758	PT-22
1968	41-20759	PT-22
1969	41-20760	PT-22
1970	41-20761	PT-22
1971	41-20762	PT-22
1972	41-20763	PT-22
1973	41-20764	PT-22
1974	41-20765	PT-22
1975	41-20766	PT-22
1976	41-20767	PT-22
1977	41-20768	PT-22
1978	41-20769	PT-22
1979	41-20770	PT-22
1979A		
1980	41-20771	PT-22
1981	41-20772	PT-22
1982	41-20773	PT-22
1983	41-20774	PT-22
1984	41-20775	PT-22
1985	41-20776	PT-22
1986	41-20777	PT-22
1987	41-20778	PT-22
1988	41-20779	PT-22
1989	41-20780	PT-22
1990	41-20781	PT-22
1991	41-20782	PT-22
1992	41-20783	PT-22
1993	41-20784	PT-22
1994	41-20785	PT-22
1995	41-20786	PT-22
1996	41-20787	PT-22
1997	41-20788	PT-22
1998	41-20789	PT-22
1999	41-20790	PT-22
2000	41-20791	PT-22
2001	41-20792	PT-22
2002	41-20793	PT-22
2003	41-20794	PT-22
2004	41-20795	PT-22
2005	41-20796	PT-22
2006	41-20797	PT-22
2007	41-20798	PT-22
2008	41-20799	PT-22
2009	41-20800	PT-22
2010	41-20801	PT-22
2011	41-20802	PT-22
2012	41-20803	PT-22
2013	41-20804	PT-22
2014	41-20805	PT-22
2015	41-20806	PT-22
2016	41-20807	PT-22
2017	41-20808	PT-22
2018	41-20809	PT-22
2019	41-20810	PT-22
2020	41-20811	PT-22
2021	41-20812	PT-22
2022	41-20813	PT-22
2023	41-20814	PT-22
2024	41-20815	PT-22
2025	41-20816	PT-22
2026	41-20817	PT-22
2027	41-20818	PT-22
2028	41-20819	PT-22
2029	41-20820	PT-22
2030	41-20821	PT-22
2031	41-20822	PT-22
2032	41-20823	PT-22
2033	41-20824	PT-22
2034	41-20825	PT-22
2035	41-20826	PT-22
2036	41-20827	PT-22
2037	41-20828	PT-22
2038	41-20829	PT-22
2039	41-20830	PT-22
2040	41-20831	PT-22
2041	41-20832	PT-22
2042	41-20833	PT-22
2043	41-20834	PT-22
2044	41-20835	PT-22
2045	41-20836	PT-22
2046	41-20837	PT-22
2047	41-20838	PT-22
2048	41-20839	PT-22
2049	41-20840	PT-22
2050	41-20841	PT-22
2051	41-20842	PT-22
2052	41-20843	PT-22
2053	41-20844	PT-22
2054	41-20845	PT-22
2055	41-20846	PT-22
2056	41-20847	PT-22
2057	41-20848	PT-22
2058	41-20849	PT-22
2059	41-20850	PT-22
2060	41-20851	PT-22
2061	41-20852	PT-22
2062	41-20853	PT-22
2063	41-20854	PT-22
2064	41-20855	PT-22
2065	41-20856	PT-22
2066	41-20857	PT-22
2067	41-20858	PT-22
2068	41-20859	PT-22
2069	41-20860	PT-22
2070	41-20861	PT-22
2071	41-20862	PT-22
2072	41-20863	PT-22
2073	41-20864	PT-22
2074	41-20865	PT-22
2075	41-20866	PT-22
2076	41-20867	PT-22
2077	41-20868	PT-22
2078	41-20869	PT-22
2079	41-20870	PT-22
2080	41-20871	PT-22
2081	41-20872	PT-22
2082	41-20873	PT-22
2083	41-20874	PT-22
2084	41-20875	PT-22
2085	41-20876	PT-22
2086	41-20877	PT-22
2087	41-20878	PT-22
2088	41-20879	PT-22
2089	41-20880	PT-22
2090	41-20881	PT-22
2091	41-20882	PT-22
2092	41-20883	PT-22
2093	41-20884	PT-22
2094	41-20885	PT-22
2095	41-20886	PT-22
2096	41-20887	PT-22
2097	41-20888	PT-22
2098	41-20889	PT-22
2099	41-20890	PT-22
2100	41-20891	PT-22
2101	41-20892	PT-22
2102	41-20893	PT-22
2103	41-20894	PT-22
2104	41-20895	PT-22
2105	41-20896	PT-22
2106	41-20897	PT-22
2107	41-20898	PT-22
2108	41-20899	PT-22
2109	41-20900	PT-22
2110	41-20901	PT-22
2111	41-20902	PT-22
2112	41-20903	PT-22
2113	41-20904	PT-22
2114	41-20905	PT-22
2115	41-20906	PT-22
2116	41-20907	PT-22
2117	41-20908	PT-22
2118	41-20909	PT-22
2119	41-20910	PT-22
2120	41-20911	PT-22
2121	41-20912	PT-22
2122	41-20913	PT-22
2123	41-20914	PT-22
2124	41-20915	PT-22
2125	41-20916	PT-22
2126	41-20917	PT-22
2127	41-20918	PT-22
2128	41-20919	PT-22
2129	41-20920	PT-22
2130	41-20921	PT-22
2131	41-20922	PT-22
2132	41-20923	PT-22
2133	41-20924	PT-22
2134	41-20925	PT-22
2135	41-20926	PT-22
2136	41-20927	PT-22
2137	41-20928	PT-22
2138	41-20929	PT-22
2139	41-20930	PT-22
2140	41-20931	PT-22
2141	41-20932	PT-22
2142	41-20933	PT-22
2143	41-20934	PT-22
2144	41-20935	PT-22
2145	41-20936	PT-22
2146	41-20937	PT-22
2147	41-20938	PT-22
2148	41-20939	PT-22
2149	41-20940	PT-22
2150	41-20941	PT-22
2151	41-20942	PT-22
2152	41-20943	PT-22
2153	41-20944	PT-22
2154	41-20945	PT-22
2155	41-20946	PT-22
2156	41-20947	PT-22
2157	41-20948	PT-22
2158	41-20949	PT-22
2159	41-20950	PT-22
2160	41-20951	PT-22
2161	41-20952	PT-22
2162	41-20953	PT-22
2163	41-20954	PT-22
2164	41-20955	PT-22
2165	41-20956	PT-22
2166	41-20957	PT-22
2167	41-20958	PT-22
2168	41-20959	PT-22
2169	41-20960	PT-22
2170	41-20961	PT-22
2171	41-20962	PT-22
2172	41-20963	PT-22
2173	41-20964	PT-22
2174	41-20965	PT-22
2175	41-20966	PT-22
2176	41-20967	PT-22
2177	41-20968	PT-22
2178	41-20969	PT-22
2179	41-20970	PT-22
2180	41-20971	PT-22
2181	41-20972	PT-22
2182	41-20973	PT-22
2183	41-20974	PT-22
2184	41-20975	PT-22
2185	41-20976	PT-22
2186	41-20977	PT-22
2187	41-20978	PT-22
2188	41-20979	PT-22
2189	41-20980	PT-22
2190	41-20981	PT-22
2191	41-20982	PT-22
2192	41-20983	PT-22
2193	41-20984	PT-22
2194	41-20985	PT-22
2195	41-20986	PT-22
2196	41-20987	PT-22
2197	41-20988	PT-22
2198	41-20989	PT-22
2199	41-20990	PT-22
2200	41-20991	PT-22
2201	41-20992	PT-22
2202	41-20993	PT-22
2203	41-20994	PT-22
2204	41-20995	PT-22
2205	41-20996	PT-22
2206	41-20997	PT-22
2207	41-20998	PT-22
2208	41-20999	PT-22
2209	41-21000	PT-22
2210	41-21001	PT-22
2211	41-21002	PT-22
2212	41-21003	PT-22
2213	41-21004	PT-22
2214	41-21005	PT-22
2215	41-21006	PT-22
2216	41-21007	PT-22
2217	41-21008	PT-22
2218	41-21009	PT-22
2219	41-21010	PT-22
2220	41-21011	PT-22
2221	41-21012	PT-22
2222	41-21013	PT-22
2223	41-21014	PT-22
2224	41-21015	PT-22
2225	41-21016	PT-22
2226	41-21017	PT-22
2227	41-21018	PT-22
2228	41-21019	PT-22
2229	41-21020	PT-22
2230	41-21021	PT-22
2231	41-21022	PT-22
2232	41-21023	PT-22
2233	41-21024	PT-22
2234	41-21025	PT-22
2235	41-21026	PT-22
2236	41-21027	PT-22
2237	41-21028	PT-22
2238	41-21029	PT-22
2239	41-21030	PT-22
2240	41-21031	PT-22
2241	41-21032	PT-22
2242	41-21033	PT-22
2243	41-21034	PT-22
2244	41-21035	PT-22
2245	41-21036	PT-22
2246	41-21037	PT-22
2247	41-21038	PT-22
2248	41-21039	PT-22
2249	41-21040	PT-22

NOTE:

Many of the PT series aircraft were sold surplus to civilians and therefore assigned the standard FAA "N" number designation.

Because these numbers change from time to time at the owners discretion, it was felt they could not be included and still represent an up to date record.

Hence, it is suggested any researcher desiring such information should consult with the nearest FAA office or the FAA Records Branch in Oklahoma City, Oklahoma.

Chapter Sixteen

Master List of Existing Ryans

Explanation

During the year 1990, the author sent out a standard questionnaire to all FAA registered owners of Ryan ST series aircraft. Only a handful replied. Therefore, information on each existing aircraft is minimal.

The remaining information was gleaned from all previous correspondence with owners over a period of about 30 years. From that information and other data gathered from historians, Ryan airplane buffs, the Oshkosh EAA convention, and other sources, the "Master List" was updated as far as is possible.

Any additions, corrections or other comments would be welcome, and it is suggested that they be submitted through the publisher.

MASTER LIST OF EXISTING RYANS
December 1994

S/N	FAA Reg. #	Owner	Remarks
110	N14954	Ben Salesburg Palo Alto, California	Oldest original ST in existence.
111	N86555	Fred Barber Stone Mt., Georgia	Was NC15955. Now being rebuilt.
112	NC14956	Larry Lee Atlanta, Georgia	Airworthy. Rebuilt original.
113	NC14957	Fred Barber Stone Mt., Georgia	Being rebuilt.
114	NC14982	Mark Hoskins Olympia, Washington	In Storage.
115	NC14983	Gordon F. Autry Denver, Colorado	Status unknown.
116	NC14984 N69094	Donald Carter Lafayette, California	Actually PT-20 s/n 352.
117	NC14985	Don Young Santa Barbara, California	Airworthy. Original.
118	NC14986	Troy Stimson Justin, Texas	Original under restoration.
124	N14987	John Richards Ventura, California	Papers only?
128	NC16039	Ted Babbini Sonoma, California	Airworthy. Original Tex Rankin airplane.
133	N14955	Bill Allen San Diego, California	Papers only.
148	N17345 N26JG	John T. Crouse Charleston, W. Virginia	Airworthy.
149	NC17346	Bill Rose Barrington, Illinois	Being restored.
151	N17348 N42X N27JG	John Gosney Centennial, Wyoming	Original PT-20 s/n 197. Now rebuilding.
154	N633X	Wm. W. Halverson Bloomington, Minnesota	Original airframe. Was NC-17351. Being restored.
156	N17352	Ed Power, Jr. Nut Tree, California	Airworthy.
157	NC17353	Creative Interiors, Inc. Wichita, Kansas	Airworthy. Original.
162	N17357	Donald Carter Lafayette, California	All original.

166	NC17361	San Diego Aero Space Museum, San Diego, Cal.	Original.
173	N17368	Bill Rose Barrington, Illinois	Built up from Guatemala STM parts. Airworthy.
174	NC17369	Argie V. Tidmore Pottsville, Pennsylvania	Original. Being restored.
177	N17364	Bill Rose Barrington, Illinois	Being restored.
184	N17360	Roger W. Sherman, M.D. Leesburg, Florida	STM from Mexico. Airworthy.
188	NC18904	Roger W. Sherman, M.D. Leesburg, Florida	Airworthy. Original.
192	N17350	Fred Spec Bradford Woods, Pennsylvania	STM s/n 192. Being restored.
195	N17349	Walter Hill Stuart, Florida	Airworthy. Original.
198	NC18902	Antique Airplane Assn. Blakesburg, Iowa	In museum.
199	NC18905	William Foley Glastonbury, Connecticut	Original. Being restored.
302	N302D	Bill Dodd Prairie View, Illinois	STM parts. Rebuilding.
304	N10535	Robert Webb Address unknown.	Status unknown.
305	N	?	STM from Guatemala?
306	N18907	?	?
312	N18922	USAF Museum Wright Patterson AFB, Ohio	PT-16 prototype. Original. In museum.
313	N96547	Bill Rose Barrington, Illinois	Mfg. plate only. No hardware.
316	N9655W	Bill Rose Barrington, Illinois	Mfg. plate only. No hardware.
324	NC62127	David B. Talton Wendell, North Carolina	To be restored. Was in fatal crash years ago.
325	N9651N	Bill Rose Barrington, Illinois	Mfg. plate only. No hardware.
329	N9652H	Bill Rose Barrington, Illinois	Mfg. plate only. No hardware.
339	NC18921	Ryan ST, Inc. Walkill, New York	Status unknown.
341	N17348	David Masters Palo Alto, California	Original PT-20
352	N69094	Donald Carter Lafayette, California	Original PT-20, with S/N 116 papers.
355	N9E	Roger France Reston, Virginia	Original. Being rebuilt.
452	N9761	James R. Bassett Toledo, Washington	Original STM-S2. Airworthy.
457	N8146	James O'Donnel Naperville, Illinois	Original STM-S2 with parts from s/n 463.
458	N17343	Bill Rose Barrington, Illinois	Original STM-S2. Airworthy.
466	N466WA	Willis M. Allen San Diego, California	Original STM-2. Airworthy.
476	N7779	Bill Rose Barrington, Illinois	Original STM-S2. Being restored on floats.
480	N	Fred Barber Stone Mt., Georgia	Original STM-2. Only fuselage. In storage.
490	N18923	Mark Hoskins Tacoma, Washington	Built up from parts of s/n 490 & 322. In storage.
494	N14911	Bob DeVries Germany	Original STM-2. In storage in California. NC14911 papers.

Chapter Seventeen

Ryan ST Series

Technical Data
PERFORMANCE - SPECIFICATIONS
Models ST, ST-A & ST-A Special
ATC #541

MODEL	ST	ST-A	ST-A SPECIAL
Engine - Menasco	B-4	C-4	C-4S (Supercharged)
Horsepower	95 hp @ 1975 rpm	125 hp @2175 rpm	150 hp @2275 rpm
Wing Span	30'	30'	30'
Length Overall	21' 5 3/8"	21' 5 3/8"	21' 5 3/8"
Height Overall	6'11"	6'11"	6'11"
Wing Area	124 sq ft	124 sq ft	124 sq ft
Fuel Capacity	24 gal	24 gal	24 gal
Fuel Consumption per hr	7 gal	8 gal	8.6 gal
Propeller Clearance — Level	23.75"	23.75"	22.25"
Airfoil Section	N.A.C.A 2412	N.A.C.A. 2412	N.A.C.A. 2412
Wheel Tread	66"	66"	66"
Tire Size (Air Wheels)	18 x 8 x 3	18 x 8 x 3	18 x 8 x 3
Tail Wheel Size	8" Pneumatic	8" Pneumatic	8" Pneumatic
Weight Empty	1023 lbs	1023 lbs	1058 lbs
Useful Load	552 lbs	552 lbs	517 lbs
Gross Load (Maximum)	1575 lbs	1575 lbs	1575 lbs
Range (Cruising)	400 mi	350 mi	350 mi
Maximum Speed at Sea Level	140 mph	150 mph	160 mph
Cruising Speed at 2000 ft	120 mph	127 mph	135 mph
Rate of Climb (Sea Level)	850 ft/min	1200 ft/min	1400 ft/min
Service Ceiling	15,500 ft	17,500 ft	21,000 ft
Landing Speed	42 mph	42 mph	42 mph
Landing Speed with Flaps Up	50 mph	50 mph	50 mph
Take-off Run with Full Load	190 yds	175 yds	145 yds

Ref: As published by Ryan Aeronautical Corp. 1937

ST SERIES STANDARD EQUIPMENT - ALL MODELS - 1937

Wing flaps with new, instant lever control
(from s/n 118; up to s/n #117 had chain and crank).
N.A.C.A. in-line engine cowling
Tail wheel swivel lock controllable from cockpit
   (later models)
Long stroke, oleo type shock absorbers
Baggage compartment with Sesame combination lock
Reserve fuel supply system (standpipe)
Impulse hand starter
   (impulse gives boost while hand "propping")
Compass
Oil pressure and temperature gauge
Fire extinguisher
Aircraft and Engine log book
Parachute type bucket seats

Tab balance controls (elevator trim tabs)
Wheel pants, wing fillets and fairings throughout
Full swiveling, pneumatic tail wheel
Full airwheels (18 x 8 x 3 Goodyear "Airwheels")
Wheel brakes, controlled from both cockpits
Wiring for position lights
Direct reading fuel gauge
Complete set of dual controls
Altimeter
Tachometer
Airspeed indicator
First aid kit
Tool kit
Aircraft and Engine Instruction Manuals
Attractive cockpit upholstering, including thick
   cushions and back pads

Ref: Ryan Brochure 1937

ST SERIES
FOREIGN SHIPMENT

All models of the new Ryan ST series when boxed for foreign shipment are carefully treated with a special cosmoline coating and wrapped as an extra preventive against salt water exposure. Wings and tail surfaces are disassembled and the plane and motor placed in one box of the following dimensions:

	English	**Metric**
Length	20' 4"	6.20 M
Width	6' 3"	1.91 M
Height	4' 8"	1.42 M
Total Weight	2400 lbs	1088 kg
Total Content	593 cu ft	16.8 M3

(Ref: 1937 Ryan Brochure)

CHINESE RYANS

(48) Ryan STC-4 Two Place Primary Trainers at US $7,816.60	$375,196.80
(2) Ryan STC-P4 Single Place Pursuit Trainers, at $10,795.41	$21,590.82
Airplane Spare Parts	$96,360.28
Spare Engines and Engine Spare Parts	$57,309.72
	$550.457.62

CHINESE RYANS

RYAN STC-4 TWO-PLACE PRIMARY-SECONDARY TRAINER
POWERED WITH MENASCO 165 hp ENGINE

Standard Equipment

Hartzell wood propeller; wing flaps; tab balance controls; wheel pants; pneumatic tail wheel with lock from cockpit; wheel brakes; oleo shock absorbers; baggage compartment; reserve fuel supply system; dual controls; 2 compasses; 2 airspeed indicators; 2 oil pressure gauges; 2 oil temperature gauges; one fuel gauge; one impulse hand starter; 2 altimeters; 2 tachometers.

Specifications

Engine	Menasco C-4S2	Horsepower	165 hp
Maximum Speed	142 mph	Cruising Speed (sea level)	128 mph
Stalling Speed	54 mph	Landing Speed (with flaps)	45 mph
Rate of Climb (sea level)	975 fpm	Service Ceiling (full load)	18,600 ft
Absolute Ceiling (full load)	22,000 ft	Weight Empty (average)	1053 lbs
Useful Load	547 lbs	Pay Load	210 lbs
Gross Weight	1600 lbs	Cruising Range (full load)	320 miles
Wing Loading	12.90 lb/sq ft	Power Loading	10.65 lb/hp
Length Overall	21' 5 3/8"	Height Overall	6' 11"

PERFORMANCE & SPECIFICATIONS
RYAN STM-2

	Menasco C-4 engine 125 hp @2175 rpm - sea level		Menasco C-4S engine 150 hp @2260 rpm - 3000'	
Performance Summary	**English**	**Metric**	**English**	**Metric**
Max. Speed - level flight (sea level)	126 mph	203 km/hr	138 mph	222 km/hr
Max. Speed - level flight (3281'-1000m)	124 mph	200 km/hr	142 mph	228 km/hr
Max. Speed - level flight (6562'-2000m)	123 mph	198 km/hr	140 mph	225 km/hr
Max. Speed - level flight (9842'-3000m)	118 mph	190 km/hr	137 mph	220 km/hr
Max. Speed - level flight (10,000'-3048m)	118 mph	190 km/hr	137 mph	220 km/hr
Max. Speed - level flight (13,123'-4000m)	114 mph	183 km/hr	134 mph	216 km/hr
Max. Speed - level flight (16,000'-4877m)	108 mph	173 km/hr	131 mph	211 km/hr
Cruising Speed (11,500' - 3505m)			136 mph	219 km/hr
Cruising Speed (7600'-2320m)	122 mph	196 km/hr		
Cruising Speed (3000'-914m)	115 mph	185 km/hr	128 mph	206 km/hr
Cruising Speed (sea level)	113 mph	182 km/hr	125 mph	201 km/hr
Rate of Climb-full power, full load (sea level)	800 fpm	244 m/min	975 fpm	297 m/min
Rate of Climb-full power, full load (10000'-3048m)	320 fpm	98 m/min	505 fpm	154 m/min
Range - full load (11,500' - 3505m)			326 miles	525 km
Range - full load (7600' - 2320m)	366 miles	588 km		
Range - full load extra fuel tanks	640 miles	1030 km	571 miles	919 km
Time of Climb To (3281' - 1000m)	3.8 min	3.8 min	4.0 min	4.0 min
Time of Climb To (6562' - 2000m)	10.5 min	10.5 min	8.25 min	8.25 min
Time of Climb To (9842' - 3000m)	19.0 min	19.0 min	13.75 min	13.75 min
Time of Climb To (10,000' - 3048 m)	19.5 min	19.5 min	14.0 min	14.0 min
Time of Climb To (13,123' - 4000m)	34.0 min	34.0 min	21.25 min	21.25 min
Time of Climb To (16,000' - 4877m)	52.0 min	52.0 min	32.0 min	32.0 min
Service Ceiling - Full Load	16,000 ft	4877 m	18,600 ft	5669 m
Absolute Ceiling - Full Load	17,200 ft	5242 m	20,800 ft	6340 m
Take-Off Run (5 mph wind) (sea level)	690 ft	210 m	680 ft	207 m
Landing Speed-power off-full load (sea level)	54 mph	87 km/hr	54 mph	87 km/hr
Landing Run with flaps (5 mph wind) (sea level)	523 ft	159 m	523 ft	159 m
Landing Run without flaps (5 mph wind)(sea level)	608 ft	185 m	608 ft	185 m

WEIGHTS, DIMENSIONS AND GENERAL DATA
RYAN STM-2

	Menasco C-4 engine 125 hp @2175 rpm - sea level		Menasco C-4S engine 150 hp @2260 rpm - 3000 ft	
Weights and Loadings	**English**	**Metric**	**English**	**Metric**
Weight Empty (average)	1081 lbs	490.0 kg	1083 lbs	491.0 kg
Oil (2 gal-125 hp) (3 gal-150 hp)	15 lbs	6.8 kg	23 lbs	10.4 kg
Gasoline (24 gal - 91 lit)	144 lbs	65.4 kg	144 lbs	65.4 kg
Instructor	170 lbs	77.1 kg	170 lbs	77.1 kg
Student	170 lbs	77.1 kg	170 lbs	77.1 kg
Tools, extra equipment, etc.	20 lbs	9.1 kg	10 lbs	4.5 kg
Useful Load	519 lbs	235.0 kg	517 lbs	234.0 kg
Gross Weight	1600 lbs	726.0 kg	1600 lbs	726.0 kg
Power Loading	12.8 lbs/hp	5.81 kg/hp	10.67 lbs/hp	4.84 kg/hp

Wing Loading	12.9 lbs/sq ft	6.3 kg/sq m	12.90 lbs/sq ft	6.3 kg/sq m
	Menasco C-4 engine		Menasco C-4S engine	
	125 hp		150 hp	

Dimensions and Areas	**English**	**Metric**	**English**	**Metric**
Wing Span	29' 11"	9.12 m	29' 11"	9.12 m
Length Overall	21' 5 3/8"	6.54 m	21' 5 3/8"	6.54 m
Height Overall	6' 11"	2.11 m	6' 11"	2.11 m
Wing Area	124.0 sq ft	11.52 sq m	124.0 sq ft	11.52 sq m
Stabilizer Area	12.0 sq ft	1.12 sq m	12.0 sq ft	1.12 sq m
Elevator Area	10.0 sq ft	0.93 sq m	10.0 sq ft	0.93 sq m
Fin Area	4.7 sq ft	0.44 sq m	4.7 sq ft	0.44 sq m
Rudder Area	7.25 sq ft	0.67 sq m	7.25 sq ft	0.67 sq m
Aileron Area	12.0 sq ft	1.12 sq m	12.0 sq ft	1.12 sq m
Flap Area	10.5 sq ft	0.98 sq m	10.5 sq ft	0.98 sq m

General Data				
Wing Incidence	3°	3°	3°	3°
Wing Dihedral	4° 30'	4° 30'	4° 30'	4° 30'
Wheel Tread	66"	167.6 cm	66"	167.6 cm
Tire Size	18x8x3	46 cm x 20 cm	18x8x3	46cmx20cm
Tail Wheel Size	8" streamline	20 cm	8" streamline	20 cm
Propeller Diameter (average)	80"	203 cm	80"	203 cm
Propeller Clearance (thrust line level)	21 7/8"	56 cm	21 7/8"	56 cm
Ground Angle	12° 38'	12° 38'	12° 38'	12° 38'
Type of Flaps	Plain	Plain	Plain	Plain
Wing Airfoil	NACA 2412	NACA 2412	NACA 2412	NACA 2412
Hourly Fuel Consumption (75% power)	8.0 gal/hr	30.3 lit/hr	10.0 gal/hr	37.9 lit/hr

PERFORMANCE & SPECIFICATIONS
RYAN STM-S2 SEAPLANE

Menasco C-4S Engine
150 hp

Performance Summary	**English**	**Metric**
Max. Speed - level flight (sea level)	122 mph	196 km/hr
Max. Speed - level flight (3281' - 1000 m)	120 mph	193 km/hr
Max. Speed - level flight (6562' - 2000 m)	118 mph	189 km/hr
Max. Speed - level flight (9842' - 3000 m)	111 mph	178 km/hr
Cruise Speed (3000' - 914 m)	107 mph	172 km/hr
Cruise Speed (sea level)	108 mph	173 km/hr
Rate of Climb-full power, full load (sea level)	700 fpm	213 m/min
Rate of Climb-full power, full load (10000')	210 fpm	64 m/min
Range - full load (11,500' - 3505 m)	246 miles	395 km
Range - full load - Extra fuel tanks	432 mi	695 km
Time of Climb To (3281' - 1000 m)	5.5 min	5.5 min
Time of Climb To (6562' - 2000 m)	12.5 min	12.5 min
Time of Climb To (9842' - 3000 m)	20.3 min	20.3 min
Time of Climb To (10,000' - 3048 m)	24.4 min	24.4 min
Time of Climb To (13,123' - 4000 m)	44.0 min	44.0 min
Service Ceiling - Full Load	12,250 ft	3740 m
Absolute Ceiling - Full Load	14,280 ft	4350 m
Take-Off Time - 8 mph (12.9 km/hr) wind	25 sec	25 sec
Landing Speed - Power off - Full Load (sea level)	59 mph	95 km/hr

WEIGHTS, DIMENSIONS AND GENERAL DATA
RYAN STM-S2 SEAPLANE

Weights and Loadings	English	Metric	Weights and Loadings	English	Metric
Weight Empty (average)	1311 lbs	595.0 kg	Extra Equipment	10 lbs	4.5 kg
Oil (3 gal)	23 lbs	10.4 kg	Useful Load	517 lbs	234.0 kg
Gasoline (24 gal - 91 lit)	144 lbs	65.4 kg	Gross Weight	1828 lbs	828.0 kg
Instructor	170 lbs	77.1 kg	Power Loading	12.18 lbs/hp	5.52 kg/hp
Student	170 lbs	77.1 kg	Wing Loading	14.71 lbs/sq ft	72 kg/sq m

Dimensions and Areas	English	Metric	Dimensions and Areas	English	Metric
Wing Span	29' 11"	9.12 m	Elevator Area	10.0 sq ft	0.93 sq m
Length Overall	22' 8 1/2"	6.92 m	Fin Area	4.7 sq ft	0.44 sq m
Height Overall	7' 4 1/2"	2.25 m	Rudder Area	7.25 sq ft	0.67 sq m
Wing Area	124.0 sq ft	11.52 sq m	Aileron Area	12.0 sq ft	1.12 sq m
Stabilizer Area	12.0 sq ft	1.12 sq m	Flap Area	10.5 sq ft	0.98 sq m

General Data	English	Metric		English	Metric
Wing Incidence	3°	3°	Propeller Clearance	26"	61 cm
Wing Dihedral	4° 30'	4° 30'	Water Angle	6 ° 23'	6 ° 23'
Float Tread	7' 1"	2.4 m	Type of Flaps	Plain	Plain
Float Type	Edo #1965	Edo #1965	Wing Airfoil	NACA 2412	NACA 2412
Propeller Diameter	80"	203 cm	Hourly Fuel Consumption (75% power)	10.5 gal/hr	39.8 lit/hr

ENGINE
Menasco 4 cylinder, air-cooled, in-line, Model C-4S,
Developing 150 hp at 2260 rpm @ 3000'

PERFORMANCE & SPECIFICATIONS
RYAN ST-3 (ST-3KR)
PT-21/PT-22/NR-1
ATC #749

	English	Metric	English	Metric
Engine - Kinner	B-5(R-440-1)		R-5 (R-540-1)	
Horsepower	125 @ 1975 rpm		160 @ 1850 rpm	
Wing Span	30'-1"	9.2 m	30' 1"	9.2 m
Length Overall	22'-5"	6.8 m	22' 5"	6.8 m
Height Overall	7'-2"	2.2 m	7' 2"	2.2 m
Wing Area	134.25 sq ft	12.5 sq m	134.25 sq ft	12.5 sq m
Fuel Capacity	24 gal		24 gal	
Fuel Consumption	9 gal/hr		10 gal/hr	
Airfoil Section	NACA 2412		NACA 2412	
Tire Size	7.00-6		7.00-6	
Tail Wheel Size	8 in		8 in	
Weight Empty	1228 lbs	557 kg	1272 lbs	577 kg
Useful Load	547 lbs	248 kg	553 lbs	251 kg
Gross Weight (Maximum)	1775 lbs	805 kg	1825 lbs	828 kg
Power Loading	14.2 lb/hp	6.4 kg/hp	11.4 lb/hp	5.2 kg/hp
Wing Loading	13.2 lb/sq ft	64.4 kg/sq m	13.6 lb/sq ft	66.4kg/sq m
Range (Cruising)	312 miles	502 km	266 miles	428 km
Maximum Speed - level flight (sea level)	120 mph	193 kph	129 mph	208 kph
Cruising Speed	109 mph	175 kph	120 mph	193 kph

	(B-5) English	Metric	(B-6) English	Metric
Rate of Climb (sea level) full load	635 fpm	193.5 m/min	850 fpm	259.1m/min
Service Ceiling - full load	12,900 ft	3932 m	15,800 ft	4816 m
Landing Speed - (sea level) power off	56.4 mph	90.8 kph	57 mph	91.7 kph
Take-Off Run (sea level) 5 mph wind	610 ft	185.9 m	480 ft	146.3 m
Endurance at Operating Speed	2.86 hrs	2.86 hrs	2.22 hrs	2.22 hrs
Absolute Ceiling	15,500 ft	4724 m		5578 m

(Ref: Ryan Aeronautical Company, 1941)

RYAN SCHOOL OF AERONAUTICS TRAINING AIRCRAFT CHRONOLOGY

School #	S/N	Registration #	Model	School #	S/N	Registration#	Model
1	210	NC18915	SC-W	9	160	NC17355	ST-A
2	200	NC18906	ST-A Special	10	152	NC17349	ST-A
3	312	NC18922	ST-A	11	151	NC17348	ST-A
4	110	NC14954	ST-A	12		NC13858	(Stinson)
5	176	NC17371	ST-A	14	118	NC14986	ST-A
6	157	NC17353	ST-A	15		NC18401	(Stinson)
7	128	NC16039	ST-A		93	NC4939	B-1 Brougham
8	116	NC14984	ST-A				

Note: Ship (school) number was usually painted on the side of the fuselage, aft of the rear cockpit on the STs.

GREAT LAKES TRAINERS
(used for primary training)

Registration number

NC11318   NC11320   NC11324   NC11715   NC313Y   NC825K   NC875K

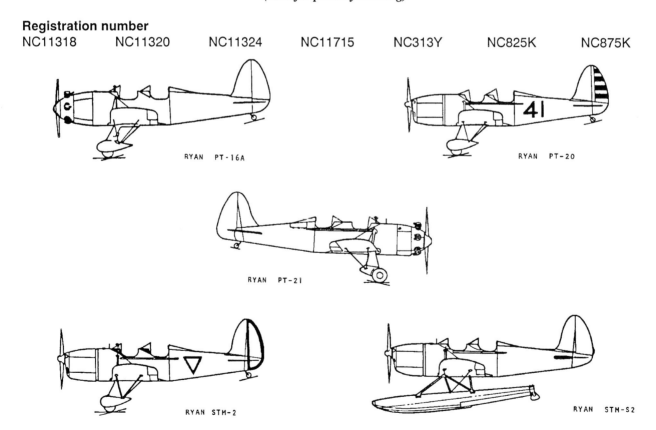

Chapter Eighteen

Ryan SC, "Sport Cabin"

One of first photos of serial number 201 in flight.

Another sleek creation of Claude Ryan was the SC, or "Sport Cabin." She was just as beautiful and as easy to fly as she was to look at, possibly a trend setter. Of all of Ryan's designs, the SC probably came the closest to looking like what we have around today.

It was a classic design like the ST and it was the first truly successful private aircraft to pioneer the all metal, cantilever low-wing, enclosed-cabin concept. One could not mistake it in the sky with those tapered and almost pointed wing tips.

T. Claude Ryan envisaged the SC in 1935-36. Later, in a personal resume of its development, he expressed his hopes, intentions and requirements— "The plane was planned from the first preliminary drawing as a production job. We wanted to develop a type of construction so simple and so practical that it could lend itself to efficient manufacture in much larger quantities than had been customary in the past.

Aircraft designers have for many years toyed with the idea of airplanes stamped all at once in one high press or poured out of some synthetic material in a simple molding operation or somehow fabricated so as to avoid the tedious hand fitting of limitless numbers of small parts. We believe that in the development of the SC we approached this ideal of a one piece airplane—

It is a much more difficult assignment to simplify a structure than to 'complexity' it...we feel it (the SC) is the most simply manufactured metal airplane and the most adaptable of any yet developed to an efficient production machine."

The airplane came at a time when the low-wing, high-performance light aircraft concept was practically unknown in the United States. The Percival and Miles companies of England were manufacturing many light airplanes of this type, but by late 1937, no comparable designs from America had progressed beyond the prototype state. As a result, the airplane received wide recognition and acclaim as a sensational airplane, in advance of its time.

It did have a distinctly European look with its cowled engine (Menasco version) and full-faired landing gear (pants). But with metal construction and the tapered wing plan, she was quite set apart from any similar foreign designs.

The designers achieved the classic SC after two years of extensive study, experiment and ingenuity.

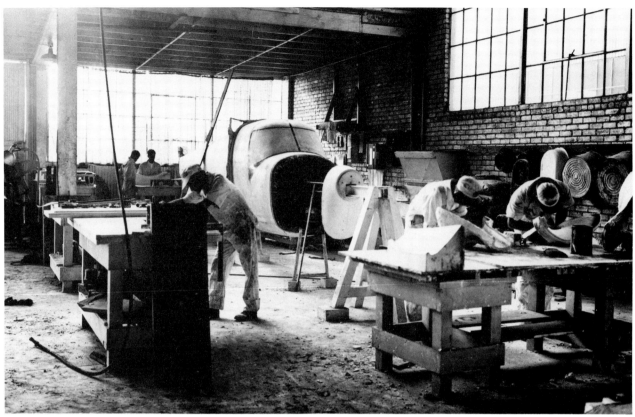

SC mock-up being developed.

RYAN AERONAUTICAL CO.

MEL THOMPASON

(Middle left) Another view of the full scale plaster mock-up showing the Menasco engine configuration.

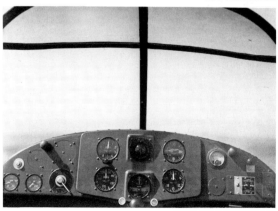

RYAN AERONAUTICAL CO.

(Lower Left) Four-piece windshield as used on the prototype only. Primer and carburetor heat knobs in upper right of instrument panel.

Every part, with few exceptions, was either a flat sheet or a drop hammer stamping. Flat sheets were all marked and drilled from steel master templates while stamped sheets were formed from dies which accurately reproduced a given part over and over again. The only major compound curves were in the engine cowling, wheel pants and fairing. Roughly 90% of the structure and covering was of single-gauge, 24ST "Alclad" aluminum.

In producing this classic, a full scale plaster model was first constructed. When the basic shape was finalized, the lines were transferred from the plaster mock-up directly to metal by progressive steps. Shells were built around the fuselage model at bulkhead points and at compound curve areas. Plaster casts were then made and from these female castings, master male castings were made.

Then the plaster patterns were used to make sand molds into which molten zinc metal was poured, thus forming one half of the die. The "punch" (female) half of the die was made by pouring lead directly over the zinc die. The complete airplane was built up of just

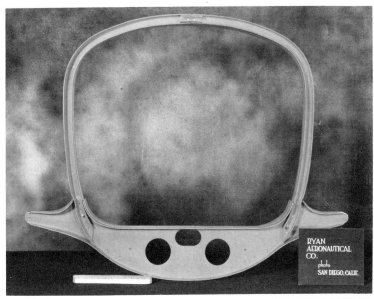

Bulkhead assembly.

RYAN AERONAUTICAL CO.

over 200 individual sets of dies from which all the necessary and essential parts of the plane were formed.

The 37'6" span wing, with tapered trailing edge, created somewhat of a gull effect as it quickly curved into the fuselage at the root. It was quite simplified in construction. The precision of the drop hammer die

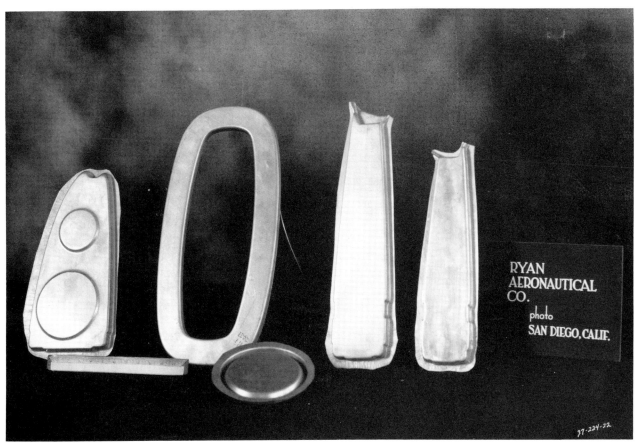

Drop hammered parts from stamped sheets before final finishing.

RYAN AERONAUTICAL CO.

(Top left) Preliminary assembly of cabin area & center section main spar in jig.

(Top right) Aft monocoque fuselage assembly.

(Below) Main fuselage components ready for assembly.

stamping process was utilized, and featured the monospar principle, and each wing panel was attached to the fuselage by three taper-bolts. The metal "monocoque spar," as it was sometimes termed, was developed by the Ryan design group, and patented by them. In reality the spar embodied approximately the full forward third portion of the wing. This nose, or leading edge portion, was assembled as a single unit with major stresses carried by the outer skin. It was further stiffened by the nose ribs and single vertical webs located about one third of the chord. Thus the entire forward portion of the wing, covered with 24ST "Alclad," formed a light-but- strong tapered box spar. The master spar swept back from root to tip about 1 1/2 degrees, due partially to the 3 degree washout in the wing, to gain added structural strength as the wing thinned near the tip to retain the correct airfoil shape. This method of construction is known today as the "D" tube spar and is used on the popular Mooney airplane.

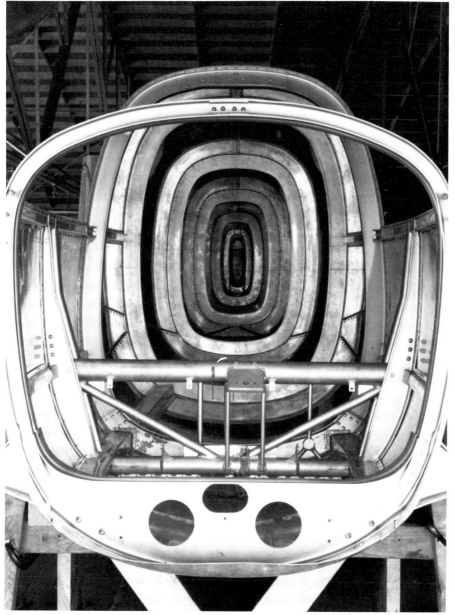

(Left) Aft fuselage assembly after mating with cabin area assembly.

some 5 sq. ft. area was installed to reduce the landing speed. It was mounted beneath the wing at a point about one-third back from the leading edge, and was a new approach to the handling of the airplane in any way. The perforations allowed some air to flow through to prevent interference of the normal tail group air flow.

The aft portion of the wing was fabric covered over strong aluminum structure (Wellington-Sears B-30 fabric with Fuller dope). The entire airplane was completely assembled and aligned on but three main jigs. A swiveling tail wheel was also provided.

These processes may seem commonplace today and in many cases old-fashioned. However, in 1936/37 such utilization of metal in a low cost private light plane was a great advance in aircraft design and construction. For its simple construction the SC was a beautifully streamlined and efficient airplane. It quickly gained a reputation as being just about the classiest private airplane to flex its wings in flight.

MEL THOMPSON

Cabin dimensions were quite attractive. The sliding hatch moved to the rear 27 inches for a ready access, leaving no obstructions to require stooping upon entering. The forward seats had an inside width of 43 inches, seating the pilot and passenger side-by-side. A third passenger occupied a single rear bench seat (the mother-in-law seat) that was 40 inches wide, and there was ample room for forty pounds of luggage. The inside length of the cabin was 74 1/2", and height was 50 3/4". The interior finish was with Laidlaw upholstery, and the entire cabin insulated and soundproofed with "Seapak." Windshield and hatch windows were of DuPont "Plasticele."

Visibility was equally good from either right or left side, with the pilot's eye level being 10 inches above the cowling line. The cowling sloped forward at an angle

The wings were formed and assembled in one continuous operation in a master jig. The trailing portion was cantilever ribbed. From root to aileron, ribs were built up from drop hammer formed cap strips and simple diagonal members (truss type). The wing had a very pronounced dihedral and washout incidence of some six degrees, in uniform change from root to wingtip. The outer ribs (non-truss, from the inboard end of the ailerons to the wing tips) were stamped, individually in one piece. In final assembly, the wing was completed on the master wing panel jig to assure alignment.

The ailerons were made of "Alclad" and steel and were fabric covered. They were balanced both statically and dynamically. A single perforated dural belly flap (lever operated) or "drag brake," split type, of

of 6 1/2 degrees to give good forward vision even in taxiing, especially in the Menasco model.

The fuselage construction was of monocoque design using thick-skin 24ST "Alclad" over rugged transverse rings (bulkheads).

The steel tube landing gear, which was attached to the wing spar, incorporated a seven-inch stroke oleo strut and was fitted with streamlined 24ST fairings and pants, which covered the Goodyear Airwheels (18x8x3) with disc brakes. Landing gear tread was 8' - 3/4".

Before assembly, the shaped aluminum was drilled for rivets, using nesting-type

(Top left) Joining tail cone and cockpit section.

(Middle left) Landing gear upper strut weldment in jig.

(Bottom left) Landing gear strut assembly on one side and fully faired-in with wheel pant on other side.

(Bottom right) Detail of tail wheel and access panel for servicing.

steel templates, thus eliminating layout work on each part. All of the pieces went together in an exact and rapid operation, fitted so accurately that only the six wing root fittings and four engine mount points had to be determined by jigging.

Needless to say, this Ryan was a remarkable airplane, highly maneuverable, responsive to the controls under all conditions yet stable enough to be flown hands off. Careful choice and use of the right airfoil, wing root NACA 23012 and wing tip NACA 23009, provided a stable center of pressure, which made the natural center of gravity coincide with the center of pressure throughout the wing. The result was a wing nearly perfectly balanced and as free as possible from flutter under all conditions. Stalls were mild, the nose dropping only slightly below the horizon, and aileron control was positive throughout. Forced loops and spins were possible with the airplanes, but they were placarded against any violent maneuver. They were definitely not intended as aerobatic machines.

Development of the SC was based on the popular acceptance of the model ST low-wing, open-cockpit "sport trainer," and interests expressed by dealers and owners for a companion cabin model.

With 100 employees and an expansion program well underway in order to triple their production capacity, it appeared the SC might be a long-time production airplane. Under the direction of Fred Rohr, with T. Claude Ryan as president, the first phase called for the production of 100 airplanes. According to Walter O. Locke, the 201 thru 300 block of serial numbers was assigned to the SC.

At this time, E.A. Smith was secretary/treasurer and Sam C. Breder was sales manager. Engineering was placed under the direction of Millard Boyd and Will Vandermeer who had previously designed the ST. The mock-up was built during the late winter and early spring of 1937, with the flying prototype being completed shortly thereafter.

All metal monocoque spar leading edge of wing in jig, with landing gear strut in place.   RYAN AERONAUTICAL CO.

Left wing assembly of prototype.   RYAN AERONAUTICAL CO.

Right wing tip to wing assembly.   RYAN AERONAUTICAL CO.

Prototype serial number 201 under construction.

ERNIE MOORE

(Right) Initial roll-out of prototype - serial number 201 being admired by Ryan employees.

RYAN AERONAUTICAL CO.

Prototype

The prototype SC-M, serial number 201, licensed first as X17372, was powered by the supercharged Menasco C-4S (150 hp) which at the time proved most adaptable from the standpoint of operational costs versus performance compromise.

After some final touching up and tuning of the engine, the airplane made its initial test flight on May 11, 1937, lasting all of 30 minutes. John Fornasero was the test pilot. According to his log book, he flew the little ship another 15 hours and 30 minutes from May 12th through the 28th. All flights were recorded as test flights.

On September 15, 1937, it received its ATC #651, and the X, or NX17372 (as seen in some photographs) was changed to NC17372. Records indicate the airplane was registered to the Ryan School of Aeronautics, San Diego, California at this time.

It was flown all that summer and chalked up an enviable performance record. The recorded facts and figures along with its sleek appearance made headlines in all the leading aviation journals. Many inquiries were received by the Ryan company office.

As fall approached the SC was pressed into service as a primary trainer at the Ryan school, being used for indoctrination into the "first feel of flight." Paul Wilcox, Ryan school instructor, even gave night training to some students during this time.

Toward the fall of 1937, it was re-evaluated with regard to upkeep costs, flight time, maintenance problems, and what effect this would have on customers and of course general sales.

Because the Menasco did give them problems, they decided to try the Warner Super-Scarab radial engine of 145 hp. The Warner proved to be easier to maintain, was less expensive to install and had a greater service life.

So in late September 1937, the airplane was rolled back into the Ryan factory and they removed the Menasco engine.

Warner engine serial number SS567, Model S-50, was installed and the airplane test flown again by John Fornasero. Test flight date is not presently known.

MEL THOMPSON.

Good front view of Menasco installation serial number 201 shortly after roll-out.

RYAN AERONAUTICAL CO.

Another view of prototype serial number 201.

RYAN AERONAUTICAL CO.

View of prototype serial number 201 with the Warner Engine installed with proverbial "bump" cowl.

RYAN AERONAUTICAL CO.

Excellent view revealing the "perforated" flap between gear legs.

With the Warner engine, enclosed in that beautiful NACA deep chord "bump cowl", fuel consumption was only slightly less than with the Menasco, but it proved more reliable, rugged, easier to maintain and cost less per unit to install. With the radial engine as power, the entire series of tests had to be repeated, and the only change found necessary was a modified wing-to-fuselage fairing. This was done in order to retain safe spin characteristics for the airplane to be CAA certified. John Fornasero once again did the early flight work, but most of the later wringing out was done by Paul Wilcox, who succeeded Fornasero in late 1937. One entry into Paul Wilcox's log book, dated September 22, 1937 stated it was a flight "for CAA tests."

So the airplane was re-designated SC-W under an entirely new ATC number, ATC #658, (issued Oct. 31, 1937), and carried NC17372, being changed from NX17372, so the airplane was actually certificated twice.

RYAN AERONAUTICAL CO.

Excellent top view of prototype serial number 201 while it still had the Menasco.

(Left) P.R. shot of designer T. Claude Ryan about to fly s/n 201.

WILLIAM WAGNER

(Right) View clearly shows easy access to engine

(Bottom) Good view of initial wing trailing edge to fuselage design. Later version was filled in with a flat fairing.

RYAN AERONAUTICAL CO.

RYAN AERONAUTICAL CO.

This prototype airplane was the only one of all the other production airplanes that had the four-piece front windshield, modified later to two-piece. All of the later production ships had the two-piece windshield and a beefed-up sliding hatch.

The company continued to fly her for training at the Ryan school, and of course on demonstration flights, and possibly even a tour of the USA for sales purposes.

On October 7, 1938, s/n 201 was sold to Mr. Fernando Gonzalez, Torreon, Coahuila, Mexico, D.F. and flown away on that day. It carried Mexican registration designation XB-AKC, according to original Ryan sales records. In all the years this particular airplane has only had four owners.

It is sad to realize the original log books have not been found covering its history up to its sale to the Mexican buyer. That feeling can be realized in a letter to the author, dated August 1966, from Walter Locke—"Old records were disposed of long ago. During and after the war, when storage space was at a premium, our then big shot controller gave orders to scrap just about everything which was not necessary or mandatory to retain govern-

ment records. Neither Mr. Ryan nor Bill Wagner or myself were even consulted. Fortunately, the then service manager tipped me off when they confiscated his files, and I succeeded in hanging on to three boxes, which contained some of the records on the ST's and SC's. But even the records on the Dutch planes (STMs) were dumped because they were in the service file. Thus it is not for lack of interest that we cannot now answer many of the questions which come to us."

Log books covering s/n 201 while serving in Mexico do exist and copies are in the hands of the author.

Eventually it carried Mexican registration designation XA-CUT. It flew around Mexico and as far south as Central and South America. It was even used to teach the first woman of Mexico to be licensed as a pilot, (name unknown). After sitting in derelict condition for many years, it was purchased by an American, Morton W. Lester, in March 1973, restored, and brought back into flying condition, finally being donated to the EAA Museum in Oshkosh, Wisconsin.

EV CASSAGNERES

Rare photo of s/n 201 shown in Mexican registration while based in that country.

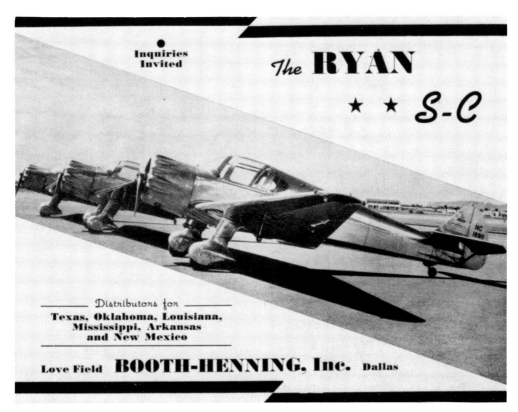

Production

Soon after the prototype sported its SC-W 145 designation, the company ordered material for another 25 airplanes to be produced in the next few months. They were planning to start deliveries in the spring of 1938.

The company had just begun production when Claude Ryan announced receipt of a new subcontract order for aircraft parts, putting the company in the position of having an over $300,000 backlog of work. And within a few months the firm received even larger orders for the STM military version of the ST trainer. These orders came in from the United States as well as some foreign governments.

Military demands leading up to WWII put the production of the PT-16 and PT-20 into full gear and therefore top priority, which had a definite effect on the SC production.

All of this absorbed Ryan's production capacity and repeat orders steadily increasing in size continued to require all of their resources and manpower.

SC production line — appears that serial number 202 is in the foreground.   RYAN AERONAUTICAL CO.

Only eleven complete SCs were built and delivered in 1938. They were s/n 202 through 212. One, serial number 213, was put together by the Ryan school in 1941, but there are no records indicating what ever became of it. It appears that 214, basically a skeleton airframe, was sold in August 1959 to a V.L. DuPont of Lancaster, California, who was attempting to build up the missing components and install a Lycoming engine. As far as can be determined, it presently exists and carries registration number N18900. There is speculation that for a time it may have carried NC305W.

It was hoped the SC could be brought back, but when war broke out, any possibilities of resuming commercial production were forgotten for the duration, at least until the end of the war.

Following the war, there was an avalanche of companies starting to build small personal airplanes at selling prices which they felt were below the level to make profits possible. Ryan decided not to go into production on any personal-type aircraft at that time. They abandoned any further plans to produce the SC, and bought the North American Navion rights starting production in 1947 on that model.

The SC, although short lived, did leave a mark in aviation history that will long be remembered. Of course, it set a trend in metal aircraft production techniques.

The initial retail price for the standard SC was $6885. With the extra equipment most customers chose to have installed, the cost was around $7500, a rather high price for the prewar market. There were no Menasco or any other in-line engine powered SCs produced or sold to a customer. All were powered with the Warner radial engine.

The SC had a top speed of about 140 mph at 5000 ft and a cruising speed of 125 mph. Landing speed was 55 mph. The metal perforated landing flap, situated between the landing gears, attached at the main spar line and manually controlled by a lever in the cockpit, was effective in giving good glide control during approach but had little effect upon the airplane's speed. It in no way changed the stability and no correction was necessary when it was extended. The sliding cockpit canopy could be adjusted in flight through intermediate positions from closed to fully open. No buffeting occurred and there was no change in trim necessary with the canopy open.

(Right) Production line of the Sport Cabins.

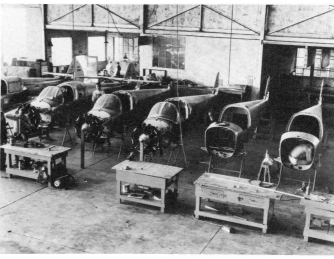

RYAN AERONAUTICAL CO.

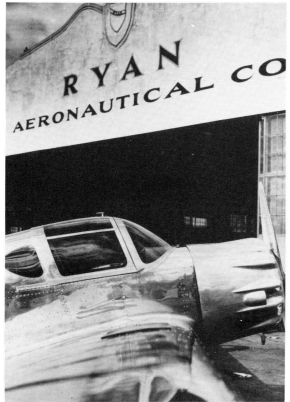

(Left) Good view of canopy assembly of a production SC.

(Below) Serial number 202 taking off from the 1938 International Air Show in downtown Chicago. Impressive performance.

RYAN AERONAUTICAL CO.

RYAN AERONAUTICAL CO.

Flight of five SCWs during filming of the movie "Wake Island."

RYAN AERONAUTICAL CO.

Due to a similarity in plan-view—with long tapered wings, fixed spatted undercarriage and general silhouette—several Ryan SCs were used in war movies to represent early Japanese Nakajima fighters, the Ki-27 "Nate". The first of these was the Paramount Pictures release "Wake Island", produced in the Fall of 1942.

The SC Goes to War

In the history of our country, few antagonists have attempted to sail the Atlantic to invade us or do territorial harm. However, in WWII, German submarines invaded the American territorial waters to torpedo our shipping. With no clear-

Serial number 202 at St. Simons Island, Georgia, during WWII Civil Air Patrol service. Notice wind driven generator and bomb racks, plus sight gauge near cockpit.

RYAN AERONAUTICAL CO.

RYAN AERONAUTICAL CO.

Serial number 202 (#19). Good view of "Bombsight" just below and forward of pilot, outside. Also notice bomb rack on belly.

RYAN AERONAUTICAL CO.

Serial number 203 at St. Simons Island, Georgia.

cut plan for retaliation, we mustered a hastily-organized group of civilian fliers—the Civil Air Patrol. C.A.P. pilots, from all walks of life, would wake up in their own homes and drive to nearby flying fields. They would take-off, to do battle with enemy in a civilians-at-war situation the country had not seen since the Revolution.

There was little money available, and limited help from local military bases. With few supply channels, and with limited community support, these flying men and women financed their squadrons partly from their own pockets to fight submarines from Maine to Florida. From about the spring of 1942 to the summer of 1943, they flew their converted civilian airplanes, first on patrol, and then in armed retaliation—relieving the regular military from this critical job in the all-important first year of the war.

The Ryan SC was one of the types pressed into service for the Civil Air Patrol, auxiliary of the U.S. Army Air Force. It appears that about 5 SCs were used in this service, serial numbers 202, 203, 207, 211, 212.

The airplanes were equipped with bomb racks, carried one or two 100 pound bombs, and flown by CAP pilots patrolling the Eastern coastline, most of it off the

coast of Georgia (St. Simons Island) and Virginia.

Roger Thiel, of Washington, D.C., owner of Ryan SC N830E, s/n 203, has taken an extreme interest in the unique civilians-at-war history of the Civil Air Patrol anti-sub era. Spending many years on this research, he has been writing a screenplay, factual articles, and now a novel on this unique chapter of American history.

In 1992, Donna and Dirk Leeward flew s/n 202 around the United States on their honeymoon, covering 10,000 miles in ten weeks and 100 flying hours. They visited 19 states and Washington, D.C. and a few Canadian provinces. The airplane is now known as the "Honeymoonmobile."

As of this writing, about 9 SCs remain in existence in the United States. The status of one in Brazil (s/n 209) is unknown. Two were lost in fires, and the final status of two others is unaccounted-for.

So the Ryan SC had a comparatively short production life, but its appearance in the late 1930s will long be remembered in the pages of history as that of one of the most advanced private airplanes to be developed during the era.

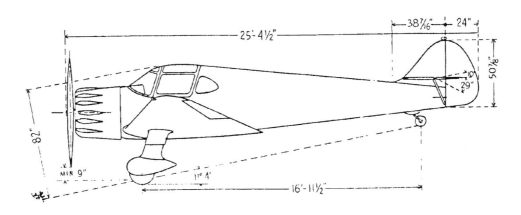

Ryan Sport Cabin Chronology

200	Re: Boyd - Not used because number did not sound good.			
201	X17372	SC-M	Menasco C-4S	Prototype. Mexico
		SC-W	Warner S-50	XA-CUT, Now in USA
202	NC18908	SC-W	Warner S-50	Civil Air Patrol ship
203	NC18909	SC-W	Warner S-50	Civil Air Patrol ship
204	NC18910	SC-W	Warner S-50	Lost in fire at San Diego Aerospace Museum
205	NC18911	SC-W	Warner S-50	In movie "Wake Island"
206	NC18912	SC-W	Warner S-50	Civil Air Patrol ship. In movie "Wake Island"
207	NC18913	SC-W	Warner S-50	Civil Air Patrol ship. Lost in fire, 1948.
208	NC18914	SC-W	Warner S-50	Firestone Co. test ship
209	PP-TEC	SC-W	Warner S-50	Sold to Brazil. Crash June 17, 1958.
210	NC-18915	SC-W	Warner S-50	In movie "Wake Island" Mexico XA-DIR, NC75395 & N147W
211	NC18916	SC-W	Warner S-50	Civil Air Patrol ship N126 & N46207
212	NC18917	SC-W	Warner S-50	Civil Air Patrol ship
213		Never assembled.		Used at Ryan School of Aeronautics
214	N305W SC	Warner		Built up from parts. N18900
215 thru 300				This block of numbers reserved for future production but never used or materialized.

Ryan SC
Standard Equipment

Split, perforated-type wing flap
Trimming tab controlled by convenient
    crank in cabin
Wheel pants, wing fillets and fairing throughout
Modified NACA type engine cowling
Full swiveling, pneumatic tail wheel
Wheel brakes, differentially actuated
    by both sets of controls
Roller-type sun curtains
Reserve fuel supply system
Eclipse electric starter
Storage battery
Exhaust manifold system
Hot air cabin ventilation system
Cold air cabin ventilation system
Cold weather carburetor system
Seats designed to accomodate chair or
    standard seat pack parachutes
Complete upholstering interior finish
Long stroke oleo-type shock absorbers
Altimeter

Tachometer
Compass
Air speed indicator
Oil pressure gauge
Direct reading fuel gauge
First Aid kit
Fire extinguisher
Tool kit
Aircraft and engine log books
Aircraft and engine instruction manuals

Optional SC Equipment

Grimes electrically retractable landing lights
International type parachute flares
Lear or RCA radio receiver
Hodges wind driven generator or Bosch
    engine driven generator
Turn and bank indicator
Sensitive altimeter

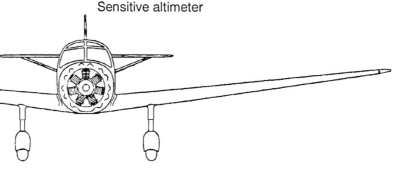

Ryan Sport Cabin ATC Numbers
Specifications and performance

RYAN SC-M
ATC 651

Engine	Menasco C-4S 150 hp
Length Overall	26 ft 7 1/8 in
Wing span	37 ft 6 in
Wing chord at root	99 in
Wing chord at tip	26 in
Height	7 ft
Wing area	202 sq ft
Wing loading	10.4 lbs per sq ft
Power loading	14 lbs per hp
Empty weight	1,300 lbs
Useful load	800 lbs
Pay load	3 people, 40 lbs baggage
Gross weight	2,100 lbs
Fuel capacity	37 gals
Oil capacity	3 gal
Max speed	152 mph (3000 ft altitude)
Cruising speed	136 mph at 3000 ft
Cruising speed	140 mph at 5000 ft
Landing speed	45 mph
Rate of climb	900 ft per minute (sea level)
Service ceiling	19,400 ft
Propeller	Hartzell wood

Menasco "Pirate" C-4S
Aircraft engine
ATC 134

Type	Air-cooled, in-line inverted
Number of cylinders	4
Bore	4 3/4 in
Stroke	5 1/8 in
Displacement	363 cu in
Compression ratio	5.5 to 1
Horse power (rated)	150 @ 2,260 @ 3,000 ft @ 33 in
Ignition	2 Scintilla or Robt. Bosch Magneto
Carburetor	Stromberg NA-R5
Fuel Consumption	9 1/2 gph @ 75% power, 2,050 rpm
Oil Consumption	.05 lbs/B.H.P./hr
Crankshaft	Prop Hub end No 10 SAE Spline
Dry weight	310 lbs
Supercharger Ratio (to crankshaft speed)	9.6 to 1
Introduced	1934

Note: Manufacturing serial number installed in the prototype SC registration number 17372, unknown at this writing.

RYAN SC-W
ATC 658

Engine	Warner "Super Scarab" 145 hp
Length overall	25 ft 5 1/8 in
Wing span	37 ft 6 in
Wing chord at root	99 in
Wing chord at tip	26 in
Height	7 ft
Wing area	202 sq ft
Wing loading	10.7 lbs per sq ft
Power loading	14.8 lbs per hp
Empty weight	1,345 lbs (standard equipment)
Useful load	805 lbs
Pay load	3 people, 60 lbs baggage, 390 lbs
Gross weight	2,150 lbs
Fuel capacity	37 gals
Oil capacity	3 gal
Max speed	150 mph at sea level
Cruising speed	135 mph at 8500 ft
Landing speed	45 mph
Rate of climb	900 ft per minute
Service ceiling	17,200 ft
Take off run	166 yards
Maximum cruising range	500 miles
Propeller	Hartzell, wood, 82 in diameter

Warner "Super Scarab"
Series 50
145 HP
Aircraft Engine
ATC 104

Type	Radial air-cooled
Number of Cylinders	7
Cycles	4
Bore	4 5/8 in
Stroke	4 1/4 in
Displacement	499 cu in
Compression ratio	5.3 to 1
Horse Power (rated)	145
Speed (rated)	2,050 rpm
Ignition	Scintilla or Bosch
Carburetor	Stromberg
Fuel Consumption	.55 lbs. per hp hour
Oil Consumption	.025 lb. per hp hour
Dry Weight (less hub & starter)	305 lbs
Height or overall diameter	36 9/16 in
Mean or effective pressure	115 lbs per sq in
Crankshaft Rotation	Counter-clockwise
Tachometer shaft speed	1/2 crankshaft speed
Engine driven generator	
Introduced	Early 1932

Note: Mfg. serial number SS567E, Warner model S-50 installed in the prototype SC registration NC17372, at the time of sale.

Warner "Super Scarab"
165 HP
Aircraft Engine
ATC 214

Type	Radial air-cooled
Number of Cylinders	7
Cycles	4
Bore	4 5/8 in
Stroke	4 1/4 in
Displacement	499 cu in
Compression ratio	6.4 to 1
Horse Power (rated)	165
Speed (rated)	2,100 rpm
Ignition	Scintilla Model MN&-DF
Carburetor	Stromberg NAR-5A 1 15/16" Vent
Fuel Consumption	.58 lbs per hp hour
Oil Consumption	.025 lb. per hp hour
Dry Weight (less hub & starter)	332 lbs.
Overall diameter	37 1/4"
Length (less starter)	30 25/64"
Spark Plugs	Champion M-4 (standard)
Crankshaft Rotation	Counter-clockwise
Tachometer shaft speed	1/2 crankshaft speed
Take-off power	175 @ 2,250 rpm
Introduced	1939

SC Pilot Report

Jim Leeward checking out the author in serial number 202, NC18908, the oldest SC-W still flying. This flight was at Bill Rose's strip in Barrington, Illinois, July, 1993.   EV CASSAGNERES

I had the surprise of my life when Jimmy Leeward, owner of Ryan SCW, s/n 202, NC18908, approached me just before the 1993 EAA convention at Oshkosh, and said — "Hey Ev, would you like to go flying in the SC?" Needless to say, I was shocked, elated and ecstatic, all at once, and I felt like when I was a kid on a bicycle hanging around the local airport when an aviator said one day — "Hey Ev, want to 'go up'?"

I figured I would just go for a "ride", in the right seat, but when Jim suggested I climb up the left side of this beautiful machine, I darn near broke both legs as I could not climb in fast enough.

After a short discussion regarding my flying background (learned to fly in 1945 in J-3 Cubs and many other tail wheel aircraft - Standard Category) Jim said go ahead and start it up. The SC has the 165 hp Warner "Super Scarab" radial engine and swings an Aeromatic propeller.

The perforated flap had been removed long ago, so no flap handle was visible as I recall. The brake system consists of a central Johnson bar between the seats, which comes straight out of the floor. With a detent, Jim suggested that for general taxiing, take-off and landing I should engage it in the second notch. That is so the pilot gets brake action as he "rudders" the particular side, or the wheel that he wishes to brake. The brakes are mechanical and may be applied from either seat position. I found no problem with the system, and actually found it similar to the early ST with its

bicycle chain crank system, a bit challenging and fun actually.

We were flying out of a beautiful grass strip, about 2800 feet long, owned by Bill Rose in Barrington, Illinois. As we taxied to the south end of the runway, we talked about the air speed numbers, and I remarked that I usually "feel" an airplane off the ground and only use the airspeed indicator (at least in this class of airplane) as a secondary reference, for general fun flying. Jim immediately put his hand over the A.S.I. and we knew where both of us were coming from. We were both taught by feel and sound, and in some cases — smell.

Before this I had only been in an SC one time, about 30 years ago, when I was given a "ride" in s/n 211, NC46207 in New Jersey, and only got to handle the controls for about 30 minutes, in the air. The owner did the take-off and landing, so I did not remember much, when I climbed into 202.

Visibility is quite good considering the Warner radial engine up front, and even better to the side of the engine. Taxiing is just like any other radial powered airplane and one would have to 'S' turn as you drove it along the taxiway. Steering it about 5 or 10 degrees either side of center gives you enough forward vision to do your job and not hit something, and to see where you're going.

As we started down the runway, I applied the throttle gently-but-firmly, and I would say we lifted off at about 70 mph, give or take. I immediately, and ever so slightly, played with the stick, to left and right, and forward and back, to get an idea what the control pressures and responses would be. I found it to be quite responsive and positive. No sluggishness in this beauty.

We climbed up to about 2500 feet above ground level (AGL), where I could play with the airplane, doing "lets get acquainted things" like steep 360 left and right turns, power on and off stalls, dutch roll, and "airborne landings" as I call them, including a side slip or two. During the power off stall, throttle and stick all the way back, the SC stayed right there until the clean and honest break at about 55 mph. It did have a tendency to drop a wing on either side as I did several of them, both with and without power. However, with some stick and rudder coordination, one can "save" it from going into a spin rather quickly, without a lot of effort.

When I decided to do a high angle of attack power on (about 1500 rpm) stall with full back stick, the break was again very clean and honest, at about 50-53 mph. Recovery — with smooth but aggressive full power and nose on the horizon — was very pleasant and the airplane gave not the slightest indication of "fighting" the pilot. Very comforting indeed.

Shortly we set up a cruise of an indicated 125-130 mph at 1950 rpm and 23 inches of manifold pressure at about 2500 ft AGL. Once it was trimmed up, with the little knob on the left wall, in smooth air that we were blessed with, the airplane just sailed off westward towards another grass strip 30 minutes away, and I just sat there with my left hand barely touching the stick.

With the canopy slid open about ten inches, listening to that Warner purr away, and enjoying the scenery, my thoughts turned to what it must have been like for John Fornasero and Paul Wilcox to fly this new Claude Ryan creation for the first time: Complete elation, as it was for me. All of a sudden I was the test pilot flying a brand new design in 1937.

As I came into the pattern for my first landing, and behind another Ryan (STM-S2), I set it up at about 90 mph, with carburetor heat on, carrying about 1500 rpm, to land behind the Ryan. I held it steady at 500 fpm descent from down wind, base and into final. I was a bit high and fast I felt, so I put her into a left slip (my favorite) and held about 85 on final and over a five foot high fence, rounding out for a nice 3 point landing on the grass. All through the approach I felt quite comfortable cutting the power well before the runway, while continuing the slip. The SC had no tendency to give up flying, and in fact I felt it would glide right past the airstrip if I let it, sort of like a Taylorcraft or Piper Supercruiser. The landing was quite soft (yes, I know it was grass) due to the good oleo gear legs and that wide gear tread. I am sure one could get this Ryan into a very short strip (perhaps 1200 - 1500 ft) once you got used to it and with that original perforated flap available. I never had to use the brakes (which I do not use in any Ryan during roll out) until I taxied back to the take-off point where I began a brief run-up and mag check.

Jim surprised me again, when he climbed out and said for me to go ahead and fly it for as long as I wished and enjoy it. I did not argue and "soloed" the SC for several more take-offs and full stop landings, some 3 point and some wheel landings.

Actually, all the landings were excellent, not because of my touch, but because of the good design. I still feel that the Ryan engineers landed the airplane rather than me. A low-time tail wheel pilot could do just as well with the SC; it's that easy, in my opinion, to fly. In fact, it appears that Jimmy Leeward's son Chad, age 18, is probably the youngest pilot to ever solo in an SC. I found it to be a dream to fly and loved every minute of it.

Interestingly, Jim Leeward, who has flown over 200 different types of aircraft over the years, says that without a doubt the Ryan SC is the most stable, especially pitch-wise, airplane he has ever flown. Vern Jobst, well known EAA pilot had the same thing to say about the SC, and could not praise it enough.

Ryan Sport Cabin - Complete Individual Histories

Ryan ST, Ryan B-5 Brougham and prototype SC, serial number 201.   RYAN AERONAUTICAL CO.

Serial number 201 shown with Menasco C-4S 150 h.p. engine.   RYAN AERONAUTICAL CO.

S/n 201

ATC	651 &658
Model	SC-M & SC-W
Registration	X17372, NX17372, NC17372, XB-AKC, XA-CUT
Date of Mfg.	May 1937
Engine	Menasco C-4S & Warner S-50 s/n SS567E
Propeller	Hartzell (for Menasco); Hartzell 714E s/n 16867, 8 bolt

Ownership history -
Ryan School of Aeronautics, San Diego, California; Fernando Gonzalez, Torreon, Coahuila, Mexico; Morton Lester, Martinsville, Virginia; Experimental Aircraft Association, Oshkosh, Wisconsin.

Final Disposition -
Experimental Aircraft Association Museum, Oshkosh, Wisconsin, 1994.

Serial number 202 at Aurora, Illinois Municipal Airport, June 4, 1967. Notice uncommon cowl.

PAUL STEVENS

Repair, Inc. Fort Wayne, Indiana, (Mr. Ralph C. Bleke); Herbert Friedrich, Frankfort, Indiana; Denny Sherman, Sherman Aircraft Sales, Fort Wayne, Indiana; Everett M. Smith, Wilmington, Delaware; Roger Thiel, Washington, D.C.

Final Disposition -
As of 1994, being restored by Roger Thiel in Washington, D.C.

S/n 202

ATC	658
Model	SC-W
Registration	NC18908
Date of Mfg.	January 1938
Engine	Warner S-50 s/n SS487E
Propeller	Hartzell 714E s/n 16747, 8 bolt
Price	$6885.00

Ownership history -
Robert H. Klein (Klein Brothers) Sky Harbor Airport, Northbrook, Illinois (price $6885.00); Civil Air Patrol, St. Simons Island, Georgia (pilot Walter Nicolazi); Turgeon Flying Service, Northbrook, Illinois; Foster Lane, Columbus, Ohio; F.S. Roth, Roth Motor Company, Cape Girardeau, Missouri; Ralph C. Immel, Dallas, Texas (he installed a Warner 165); Kenneth F. Green, Dallas, Texas; James A. Steele, Lisle, Illinois; James Leeward, Leeward Air Ranch, Ocala, Florida.

Final Disposition -
Leeward Air Ranch, Ocala, Florida, 1994.

S/n 203

ATC	658
Model	SC-W
Registration	NC18909, N830E
Date of Mfg.	February 1938
Engine	Warner S-50 s/n SS489E
Propeller	Hartzell 714E s/n 16798, 16809, 8 bolt
Price	$6885.00

Ownership history -
DeMorr Aeronautical Corporation, Paoli, Pennsylvania; It was actually shipped via railroad, crated. Priced at $6885.00; Walt Nicolai, Civil Air Patrol, St. Simons Island, Georgia; J.E. Stephens, New Orleans, Louisiana, Consolidated Aircraft

Serial number 203, NC18909 at Floyd Bennett Field, L.I., New York.

WARREN SHIPP

S/n 204

ATC	658
Model	SC-W
Registration	NC18910
Date of Mfg.	February 1938
Engine	Warner S-50 s/n SS496E
Propeller	Hartzell 714E s/n 16807, 16769, 8 bolt
Price	$6885.00

Ownership history -
Booth-Hening, Inc. Love Field, Dallas, Texas; Jerry Sass, Oklahoma City; George Carter, Chicago, Illinois; Ronan and Kunzl (A. Edward Kunzl). Was in accident, nose over upon landing, fuselage replaced with new one; Rohn-Howard Aviation Company, Peoria, Illinois (Mr. R.G. Howard); Clifford Witt, San Francisco, California; William L. Meyers, Port Angeles, Washington; San Diego Aerospace Museum, California.

Interesting photo of s/n 204, NC18910 when it was up for sale a number of years ago.

MRS. W.P. CUTTER

Final Disposition -
Burned in fire and completely destroyed on February 22, 1978, at the San Diego Aerospace Museum; in San Diego, California.

S/n 205

ATC	658
Model	SC-W
Registration	NC18911
Date of Mfg.	April 1938
Engine	Warner S-50 s/n SS497E, Cont. E-185, 205 hp
Propeller	Hartzell 714E s/n 16807, 8 bolt Beech Series 215
Price	$?

GEORGE E. CULL

Serial number 205, NC18911 September 1939 at San Francisco Bay Aerodrome, Alameda, California.

RYAN AERONAUTICAL CO.

Serial number 205 with a modern Continental E-185, 205 hp flat engine, and new paint scheme. Notice non-authentic wheel pant. T. Claude Ryan in cockpit and owner/pilot "Tex" Hilley on wing.

Ownership history -
George A. Turner, Palm Beach, Florida; William L. Plummer, General Aircraft Company, Glendale, California; Ray Clever, Whiteman Manufacturing Company, Los Angeles, California; James A. McPhereson, Los Angeles, California; Monroe S. Decker, Decker Manufacturing Company, Los Angeles, California; J.D. "Tex" Hilley, Hawthorne, California; he installed a Continental E-185-9, 185 hp flat engine. Next owner Richard C. McDonald, Vacaville, California; James K. Wickersham, Danville, California.

Final disposition -
Owned by James K. Wickersham, Danville, California, as of 1990.
Note: Was used in movie "Wake Island" as a Japanese dive bomber.

S/n 206

ATC	658
Model	SC-W
Registration	NC18912
Date of Mfg.	April 1938
Engine	Warner S-50 s/n SS279E (1989 Warner 165)
Propeller	Hartzell
Price	$?

Ownership history -
Warner Aircraft Corporation, Detroit, Michigan (this is the Warner engine manufacturer); it appears it was flown back to Detroit by Warner pilot L.A. Faunce; Mr. Neuweller, Allentown, Pennsylvania; Robert H. Silverman, Philadelphia, Pennsylvania; Civil Air Patrol, Parksley, Virginia; William Charney, Specialty Engineering & Mfg. Co., Chicago, Illinois; Fred C. Culver, Hudson, Michigan; stored for a time at Turgeon Flying Service, Northbrook, Illinois; Brad J. Larson, Minneapolis, Minnesota and later Santa Paula, California.

Final Disposition -
Owned by Brad J. Larson, Santa Paula, California as of 1994.

Serial number 206, NC18912 at Detroit's Michigan City Airport 1938/39.   WILLIAM WAGNER

Primary instrument panel of s/n 206.   WILLIAM WAGNER

S/n 207

Model	SC-W
Registration	NC18913
Date of Mfg.	August 1938
Engine	Warner S-50 s/n SS564E
Propeller	Hartzell 714E s/n 16798, 16744, 8 bolt
Price	$6885.00

Ownership history -
Beebe Air Service, Hastings, Nebraska; Dr. R.C. Foote, Hastings, Nebraska; Don E. Pratt, President P-T Air Service, Inc., Hays, Kansas; Civil Air Patrol, location unknown; C.H. Springer, J.B. Kidd Motors Inc., Springfield, Missouri; G.M. McJunkin, manager Ponca City Municipal Airport, Ponca City, Oklahoma.

Final Disposition -
Burned up and destroyed in fire on September 16, 1948 at Ponca City, Oklahoma while being rebuilt.

KENNETH E. LENZ
Serial number 207, NC18913 at Tulsa, Oklahoma Municipal Airport June 1948.

S/n 208

ATC	658
Model	SC-W
Registration	X18914, NC18914
Date of Mfg.	August 1938
Engine	Warner S-50 s/n SS565E
Propeller	Hartzell 714E s/n 16925 8 bolt
Price	$7606.03

Ownership history -
Firestone Tire & Rubber Company, Akron, Ohio. They supplied their own wheels, brakes, tires and tubes (installed by Ryan); airplane used for experimental purposes by Firestone, flown by Firestone pilot E.J. Quigley of the Aeronautic Division; Ross J. Thomas, Jr. of Thomas Memorials at Homestead, Pennsylvania; Marshall, Michigan, owner name unknown; Mr. N.J. Bossard, location unknown; Holland Air Service, W.B. Blain, Holland, Michigan; Marilyn Himes, Vans Air Service, St. Cloud, Minnesota and Frederick Hall (Univer-

PETER C. BOISSEAU
Serial number 208, NC18914 while owned and flown by Firestone Tire & Rubber Co. of Akron, Ohio. Photo at Cleveland, Ohio, September 5, 1938.

sity of Maryland) Frederick, Maryland; F.D. "Dee" Barnard, Ann Arbor, Michigan; Richard Roy Dehr, address unknown; Joel McNeal, El Cajon, California; Horace Barbetti & Jim Feick, Van Nuys, California.

Final Disposition -
Airworthy and owned by Horace Barbetti & Jim Feick, Van Nuys, California as of 1994.

S/n 209

ATC	658
Model	SC-W
Registration	PP-TEC (exported to Rio de Janeiro, Brazil)
Date of Mfg.	July 1938
Engine	Warner S-50 s/n SS563E
Propeller	Hartzell 714E s/n 16797, 8 bolt
Price	$7237.00

Ownership history -
Dr. Sergio Rocha Miranda, Rio de Janeiro, Brazil, South America; David James McMenamin, Uberaba Mines, Brazil (had two joint owners - Dr. Paulo Samplo, President of Panair of Brazil and his brother-in-law, an Air Force pilot).

Final Disposition -
Was involved in accident June 17, 1958 but details not known. Present status unknown as of 1994.

Serial number 210, NC18915 at San Diego.   EV CASSAGNERES

S/n 210

ATC	658
Model	SC-W
Registration	NC18915, N75395, N147W Mexico XA-DIR
Date of Mfg.	November 1938
Engine	Warner S-50 s/n SS364E
Propeller	Hartzell 714E s/n 16352, 8 bolt
Price	Unknown

Ownership history -
Ryan School of Aeronautics, San Diego, California, used for flight training (it was picked up at the factory and taxied across the field to its "new owner"); Paramount Pictures, Inc. Hollywood, California for use in the picture "Wake Island"; Herbert L. White, California Aircraft Corporation, Van Nuys, California; J.F. Yoas, Sanderson, Texas; M.G. Michaelis, Jr., Eagle Pass, Texas; Joel Leach Jr., of Markham, Illinois; Claude R. Bridges, Ellisville, Missouri; Darol R. Curry, Midland, Texas; Dr. David R. Conoley, Midland, Texas; Fred Sorenson, Pensacola, Florida.

Final Disposition -
As of 1994 owned by Fred Sorenson, Pensacola, Florida. Has Warner 185 of 200 hp.

S/n 211

ATC	658
Model	SC-W
Registration	NC18916, NC126, N46207
Date of Mfg.	May 1938
Engine	Warner S-50 s/n SS498E (Menasco C-4S #302)
Propeller	Hartzell 714 s/n 16786
Price	$5465.00

Ownership history -
Booth-Henning, Inc. (Doc Booth & Al Henning) Love Field, Dallas, Texas; Jerry B. Sase, Oklahoma City, Oklahoma; Oklahoma Air College , Cimarron Field, Oklahoma City, Oklahoma; John H. Burke, President; Headquarters Squadron, Caribbean Wing, Air Transport Command, Morrison Field, West Palm Beach, Florida, used for coastal patrol, flown by F.D. Maulden, 2nd Lt. Air Corps, registered as N126; Sara Flying Service, Central Airport, Los Angeles, California; Bernie Hill, North Carolina; Glenn Rossman, Portland, Maine; F.J. Kirk Moulding Company, Clinton, Massachusetts; Joe Wahlin, Glendale, California; Kenneth Nill, Oceanside, California; Walt Saunders, San Diego, California; Carl Overstreet, Virginia; Colgate Darden, Aiken, S. Carolina; Don Plackard, Indiana; Randolph Wesson, Alexandria, Virginia; Harold G. Scheck, Paramus, New Jersey (this author flew it at that time); Ernest Moritz, Chicago, Illinois; R.K. King, Egger, Houston, Texas; Douglas Koeppen, New Milford, Connecticut; Kenneth L. Senter, MD, Glendale, California.

Final Disposition -
Crash May or June 1989. Kenneth Senter still the owner as of 1989.

(Top) *Serial number 211, NC18916 at Cleveland, Ohio, September 4, 1938. Notice owner name Jerry Sass, near cockpit entry.*

(Middle) *Serial number 212, NC18917 at Bridgeport Municipal Airport, Bridgeport, Connecticut, 1946. Owned and flown by Alan Wheeler.*

(Bottom) *Another view of serial number 212, NC18917 at Bridgeport, Connecticut, 1946.*

PETER C. BOISSEAU

WARREN SHIPP

ALAN WHEELER

S/n 212

ATC	658
Model	SC-W
Registration	NC18917
Date of Mfg.	January 1939
Engine	Warner S-50 s/n SS566E
Propeller	Sensenich 82R s/n 832
Price	$2197.22 (to Ryan School)

Ownership history -
Apparently the airplane was used for about 45 hours by the Ryan company at the factory, then put in temporary storage then sold disassembled to the Ryan School of Aeronautics, San Diego, California and delivered via truck. In 1942 sold to Tom Daniel, Jr., St. Simons Island,

Georgia and flown by Major T.H. Daniel, Jr. Base Commander, Patrol No. 6; Everett R. Ingles, Ashville, North Carolina; Marie F. Thompson, Clinton, Indiana; Opal Hall, Bedford, Indiana; Morris P. Frost, Falmouth, Massachusetts; Dr. Richard P. Austin, Bedford, Indiana; Alan S. Wheeler, Huntington, Connecticut; Gene Cavoli, Cavoli's Flying Service, Buena, New Jersey.

Final Disposition -
Last owner was Gene Cavoli, as of January 1950. The airplane was "destroyed" but it is not known if by crash or some other way. Could still exist?

S/n 213

ATC	658
Model	SC-W
Registration	-
Date of Mfg.	-
Engine	-
Propeller	-
Price	-

Ownership history -
This airplane consisted of just major parts left in storage at the factory. It was never assembled but was used at the Ryan School of Aeronautics for training purposes. It appears as though some of the parts could have been sold off to owners of SCs.

Final Disposition -
SEE ABOVE
Note - Fuselage may have been the "new one" that went to s/n 204.

Rare photo of s/n 214, N18900.   MAUNO SALO

S/n 214

ATC	658
Model	SC
Registration	N-305W, N18900
Date of Mfg.	?
Engine	Cont. E-185, 205 hp
Propeller	?
Price	?

Ownership history -

The airplane was sold in parts, a set of wings and a fuselage shell, for the price of $100.00 to Southern California Air Motive, Inc., Walter R. Saunders, Gillespie Field, near San Diego, California. A letter to this author from Vernon Lee DuPont, Plattsburg, New York in 1965 indicated he had ended up with these parts and was starting the long job of building up this airplane. A basket contained parts for the landing gear and tail surfaces. Then in 1966 or 67 he moved to La Mesa, California after trucking the parts on a trailer behind his car all across the country. In January 1968, he sold the complete (what there was of it) airplane to Gary J. Papas, Compton, California. Papas installed a Continental 205 hp flat engine and hydraulic brakes, wing fuel tanks and reserved the registration number 305W. In about May 1972, Papas finished the airplane into airworthy condition and licensed it under N18900 and it flew for the first time in its life.

Final Disposition -

Present status unknown as of 1994. Possibly owned by John Winebresser of San Pedro, California.

From Chapter 1, Page 1

<u>AGREEMENT</u>   WITNESSETH:

WHEREAS Ryan has designed the airplane, the three-view drawing of which is hereto attached, and; desires to have the engineering and design work completed thereon, and

WHEREAS the said Boyd is a competent engineer to complete the same, NOW THEREFORE IT IS AGREED AS FOLLOWS:

First: Boyd hereby agrees to do all the required engineering and design work on that certain airplane, the three-view drawing of which is hereto attached, said work to be done in a space provided and in a manner satisfactory to Ryan. Boyd will well and truly work on said design, engineering, supervision of building and testing of said airplane, giving his full time thereto, without delays, and will complete the same as soon as possible. Boyd agrees to provide the services of a qualified aeronautical engineer, as assistant or associate, to devote his full time to the work covered in this contract until completed. Said engineer is to receive his compensation from Boyd, and Boyd is to be fully responsible for same.

Second: Boyd agrees to furnish at his own expense all draftsmen if, and when, required.

Third: Boyd agrees to furnish at his own expense all drafting supplies required by him to do said fore-going work.

Fourth: Boyd agrees, with the cooperation of Ryan and in a manner approved by him, to carry said design to completion, to obtain the approval of the United States Department of Commerce for said design, and either an A.T.C. rating or a Group II rating, and to cause said ship to be eligible for an NC license, and until the first plane receives said license; Boyd further agrees to supervise the construction of the first airplane to the extent required to insure complete understanding by the foreman and all workmen of the detail of construction and assembling and tests.

Fifth: Boyd further agrees to make all stress analyses and all weight, balance, performance and other design calculations in accordance with the matters approved by the Engineering Section of the United States Department of Commerce: to make all detailed drawings of every part of said airplane design, assembly drawings and other necessary or required drawings in connection with the construction of said airplane and the approval of said design, and that all of said drawings and designs shall at all times be the sole and exclusive property of Ryan: that the said design will not be used or sold by Boyd, his associates or assistants for any purpose, or placed in the hands of any other party at any time for the building of all or any part of other airplanes; and that all design information will be treated by Boyd and his assistants and associates as strictly confidential information belonging to Ryan.

Sixth: It is recognized by Boyd that the design of the airplane referred to and shown in the three-view drawing hereto attached has heretofore been developed and worked out, and is the original design of Ryan, and that the original finished design will incorporate both the ideas and experience of Ryan and Boyd; and that Ryan will be recognized as the designer of said plane and Boyd as the chief engineer responsible for all engineering, and that Boyd would at no time attempt to claim the entire credit for creating the design.

Seventh: Boyd will complete all of the foregoing work including the engineering and building of the first plane, its complete testing for the Department of Commerce, and procure the NC license for said plane and the approval by the Department of Commerce, within a period of not to exceed four calendar months from and after the date of the execution of this agreement, and Boyd states that he can do the same in three months barring unusual delays beyond his control.

Eighth: Boyd agrees to furnish all of the foregoing as set forth in this contract for an outside total sum of not to exceed One Thousand Dollars ($1,000.00), including all bonuses described below. Ryan agrees to pay to Boyd a payment of One Hundred Dollars ($100.00) for each month he is working alone, and Two Hundred Dollars ($200.00) for each month during the time that he and a full time associate engineer work on said project; payment of said sums or proportionate sums then due to be made on the 2nd and 17th days of the respective month, beginning on <u>September   2nd   </u>, 1933, being first such date after said work has actually started, and continuing for three months, when said work is expected to be completed. If work has proceeded with due diligence in the opinion of Ryan but has not been completed within three months from <u>August 21st</u>, 1933, then payments at the same rate will continue until said work is completed, with a total outside sum required to be paid of One Thousand Dollars ($1,000.00), (including all payments advanced for drafting supplies or any other special purpose). In the event Boyd has not completed said work within four months from ___August 21st___, 1933, Boyd will thereby forfeit all claims to any bonuses described below. If, in such event as all of the foregoing work herein contracted to be performed being not completed by or before the entire One Thousand Dollars ($1,000.00) total maximum payment has been paid to Boyd, then Boyd together with assistant or associate engineer agree to continue diligently, devoting their full time and energy to complete same at the earliest possible time, and until the final completion of all engineering, construction, and testing of said plane, and said design of said airplane has been approved and the license issued by the United States Department of Commerce without further payments or obligations, or additional amounts by Ryan.

Ninth: It is hereby provided that if said work is completed in a satisfactory manner to Ryan before the expiration of three calendar months, a bonus of One Hundred Dollars ($100.00) will be paid to Boyd by Ryan. It is further provided and agreed that if said work is completed in a satisfactory manner before the expiration of four calendar months, and should the total cost of the material used in the construction of said airplane (not including motor, propeller, labor or overhead) have been held to within not to exceed the sum of Six Hundred Dollars ($600.00), then Ryan will pay Boyd in addition to all of the previous payments provided for by this contract, a bonus of One Hundred Dollars ($100.00); and further should Boyd's services be performed and completed in a manner satisfactory to Ryan and the performance of the finished airplane exceed or meet the specifications which are set out in detail in Exhibit A, hereto attached, and by this reference made a part of this contract, or should the performance of the finished airplane fail to meet the said performance specifications by less than five percent (5%) on any one item of said performance specifications, then Ryan will pay Boyd, in addition to all of the payments previously provided for by this contract, a bonus of One Hundred Dollars ($100.00). In no event, however, shall anything in this contract be construed to cause the total of all payments, including bonuses, advances for drafting supplies or any other purposes, to exceed the total maximum cost for foregoing engineering work, etc. herein contracted to be done, to exceed the maximum amount of One Thousand Dollars ($1,000.00); Boyd hereby guarantees and agrees that this will be the maximum sum to cover all costs for said work.

Tenth: It is understood that Boyd is an independent contractor and not an employee of Ryan, and that the manner and time of payments as herein specified are convenient for both parties but are not and shall not be construed as salary or wages; and that any assistant or associate of Boyd shall likewise not be deemed an employee of Ryan but shall be deemed an associate of Boyd.

Eleventh: If, at any time before sixty percent (60%) of said work covered in this contract is completed, it be necessary or desirable in Ryan's opinion to discontinue this work and cancel this contract, the work provided to be performed shall be discontinued and this contract cancelled by Ryan and the sums paid by Ryan to Boyd up to the date of said cancellation and discontinuance shall be full payment to Boyd for his services under and pursuant to this agreement.

WITNESS our signatures at San Diego, California, this August ___21st___, 1933.

Millard C. Boyd /s/

WITNESS:

T. Claude Ryan /s/

Orva Johnson /s/

About the Author
Ev Cassagneres

Ev Cassagneres has written a number of articles on Ryan (and other aircraft) for aviation publications in this country as well as abroad, and is internationally recognized as the Ryan Aircraft Historian. His personal archives are now considered the largest of Ryan memorabilia in the world. The collection includes a library of over 3000 photographs of Ryan aircraft, many still unpublished.

Ev is one of the 13 founding members of the Connecticut Aeronautical Historical Association, the organization that operates the well known New England Air Museum. He is author of the book "THE SPIRIT OF RYAN" which is an in depth historical work of the Ryan Aeronautical Corporation history.

Ev is a former bicycle racer, having retired undefeated as the 7 time Connecticut Senior Champion. He holds the national cycling record for the 200 mile distance.

Born February 7th, 1928, Ev's interest in aviation dates from his childhood. He has been a licensed pilot (Commercial, SMEL, instr.) for 50 years and has flown over 50 types of aircraft, many of the antique/classic variety. He is a U.S. Army veteran whose service from 1950 through 1952 included duty in Korea. He was awarded 2 Purple Hearts while in Korea.

Ev's interests include more than aviation — sailing a rare 1945 wood/canvas canoe, windsurfing, hiking, swimming, down hill and cross country skiing, cycling, ethnic and contra dancing, black and white photography, camping, travel, smoking cessation program chairman for over 25 years, building model ships, ethnic and classical music, engineering drafting (his profession).

He is president of his own engineering and drafting service, known as Aero-Draft.

RYAN AERONAUTICAL COMPANY

Author (left) with T. Claude Ryan in San Diego — June 1968.

He has been acquainted with Anne and Charles A. Lindbergh as a result of Lindbergh's interest in Ev's research on the Spirit of St. Louis as built by Ryan. Lindbergh, before his death, was of help in Ev's project. Ev is presently working on the first book to be written of the history of the "Spirit of St. Louis" airplane.

Ev was known throughout the northeast as "SOLO" the flying clown, where he had performed the exciting comedy act with a standard Piper J-3 Cub for many years. He actually got his start by Flying Cole Palen's 1936 Aeronca C-3 at Rhinebeck, New York back in the sixties, in a comedy routine.

He lives in Cheshire, Connecticut and is proud of his two children, Kirsten and Bryan.

RYAN AERONAUTICAL COMPANY

Ev Cassagneres flying s/n 117 NC-14985 over the Connecticut countryside.

Individual histories of Ryan ST Aircraft and compilations of the background of each s/n are available by contacting the author through the Publisher at:
Flying Books
1401 Kings Wood Rd.
Eagan, MN 55122.

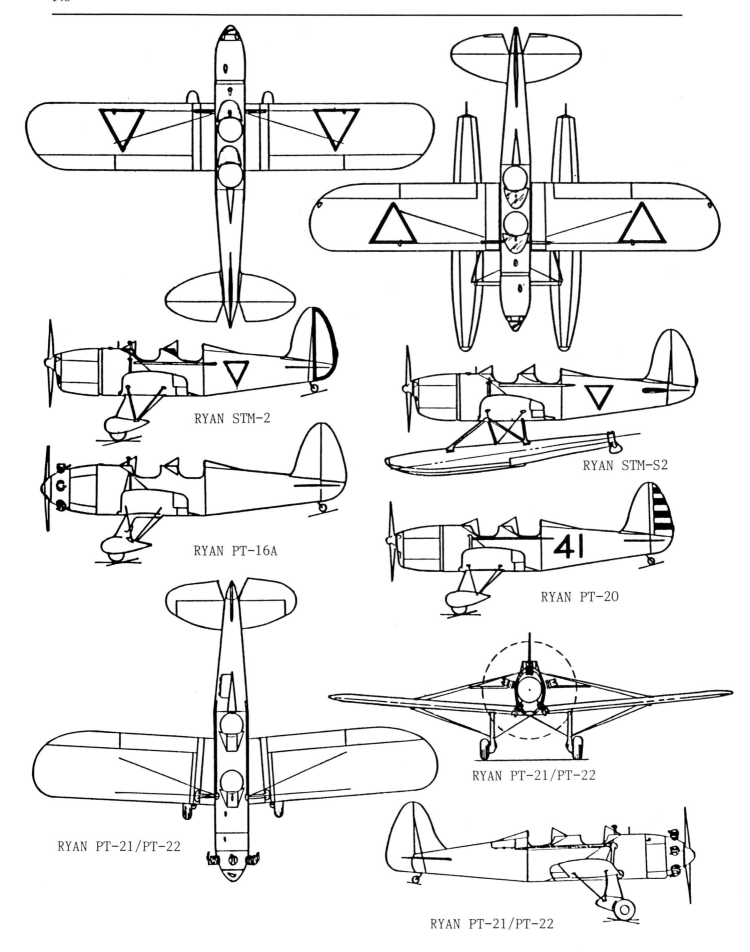

RYAN STM-2

RYAN STM-S2

RYAN PT-16A

RYAN PT-20

RYAN PT-21/PT-22

RYAN PT-21/PT-22

RYAN PT-21/PT-22